CONTEMPORARY
QUILT AR

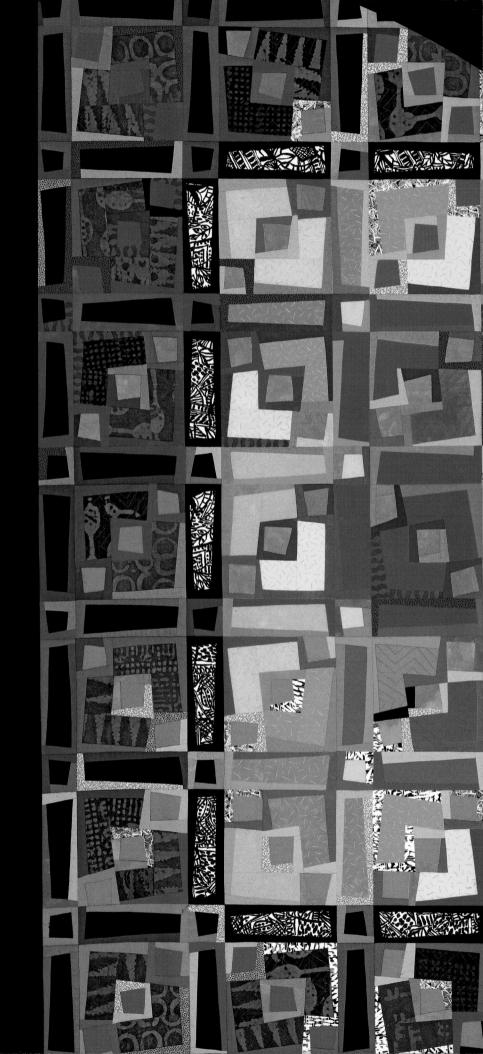

INDIANA
UNIVERSITY
PRESS

BLOOMINGTON

AND INDIANAPOLIS

CONTEMPORARY QUILT ART

An Introduction and Guide

KATE LENKOWSKY

This book is a publication of

Indiana University Press
601 North Morton Street
Bloomington, IN 47404-3797 USA

http://iupress.indiana.edu

Telephone orders   800-842-6796
Fax orders   812-855-7931
Orders by e-mail   iuporder@indiana.edu

The paper used in this publication meets the
minimum requirements of American National
Standard for Information Sciences—Permanence
of Paper for Printed Library Materials,
ANSI Z39.48-1984.

Manufactured in China

Library of Congress Cataloging-in-Publication Data

Lenkowsky, Kate.
  Contemporary quilt art : an introduction
  and guide / Kate Lenkowsky.
      p. cm.
  Includes bibliographical references and index.
  ISBN 978-0-253-35124-1 (cloth)
  1. Art quilts—United States. I. Title.
  NK9112.L443 2008
  746.460973—dc22
                                        2007035467

1 2 3 4 5 13 12 11 10 09 08

For Les, with love

Anna Torma, *Jardin du Wiltz III,* detail, 2006.
Hand embroidery on linen base, silk thread;
quilted. Photo: Natalie Matutschovsky

CONTENTS

PART THREE | A GUIDE FOR BUYERS & COLLECTORS

PREFACE

Artists have been using quilts as an art medium for more than forty years. Quilts are especially useful for the formal exploration of color, shape, line, movement, and texture, while the characteristics of cloth and the quilt's layered structure contribute to the meaning, intent, and expressiveness of quilters' work. Yet there are those who believe that quilts, constructed from the material of everyday life and bearing the burden of domestic use, cannot be art. To dismiss them so peremptorily is to deprive oneself of the pleasure of some extraordinary works of art.

Artists who make quilts differ somewhat from their colleagues. Many feel a special connection to cloth and to the process of making art. For them, the making of art is more than a mechanical act. And the cloth itself is tied to the meaning of their work.

Why choose cloth and quilts over paint, stone, or metal, the artistic media that fill our art museums and galleries? Each of these materials speaks with its own language. Cloth has an ancient and intimate association with humans, with their needs and their activities. In the artist's hands cloth becomes a metaphor for human touch, memory, time, or family; for warmth, passion, the bed. It can signify status or domesticity, fashion or "anti-fashion." It is used for decoration yet also serves as the symbol of nationhood and revolution.

Couldn't a painter pick up a brush and execute a painting which has the same associations, which evokes the same emotions? Art students are taught how to draw draped fabric in their first drawing class. But in art history, they learn of the still life paintings of Cezanne. The artist did not represent the drape or fluid lines of the tablecloth. He presented the cloth as abstract form; his subject became the paint itself.

Artists working with cloth are not only employing the symbolism and metaphorical associations of cloth. Cloth, like Cezanne's paint, is "material" in the most basic sense. It invites the viewer to touch. It can be pieced

Sue Benner, *BODY PARTS*
(Zebra Sleeve, Paisley Sleeve), 2006,
81 × 61. Silk and cotton, dyed and
painted; found fabrics, fused,
mono-printed, machine quilted.
Photo: Eric Neilsen

or collaged and presented in multiple dimensions. It can be draped or made taut, ruffled, pleated, plaited, or woven. It is pliable but can be stiffened. It is opaque, translucent, or transparent; it can reflect or absorb light. It can be dyed, painted or printed, molded, cut, and frayed. Its texture ranges from soft and sensual to cold, smooth, and hard. Cloth can be recycled. Woven, it is a ready-made grid. If these were not reasons enough, technology supplies artists with a steady stream of new fibers and fabrics to be investigated for their art potential, materials originally developed for use by fashion and industry.

The professional artists whose work is portrayed in this book have chosen to work in a particular form of fiber art—the quilt. Their reasons vary, but they have all found that cloth or the physical structure of the quilt to be important to their art. They do not all think of themselves as quiltmakers because their explorations do not necessarily begin with the intention of making a quilt. They arrive at this form when their art interests or ideas coincide with it, but they may work in other forms also. The layers of a quilt allow for the exploration of dimension and illusion in space, perspective, or color. By using transparent organza rather than opaque cotton, an artist might focus the viewer's attention on the quilt's interior. The layers themselves, or the seam lines with their sharp or modulated juxtapositions of color, take on meaning. The interaction of the pieced seams with color imbues the quilt surface with movement and energy. Stitching, too, can generate energy or imply a quieter gesture or presence. Even the fundamental elements of traditional quilt construction, such as block design and layering, have been adapted by artists using non-cloth materials, such as Mylar, metal, and recycled products of industry.

The possibilities of the studio quilt as an art form should be obvious to anyone. For the professional observer, there is more. "What really amazes me about quilting," says video artist and teacher Cecilia Dougherty, "is the use of combinations of patterns of fabric, placement, stitching, etc., in a three-dimensional object that contains elements of visual surprise, trompe l'oeil, landscape, optical illusion, creation of imaginary multi-dimensionality, that are all integrated in the quilt's materiality and seem to transcend it at the same time."

Despite the excitement that accompanied the development of the art form, and the considerable accomplishments of its artists since then, studio quiltmakers have received little attention from the art world in this country. A majority of fine art museum directors, curators, gallery owners, and art reviewers continue to associate their art with "women's work" or with the kind of craft more aptly called *kitsch*. The public, which crowds museum exhibitions of quilts, including the most avant-garde work, seems reluctant to buy them, mistakenly fearing that they will be hard to maintain or not last long. A few artists have been successful at promoting their work. But after years of unfulfilled hopes, some of the best have resigned themselves to this neglect and turned their attention fully to their art and to teaching.

This book is intended to encourage readers to look at studio quilts with an open mind, learn about them, and consider them when buying art for your homes and offices. You need not be a collector. A few simple maintenance measures—little more than is required to care properly for any art—can give you a lifetime of enjoyment.

In the following pages—which need not be read sequentially—the story of the emergence of this new art form is told. Part 1 begins with a description of the designs and methods of constructing traditional quilts and quickly proceeds to an account of the social, historical, and art developments in the twentieth century which led to the evolution of contemporary quilts. Part 2 contains essays about and illustrations of the work of the genre's most prominent artists exhibiting in this country. Part 3 is a guide for buyers and collectors. I have tried to provide information on almost every subject of potential interest, including educational and market resources, museum collecting, private and internet galleries, and quilt exhibits ranging from local guild shows to international exhibitions. Advice for buyers from artists, curators, collectors, and art consultants can be found in this section as well as suggestions for successfully commissioning work and using art consultants. Information about caring for and displaying your art and obtaining appraisals and insurance is included. Finally, the reader will find a useful listing of some museums with contemporary quilts, artists' websites, informative publications, a glossary, and biographies of the featured artists at the back of the book.

Contemporary Quilt Art: An Introduction and Guide is comprehensive in scope but can be only a guide. Approach your search in the same spirit as craft collector Robert Pfannebecker did when he began collecting in the 1950s. You will have a wonderful time. "I've had an enormous amount of fun doing what I've done," he said in an interview for the Smithsonian Institution archives in 1991, "and I've met an incredible group of people. For me, it's been a really exciting experience to know the people and live with the work. . . . I still find it an incredibly exhilarating thing to do."[1]

Patricia Malarcher, *Lift*, 1999,
66 × 36. Fabric, Mylar; collage.
Private collection

ACKNOWLEDGMENTS

Many people have offered encouragement and provided assistance while the research and writing of this book were underway. It is not possible to name them all, but without their contributions, it could not have been written. I am especially grateful to the artists for their trust and cooperation. All illustrations in the text not otherwise credited were provided by them.

Penny McMorris, Patricia Malarcher, Michael James, and Robert Shaw gave support and advice from the beginning to the end of the project. Penny, Patricia, Bruce Cole, art historian and chairman of the National Endowment for the Humanities, Cecilia Dougherty, Carolyn Ducey, David J. Hornung, Paul Smith, director emeritus of the Museum of Arts and Design, all reviewed and commented on parts of the manuscript during various stages of the writing and raised issues for consideration. The responsibility for any errors that might persist, however, and for all the opinions expressed in this book, is mine.

At the very beginning, I was received with enthusiasm by collectors Hilary and Marvin Fletcher when I arrived in Athens, Ohio, to interview them. Hilary, project coordinator of *Quilt National,* passed away in August of 2006. But her enthusiasm for the art, the artists, and a book to be written expressly to interest the public in quilt art was energizing. In addition to the Fletchers, many other collectors have shared their motivations, opinions, and interests, and have offered suggestions for readers about buying and collecting. These include Nancy and Warren Brakensiek, Camille J. Cook, Virginia McGehee Friend, Michele Hardman, Maureen Hendricks, Ardis and Robert James, Kathleen and Bob Kirkpatrick, Jackie Levinson, Robert Pfannebecker, Colleen Piersen, Sarah Reynolds, Eleanor Rosenfeld, Thelma Smith, Del Thomas, and John M. Walsh III.

Shelly Zegart, a founder of the Alliance for American Quilts, and Yvonne Porcella suggested fruitful areas of research and led me to other knowledgeable individuals, including Leatrice Eagle, former president of the board of the American Craft Council. Martha Sielman, executive director of SAQA, was a consistent source of assistance and encouragement, and Carolyn

Vehslage, Sue Pierce, and Patricia Klem provided information and guidance when it was needed.

Museum directors and curators who graciously fielded a barrage of wide-ranging questions were Arlene Blackburn, Doris M. Bowman, Inez Brooks-Myers, Carolyn Ducey, Mark Leach, Melissa Leventon, Michael W. Monroe, Pauline Pahl, Niloo Imani Paydar, Bruce Pepich, Jane Przybysz, Dixie Rettig, Judy Schwender, Jacquelyn Day Serwer, Martha Spark, Rebecca A. T. Stevens, Judith Trager, and Robin Treen. Several curators offered suggestions for readers about evaluating works of fiber art.

Carolyn Mazloomi and Carole Lyles Shaw directed me to readings about African and African American textile art, opening up a new vista in the visual arts for me. Bets Ramsey confirmed my evolving views of the importance of developments in needlework prior to the emergence of the new quilts. And from "techno textiles" expert Marie O'Mahony came the unexpected prediction that people would someday recognize the value and beauty—the patina of time—of faded, naturally dyed cloth. Karey Bresenhan, of Quilts, Inc., gave me an interview in the middle of the International Quilt Festival and promptly answered all my subsequent questions.

Art educators and historians who contributed to my education were Pat Autenrieth, Susan Brandeis, Nancy Crow, Linda Fowler, Bernard L. Herman, David J. Hornung, Michael James, Katie Pasquini-Masopust, Anne McKenzie Nicolson, Jean Robertson, Arturo Alonzo Sandoval, and Sandra Sider.

Sharon Ewing, Rick Gottas, Robin Hallar, Bruce Hoffman, Sherry Leedy, Lynn Noble, Jane Sauer, and Jodi Walsh, all owners or directors of art galleries, provided information about gallery operations and the challenges of the marketplace. The views expressed in the text, however, are not necessarily shared by all.

Appraisers Leatrice Eagle, Shelly Zegart, Julia Zgliniec; art consultants Penny McMorris, Maxine Manges of MKM Fine Art, and Judith Lepow of Galman Lepow Associates; and insurance executives Bill Lyle, Christine Johnson of Phoenix, Arizona, and Ida Ziewacz of AXA Art all contributed to my understanding of these specialties as they relate to quilt art.

Friends and fellow quiltmakers Marilyn Hamaker, Betsy Harris, and Judy Pleiss gave me both practical help and useful suggestions. The enthusiasm of Robyn Krauthammer and Suzanne Garment for the project when it was only an idea was more important than they probably realize.

A special thank-you is due to my editor, Robert J. Sloan at Indiana University Press, who first suggested a book about quilts, and to the staff at the Press, including Anne Clemmer, Bernadette Zoss, Dan Pyle, Miki Bird, Pam Rude, and freelancer Jane Curran, for patiently leading me through the process of putting it together.

Most important has been my family, especially my husband, Les. His continuing support and his confidence in me have been invaluable. Without his gentle but insistent reminders, I would, no doubt, still be conducting the research.

NOTE ON TERMINOLOGY

Ludmila Uspenskaya, *Arcanum,*
2002, 37 × 36. Silk and cotton.
Hand-painted, wax resist; collage,
machine and hand quilted.
Photo: Karen Bell

The terms *quilt art, studio quilt, studio art quilt,* and *art quilt* are often used interchangeably. Preference is given to *studio quilt* in this text. All four terms are used for exhibits and published material about this art form. Strictly speaking, the terms *fiber* and *textile* are not interchangeable, although artists sometimes use them this way, as in *fiber art* and *textile art.* See the glossary for a definition of these terms. Art made with textile techniques is often included in the category of textile art, even if it is made with materials such as metal.

All terms appearing in bold typeface are defined in the glossary.

Anne McKenzie Nickolson,

Who Will Lead Us?

detail

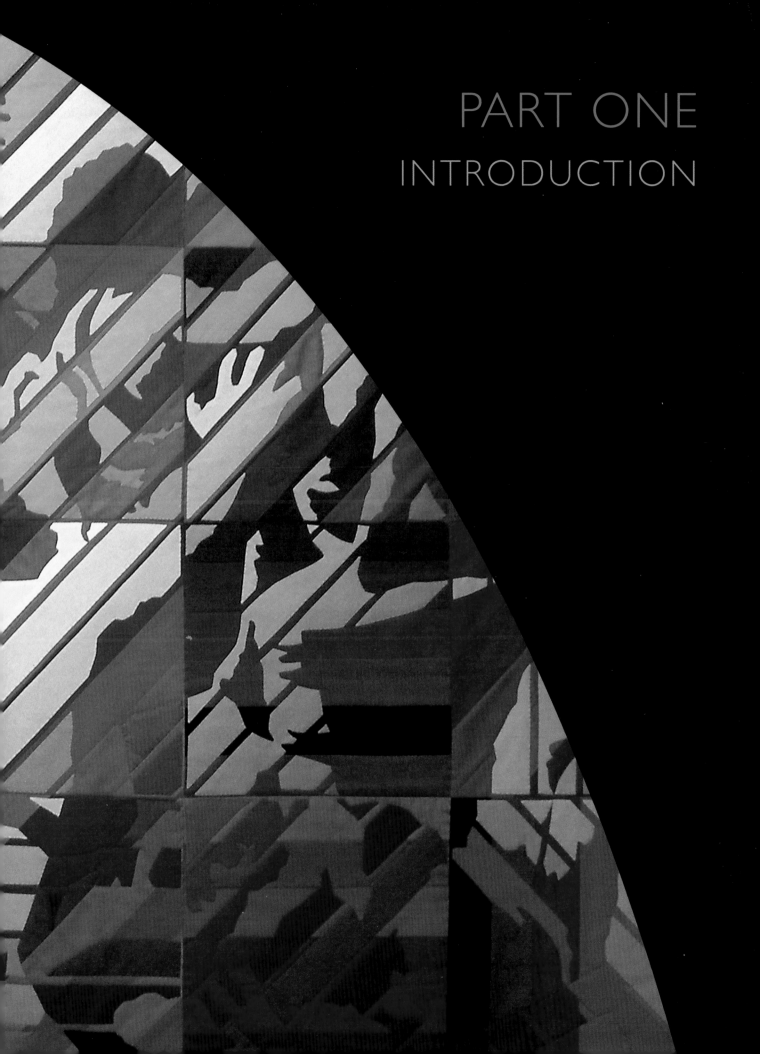

PART ONE
INTRODUCTION

Basket of Flowers,

c. 1860–1880, 80 × 86.

Cotton, appliqué. Ardis and Robert James

Collection, International Quilt Study Center,

University of Nebraska–Lincoln, 1997.007.0013

A New Art Form Evolves from a Traditional One

Studio quilts differ from traditional ones in several ways. Their structure is related to the bed quilt but sometimes departs from it in such a radical way that a viewer might wonder why a particular "quilt" is even called a quilt. Their aesthetics range from explorations of traditional design to the avant-garde. Their material components might include not only natural cotton, silk, wool, and linen, but also synthetic fabric, metal, and manmade, found, and organic objects. The most important distinction, however, is the intent of the artist.

Tradition   Because they have roots in both traditional quilts and fine art, a full appreciation of studio quilts requires familiarity with both. Traditional quilts typically, but not always, have three layers, with the center layer providing warmth.[1] These are held together by decorative stitching (the quilting) or by knots, which are evenly balanced across the surface. In the past, quilting motifs varied by era and region. They might be elaborate or simple. Geometric cross-hatching, meandering feather vines, and wreaths were, and still are, commonly used.

There are three kinds of traditional quilts: whole cloth, appliquéd, and pieced. The first is made by joining pieces of identical fabric together and then quilting them densely. The design is conveyed solely through the quilting stitches. Contemporary artists might also use this type of quilt surface as the ground for paint or image transfer processes such as **screen printing** and computer-manipulated digital image printing.

Original designs are found most often in appliquéd quilts. Floral imagery abounds, but there is also a narrative tradition associated with this kind of quilt. Making one is not unlike constructing a collage, although the overall effect is very different. Each element of the design is broken down into components which are cut and stitched carefully into place.

Pieced quilts are based on abstract designs. They are constructed by stitching together (piecing) small bits of fabric to form "blocks." These blocks have names which relate to everyday objects or to religious and historical events (for example, Flying Geese, Jacob's Ladder, Burgoyne Surrounded). They are joined to form the top layer of the quilt and are surrounded by one or more borders. Repetition of pattern and symmetry in the composition are common in pieced quilts. A variation is the "crazy quilt," popular during the Victorian era, for which fabrics were generally cut and pieced together in a manner that looked like shattered glass. They were then embellished with embroidered stitches and designs.

An important means by which quiltmaking traditions were preserved was the criteria of excellence established by judges in state and regional agricultural fairs. Here, quiltmakers competed with one another for awards. Judges looked for tiny, even stitches and perfectly matched corners and points. If the quilts were appliquéd, the stitches were to be invisible, the curves smooth with no bulges or puckers, and the points sharp without frayed edges. Furthermore, the quilts were to hang without rippling. In contemporary competitions of traditional quilts, these criteria are still applied, although innovation and artistry are rewarded, and new standards have been developed for machine quilting. Nonetheless, the quilts must demonstrate clear links to tradition and excellence in technique and craftsmanship.

Traditional quilts and quiltmaking have been studied and written about extensively, although there are myths that persist. What is clear is that quiltmaking was a leisure-time activity for some women and a matter of necessity for others; that elegance and artistry were not determined by income level or ethnic group; and that despite a tendency to rely on existing patterns, innovation flourished.

Michael Cummings, *I'll Fly Away,* 1991, 94¼ × 48.
Cotton, linen, blends, and canvas; pieced and painted;
hand-sewn embellishments including antique buttons,
African beads, and cowrie shells. Collection of the
Museum of Arts and Design. Museum purchase
with funds provided by the Horace W. Goldsmith
Foundation. Courtesy of the artist

Burgoyne Surrounded, 1900–1920, 86 × 69.
Cotton, pieced. Robert and Ardis James Collection,
International Quilt Study Center, University of
Nebraska–Lincoln, 1997.007.0395

Early Innovations   *Wild by Design: Two Hundred Years of Innovation and Artistry in American Quilts*, a scholarly book published by the International Quilt Study Center at the University of Nebraska–Lincoln, is filled with innovative and unconventional quilts.[2] Many more are illustrated in Robert Shaw's history, *Quilts: A Living Tradition*.[3]

Possibly the most famous of these, and among the most valuable, are two Bible quilts made by Harriet Powers in 1886 and 1898. Powers was a former slave living in Athens, Georgia.[4] Examples of some innovative twentieth-century appliqué quilts include the humorous yet pointedly political quilt *Prosperity Is Just around the Corner* (1930–1933), made by Fannie B. Shaw; Berthe Stenge's *The Quilt Show* (c. 1943); and the quilts designed by Ruth Clement Bond. Art historian Bernard Herman notes the sophistication of Stenge's content, calling it a conversation about quiltmaking and design.[5] Bond was an African American English professor and the wife of a sociologist hired by the Tennessee Valley Authority, who started a home beautification program for the wives of the sharecroppers working under her husband's direction. Bond had little experience quilting, but these women knew how to sew. Using her dynamic—and very contemporary—appliqué designs, they made quilts that remind us of the contributions of African Americans to a great and historic public works project in the segregated South.[6]

Above. Delectable Mountains variation, c. 1865–1885, 76 × 75; cotton, pieced. Robert and Ardis James Collection, International Quilt Study Center, Lincoln, Nebraska

Below. Ruth Clement Bond (designer) and Rose Marie Thomas (maker), Tennessee Valley Authority Appliqué Quilt Design of Man with a Black Fist, 1934, 12¾ × 10¾; cotton; pieced, sewn. Collection of the Museum of Arts and Design. Gift of Mrs. Rose Marie Thomas (maker), 1994. Courtesy of Jane Bond-Howard

Unique among the Crafts Quiltmaking is a time-consuming and labor-intensive craft. Why has it survived for so many years? One reason is that it requires the simplest of tools and is easily carried out in the home. For many generations it met a need for creative expression when women had few other outlets. For many, the family's need for warmth was of primary concern, but the opportunity to make something of interest and beauty was not lost by even the poorest makers. Quiltmaking is, as Robert Shaw has written, "the democratic art." If there was no money for new fabric, old fabric was used, and in the effort to salvage worn cloth, creativity flourished.[7]

The craft's resilience also comes from its communal nature. It has always been a social and civic enterprise as well as a familial and personal one. The "quilting bee" is a tradition most people are familiar with. But the response of today's quilt guilds to community needs has never been stronger. Hospitalized children, disaster victims, even families of soldiers killed in war have been comforted with quilts made through the group efforts of countless guilds.

Precisely because it is family-centered and its practitioners are mostly women, the history of quiltmaking deviates somewhat from the history of other American crafts. For nearly one hundred and fifty years, most commerce related to quilts has involved the sale of patterns and fabric. It cannot be compared to commerce in other handcrafts such as furniture, pottery, and glass, which were made in studios of artisans and sold for immediate use. Nor can it be compared with weaving. While some weaving took place in the home, its market was always broad based, and in the first half of the twentieth century, when most craft declined, some weavers found a market for their one-of-a-kind designs in industry.

This distinction is important. In their book *The Art Quilt*, historians Penny McMorris and Michael Kile trace the origin of studio quilts back to the Arts and Crafts movement founded in Britain in the mid-1800s.[8] The influence, however, was indirect; quiltmakers were not included among the artisans assisted by the movement. The Arts and Crafts movement had two purposes. One was to restore beauty—a victim of the new manufacturing processes—to functional objects. The second, and equally important, objective was to restore dignity and jobs to craftsmen, both lost with the advent of the Industrial Revolution. Craft studios were set up in Britain and across America to carry out these objectives. While now better known for the style associated with it, Arts and Crafts was just as much an economic movement as an aesthetic one.[9]

As McMorris and Kile point out, however, the aesthetics of the movement, which emphasized simplicity and the beauty of natural and unadorned materials, were promoted by nationally circulated women's magazines. The heavily embellished crazy quilts of the Victorians lost favor to the simpler designs of earlier times.

The authors document the path of American quiltmaking through the social, economic, commercial, and artistic history of the early twentieth century. They focus attention particularly on how change in these areas affected the levels of interest in quilts and the creativity of the quiltmakers. Improvements in manufacturing processes and in the chemistry of dyeing led to a greater variety of dye colors and printed fabrics, noticeable in quilts from the 1930s, but there was also an increasing reliance on published patterns and mail-ordered kits with pre-selected and pre-cut fabric. By the late 1930s, these developments led to a reduction in both creativity and interest in quiltmaking.

The Arrival of Modern Art and Some Talented Immigrants

Before quilt-making declined, however, other events of the late nineteenth and early twentieth centuries were taking place that were to affect all American visual arts by the late twentieth century. While American women were making quilts, competing in fairs, and helping to keep their families warm, the fine arts were undergoing a radical transformation. Beginning in Europe in the late nineteenth century, and slowly spreading to this country, modern art was dramatically altering painting and sculpture. The elements of composition—line, light, mass, color, shape, and form—took on greater importance to the artists than the objective representation of figures and scenes. They began to dismantle and reconstruct objects and scenes according to their own visions or ideas. They experimented with both representational and non-representational abstraction. They explored the expressiveness of the elements of art without any reference to figures or scenes. They substituted the texture of real objects like paper, cloth, and wood for paint, and they invented **collage**. The materials themselves became objects of interest.

The radical nature of European art reached even greater heights as the continent went through the long and devastating years of World War I. Mondrian's flat, bold, and impersonal geometric art, the anarchic artistic statements of the Dadaists, and the strange imagery of the Futurists and Surrealists slowly began to influence American artists. As Nazi power spread over Europe in the 1930s and 1940s, many of these artists fled to the United States. Among them were some of the architects, sculptors, painters (Lyonel Feininger, Vassily Kandinsky, and Josef Albers), and craftspeople (Anni Albers) who studied or taught at the Bauhaus School.[10] Albers's book *The Interaction of Color,* published many years later in 1963, became a classic text and is still used in art schools across the country. None of these events in the history of modern art were of importance to traditional quiltmakers. But their influence would be felt by the many art students who enrolled in school during the 1950s and 1960s. By the 1970s, some of these artists were making quilts.

At the end of World War I, a small stream of talented European textile artists also began arriving in America. Among them was an accomplished tapestry maker from Sweden, Loja Saarinen, wife of architect Eliel Saarinen. Loja established the weaving program at the new Cranbrook Academy of Art in Michigan in the 1920s. Cranbrook's weaving students were to play an

Arturo Alonzo Sandoval, *Pattern Fusion No. 2,* detail, 2004, 60½ × 60¾.
Machine stitched and interlaced; recycled auto industry Mylar, recycled library
35mm microfilm, netting, monofilament and multi-colored threads, plaited braid,
Pellon, polymer medium, fabric backed. Sandoval began using recycled materials
in his fiber art in 1969. His *Cityscape No. 2* is in the collection of the Museum of
Modern Art, NYC Collection; gift of Jack Lenor Larsen.

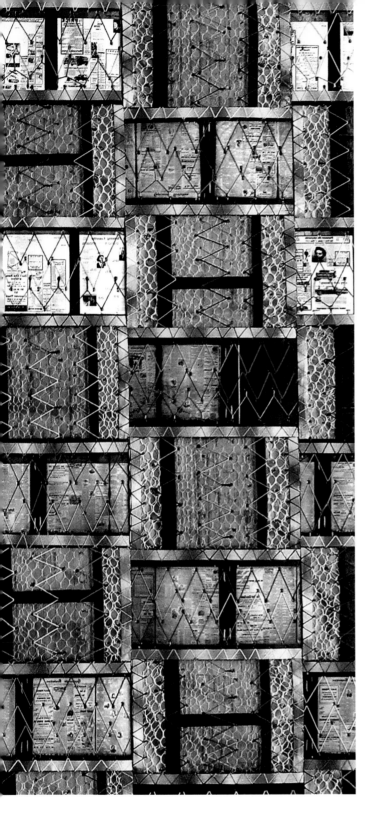

important role in the revival of fiber art in the years after World War II. Another prominent immigrant weaver was Anni Albers, the wife of painter Josef Albers and a student at the Bauhaus. Anni Albers taught at Black Mountain College in North Carolina and in workshops across the country. A third immigrant, who arrived here even earlier than Saarinen and Albers, was the talented Hungarian embroiderer Mariska Karasz. Karasz worked in clothing construction and costume design. She firmly believed that needlework could be an art form, and in the 1940s and 1950s she wrote several instructional books which encouraged American women to "abandon ready made patterns and produce their own designs."[11]

The Return of Studio Craft   Despite efforts to sustain it, by the 1940s there was real concern that quiltmaking would disappear; it was a fear that pervaded many of the crafts. The cost of handcrafted objects had become prohibitive during the economic Depression. By the time the Depression was over, manufactured goods were better designed and less costly. "Homemade" took on an association with poverty that "storebought" did not have. Moreover, the country's participation in World War II and the entry of women into the workforce left them with little time for leisure activities like quiltmaking even if they were interested.

The end of World War II, however, brought about startling and unpredicted developments. Given access to higher education by the GI Bill of Rights, thousands of returning veterans enrolled in school. Colleges and universities around the country expanded to meet their needs. Art historian Edward Lucie-Smith, in a historical essay written for the catalog of the 1986 Museum of American Craft exhibit "Craft Today: Poetry of the Physical," pointed out that the government ran craft programs during the war for soldiers and that many were exposed to craft in rehabilitation therapy during and after the war. With no restrictions on their course of study, some of the veterans "opted for craft training within a university framework." The result, he noted, was that not only were there more specialized art courses added to the curriculum, but there was also "an expansion of their scope and quality." This growth continued until the end of the 1960s.[12]

The new classes needed teachers, and the graduates quickly found academic positions of their own. The creativity in craft in the decades that followed was extraordinary. No longer was it necessary for these teaching craftsmen to rely on sales to support themselves. They returned to making one-of-a-kind objects and, with institutional support, experimented freely. Lucie-Smith suggests that the physical proximity of the craft programs to the art departments in many universities fostered the growth of "personal expression" in craft.

Market interest in craft remained low, despite the institutional support. The American Craftsmen's Cooperative Council and the American Craftsmen's Educational Council (ACEC), founded in 1943, worked together to "provide education in handcrafts and to further and stimulate public interest in and appreciation of the work of handcraftsmen." A driving force behind both organizations was Aileen Osborn Webb. Since the onset of the Depression, Webb had directed her philanthropy and organizational skills to the aid of craftsmen. In 1953 the ACEC sponsored the first of many national and regional competitions, giving recognition to the accomplishments of young artisans. Three years later, Webb founded the Museum of Contemporary Crafts (MCC) in New York City, the first museum to focus exclusively on contemporary works. Its primary aim was "to raise standards and stimulate interest in American craft."[13] The museum immediately started exhibiting the work of the new craft artists, including those in textile arts, and organized traveling exhibitions.

A New Spirit Emerges in Textile and Fiber Art For weavers (weaving being the only textile art taught at the university level) the experimental spirit of the 1950s and 1960s was liberating. Weaving is bound by rules and procedures; some were now challenging themselves to break the rules, to answer the question: What would happen if . . . ? One answer was off-loom woven construction, sometimes monumental in scope, and often three-dimensional. Artist and weaver Lenore Tawney, renowned for the expressiveness of her work, invented a means which allowed for altering the space between **warp** threads. Her invention enabled her to break out of the rigid rectangularity of traditional loom weaving and to create transparent woven constructions. Even the humble craft of basketry, an ancient off-loom woven form, was re-invigorated with fresh ideas from artists and teachers such as Ed Rossbach, a former Cranbrook student who experimented with recycled, common materials. Rossbach's books "strongly contributed to the emergence of artists who use basketry techniques to create sculptural forms."[14]

Although never part of craft studies in this country, embroidery in its classic form is also subject to rules and judged by strict criteria. It, too, was "loosening up." A memorial retrospective of Mariska Karasz's work was held at the MCC in 1961. In 1965 another MCC exhibit featured works of fabric collage. By the end of the decade, "stitchery," an art form combining embroidery and abstract fabric collage, seen in Paris in 1939, had become popular.[15] American embroidery received another boost in the late 1960s from Con-

Lenore Tawney,
The King I, 1962, 148 × 31.
Linen; woven.

B. J. Adams,
August Plenitude, 1998, 46 × 28.
Free-motion machine embroidery over
hand-painted cotton, pleated, quilted.

stance Howard, an embroiderer and retired director of the textile department at Goldsmiths College in London. Howard, who was well-known for her rule breaking, made regular trips to the United States and taught in workshops on both the East and West coasts.[16] Several American artists now making studio quilts took classes with her, including Joan Schulze and B. J. Adams.

By the 1970s, the experimental spirit had spread to quiltmaking. It was not only veterans but also women who benefited from the expansion of craft studies and the expanded art departments in the universities. The number of women in the arts was increasing. As early as 1956, Jean Ray Laury, a design student at Stanford University, submitted a quilt to meet her degree requirements. The quilt had a traditional block layout; the appliquéd designs in each block were utterly untraditional. In the years that followed, Laury became a prolific author and designer. Her first platform was *House Beautiful* magazine, a nationally circulated women's magazine. Laury's audience, like Karasz's, consisted mostly of homemakers, not people who intended to make a career of quiltmaking. She believed women needed a creative outlet. To be creative, she wrote, one needed enthusiasm, patience, and inventiveness.[17] Her greatest concern was not what they produced. "[S]he encouraged so many of us to pursue our own creative dreams and more importantly, to take our work seriously," said studio quilt artist Sue Pierce.[18] Laury's own work is contemporary, often humorous, and it frequently carries a message. Quilts attract an audience which would not otherwise pay attention, she believes. In 1960 Laury's wall hangings were exhibited at the Museum of Contemporary Crafts. In 2006 the San Jose Museum of Quilts and Textiles had a retrospective of her work. She has been teaching, writing, creating, and exhibiting her work for more than forty years.

The "New" Modern Art Takes Center Stage Despite the excitement within their own community about the new direction that craft was taking, academic craftspeople did not receive the public attention that artists working in the "higher" art forms did. American artists, critics, and historians have always engaged in discussions, debates, and polemics about the nature of art, its purpose, and its content. **Abstract Expressionism**, which emerged in the 1940s, was thought by some to be the first truly American art movement. The painters associated with it conspicuously rejected representational art. They found their inspiration and imagery by looking within their own psyches. Abstraction dominated to such an extent that figurative and landscape artists were virtually ignored by the critics. From Abstract Expressionism, several other movements evolved—**Color Field painting**, **Minimalism**, and **Post-Minimalism**. "Decorative" became a pejorative term. Formalism, or the study and critique of art based solely on the formal elements of its composition, prevailed. By the mid-1960s, however, this tide was turning. These movements were called "elitist" and were criticized for being too removed from everyday life. **Pop Art** offered a different view al-

together. Its artists resurrected representational art, but their imagery came from commerce, mass production, and street culture. Pop Art ushered in a new era, which has persisted into the twenty-first century, and radically transformed the landscape of American art. The ideas underlying all these art movements and the visual images they spawned were soon familiar to art students working in all media.

Fiber and Textile Art Begin to Flourish   Even without art world attention, craft continued its widespread revival. In the 1950s a textile arts community was taking root and beginning to flourish in the San Francisco Bay area of California. In 1952, weaver and ceramicist Ed Rossbach joined the faculty of the University of California–Berkeley. A few years later, his wife, artist Katherine Westphal, was named the director of the new design department of University of California–Davis. Through their art and teaching, they soon became influential figures in what is now called the Fiber Art movement. Collections of African, non-Western, and twentieth-century Italian textiles from the decorative arts and anthropology departments of California universities were already available to students for study. These were supplemented by samples and photographs of textiles, textile-dyeing processes, and construction methods which Rossbach and Westphal brought back from their global travels. By the mid-1970s, non-Western techniques for **dyeing** fabric (**ikat**, **batik**, and **shibori**) were being taught all over the country to eager textile students and artists.

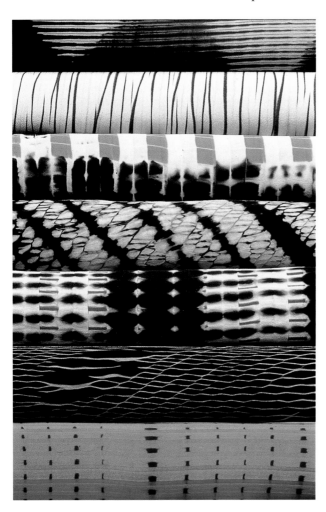

Ana Lisa Hedstrom, examples of **arashi shibori** on silk.

The collections, samples, and slides were inspiration for students and artists and influenced their art (and clothing) almost immediately. Native American textiles and the newly discovered **molas** of the San Blas Island Indians had a similar effect. Ancient methods of textile construction and dyeing were revived, experimented with, and updated, giving them a more contemporary look. It was not only the construction, aesthetics, and colors of these items which were of interest, but the signs and symbols in their imagery. Some artists appropriated this imagery as decoration; others sought to evoke its meaning.

Westphal, like her husband, was an experimenter. She was trained as a painter but worked with numerous media, often mixing them. Her focus, however, was on art, not the media or the technique, and she taught her students this way. "My work represented solutions to certain problems," she says. "Sometimes, not always, a quilt was the best solution."[19] A retrospective of her work in the early 1990s included vessels, collage, printed fabric, quilts, and books. The artist had painted, printed, and even photocopied imagery onto the surfaces of these objects, which dated back to the early days of her career. In a 1993 essay, Westphal wrote that all artists learn from the visions of other artists. She cited, in particular, Robert Rauschenberg, who was "using the **frottage** method of rubbing a newspaper image into a surface" in the early 1950s, and Andy Warhol, who used serial silk-screened images in the 1960s.[20] Westphal was not part of the community of quiltmakers on the West Coast. Nonetheless, her pioneering efforts and the work of those who followed in her footsteps have played an important part in the history of the studio quilt. Her quilts are in the collections of the Renwick Gallery of the Smithsonian American Art Museum, the Museum of Arts & Design in New York City, the de Young Museum in San Francisco, and the Museum of Fine Arts, Boston.

"Homemade" Makes a Comeback and Quilt Guilds Proliferate

It was not until the 1960s that the public's interest in handcraft finally began to rise, spurred by the development of a counterculture whose members found they could sustain their "back to the land" lifestyle by making and selling craft items. Hippie culture became a "springboard" for a new, handmade art form, Artwear, which emerged in the early 1970s on both the East and West coasts.[21] In New York City and elsewhere, galleries began to sell antique quilts and to secure nationwide attention for them in antique and interior design magazines. Both professionally trained artists and craftspeople participated in this revival and benefited from the expanding markets.[22]

The renewed interest in craft led to a great revival of traditional quiltmaking, later heightened by the upcoming Bicentennial, a revival that still shows no signs of abating. Beginning with the founding of the National Quilting Association in 1970 and followed in 1975 by the first annual International Quilt Festival—it was national at the time—in Houston, Texas, and the Quilt Market, a trade show in 1979, quiltmakers were beginning to make their presence felt. Quilt shops opened all over the country. Textile companies were persuaded to renew production of the all-cotton fabrics favored by quiltmakers and were soon designing fabric just for them. Time-saving tools like rotary cutters were introduced. Guilds proliferated, offering fellowship, educational workshops, and exhibit opportunities to enthusiasts. In 1985 another major annual quilt competition was announced by the new American Quilter's Society (AQS) in Paducah, Kentucky. Six years later, AQS opened a museum. The *Quilter's Newsletter Magazine*, founded in 1969 as a service for the customers of Bonnie Leman's mail-order business, had an initial circulation of 5,000.[23] Today the newsletter has a circulation of 194,000 under the title *Quilters Newsletter*, and it is only one of numerous quilt magazines. Market research recently found that there were more than 27 million Americans who participated in some form of quiltmaking in 2006. The total value of their spending amounted to $3.3 billion.[24]

A New Art Form Begins to Evolve: Early Influences and Challenges

The momentum to move beyond the traditional in quiltmaking did not pick

up until the 1970s, although there were several artists who did so in the 1960s. One of these was Radka Donnell, a painter born in Eastern Europe who obtained an MFA from the University of Colorado. While raising two daughters, Donnell began to make quilts; for her these proved to be a medium for "artistic and political liberation." Quilts connected her American identity with her Balkan and ethnic roots. "With my work on quilts I was distancing myself from the scene, the intention, and the rhetoric of Western art," she wrote.[25] Donnell "found in the quilt a powerful but hidden history of female artistic expression that paralleled the more accepted world of male-dominated High Art."[26] The artist worked hard on behalf of women's art at a time when feminists in the academic art world were distrustful of the domestic associations of quiltmaking.[27] By the early 1970s attitudes were beginning to change. The New York abstract painter Miriam Schapiro, living in California at the time, began using lace and chintz, along with sewing, quilting, and appliqué in her art, works she termed "femmage." The suspicion of feminist academics eventually gave way to praise and encouragement for women who used domestic materials and forms in their art. Although only a small percentage of studio quiltmakers were influenced by the **Feminist Art Theory** that arose in the 1980s, the feminist movement was of major importance to the development of studio quilts.

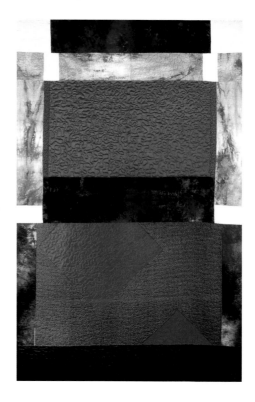

Radka Donnell, *Praise the Goddess,* 2000, 72½ × 52½. Cotton, synthetic fabric; tie-dyed, hand and machine pieced, machine quilted by Joannie Decker. Collection of the Museum of Arts and Design. Gift of Polly and Mitko Zagoroff-Drinkwater, 2003. Courtesy of the artist

In addition to Donnell, Westphal, and Laury, other artists who made or designed quilts in the 1960s were Charles and Rubynelle Counts, M. Joan Lintault, and Therese May. Best known for their pottery, the Counts had studied in California with Marguerite Wildenhain, the noted Bauhaus-trained potter who emigrated from Holland in 1940. They settled in Rising Fawn, Georgia, where they produced and sold pottery. But they also

Facing page. Katherine Westphal,
Unveiling of the Statue of Liberty, 1964,
92¾ × 66½. Batiked, quilted, and embroidered fabric.
Collection of the Renwick Gallery, Smithsonian Museum
of American Art, Washington, D.C. Gift of Katherine
Westphal Rossbach. Courtesy of the artist

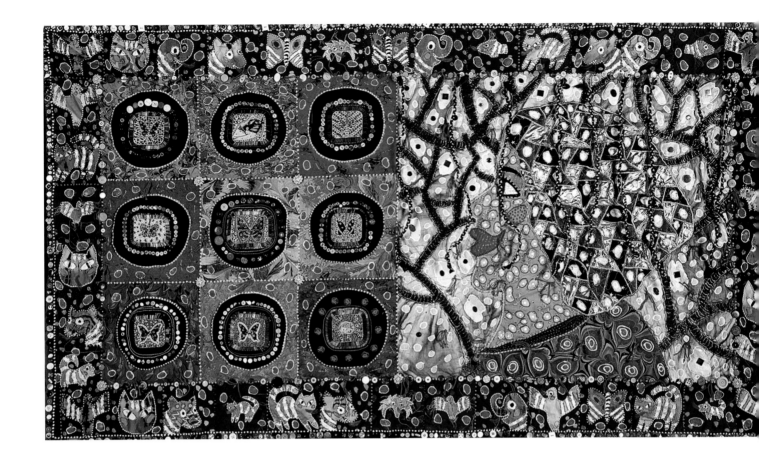

Therese May, *Contemplating the Ninepatch,* 1994, 92 × 50. Fabric, thread; machine appliqué, paint, buttons, beads, braids, polymer clay. May has used the quilt as an art form since the late 1960s.

designed distinctive quilt tops which were stitched and quilted by a group of local women known as the Rising Fawn Quilters. Robert Shaw traces the paths taken by all these pioneers and discusses the ideas and beliefs which guided and sustained them. He quotes from M. Joan Lintault's writings: "I never wanted to be a traditional quiltmaker. I wanted to use all the elements of art that I was taught by using the thread as line, fabric as shape, and color as a painter" (see Lintault's *An American Graveyard*). Addressing a concern of artists to this day, she adds, "I could never understand why there was this deep prejudice against artists who used fabric and fiber. I still don't understand it."[28]

Museums Play a Role In the mid-1960s, at a time when **Optical Art** was popular with the public, the Newark Museum in New Jersey held what may have been the first quilt exhibit to draw attention to the similarities between quilts and contemporary art. *Optical Quilts* demonstrated how quiltmakers had been creating the illusion of movement in their work for decades. But it was two exhibits in the 1970s that played key roles in the development of studio quilts. These were the 1971 exhibit at the Whitney Museum in New York City entitled *Abstract Design in American Quilts* and the 1976 exhibit at the Museum of Contemporary Crafts entitled *The New American Quilt.*

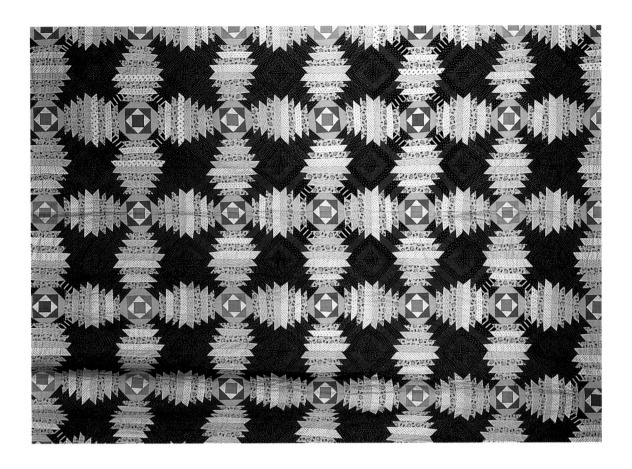

Pineapples, detail, c. 1875, 92 × 87, cotton; pieced. Collection of Jonathan Holstein

Jonathan Holstein and Gail van der Hoof curated the first of these from antique pieced quilts in their own collection. In his "biography" of the exhibition, written in 1991 when the original exhibit was re-mounted in Kentucky, Holstein wrote: "[I]t introduced American artists, particularly younger artists, to an indigenous American design form which carried no art historical baggage and which pre-dated the birth of similar modes of expression among European abstractionists and non-representational painters."[29] "The notion that quilts could be art and quiltmakers artists," observed Robert Shaw, "touched a nerve with a number of young academically trained painters, weavers, ceramicists and other visual artists."[30]

In the exhibit, Holstein and van der Hoof focused attention on the aesthetics of these quilts and pointed out their strong similarities to contemporary abstract painting. The exhibit drew huge crowds, but the reaction was not all favorable. The curators were criticized by feminists for focusing narrowly on the aesthetics and providing no information about the makers, and by traditional quiltmakers for choosing quilts which did not meet the traditional criteria for excellence. Nonetheless, the quilts were given recognition by notable art critics and caused a stir in the art world.[31] As both Holstein and Shaw have suggested, the show energized both artists and quiltmakers who saw it. They quickly recognized the potential of the quilt as a medium for art. Because the exhibit traveled to other museums in America and Europe after closing in New York, the discussion about the aesthetics of the quilts and related issues was widespread.

The Whitney exhibit presented a new way of looking at antique quilts. It did not present new quilts and did not influence everyone who later used cloth and quilts as an art medium. In her history of the art quilt in Ohio, Gayle F. Pritchard notes that few studio quiltmakers in that state saw the exhibit. She suggests that its greatest impact may have been due to the mass media coverage and the resulting dialogue about this newly discovered "art" in reviews and critical writing.[32] With the quilts displayed in a museum context, completely removed from any functional purpose, and exhibited vertically on the walls, their existence, and the resulting implications, could not be ignored by the art world.

The New American Quilt exhibit in 1976 was, as its title states, about new work, not antiques. Paul J. Smith, a young artist who had been working at the Museum of Contemporary Crafts in New York since shortly after its opening in the mid-1950s, was named the director in 1963. During his twenty-four-year tenure, Smith traveled throughout the country, seeking out promising craft artists. He organized and curated countless exhibits of their work. His vantage point, as the director of the only museum of its kind at the time, was unique, and the exhibits reflected what was happening in all the craft media during those important years. In the early 1960s, Smith exhibited the work of Jean Ray Laury. In *The New American Quilt*, thirty-eight works by twenty-four artists, including Teresa Barkley, Helen Bitar, Lenore Davis, Radka Donnell, Gayle Fraas and Duncan Slade, Susan Hoffman, M. Joan Lintault, Molly Upton, Wenda F. von Wiese, and Katherine Westphal, were shown. The artists in this exhibit represented some of the best in the field in the early 1970s.

Interest in contemporary quiltmaking grew rapidly in the late 1970s, and some gallery directors were paying attention. Radka Donnell, Molly Upton, and Susan Hoffman had an exhibit of their work at the Carpenter Center for the Arts at Harvard University in 1975.[33] That same year, a non-competitive quilt exhibit that was part of the Massachusetts Bicentennial celebration was filled with contemporary works.[34] All these exhibits, especially those in museums and galleries, reinforced the validity of the quilt as an art form.

Old Skills Are Revived Decades of neglect, however, meant there were neither proficient quiltmakers to teach nor instructional materials for those now eager to learn the fundamentals. Most people relied on the pictures of block designs in *The Romance of the Patchwork Quilt*, a book written in 1935 by Carrie A. Hall and Rose G. Kretsinger. In 1973 quiltmaker Beth Gutcheon published an instructional book, which began to fill the gap, and followed it a few years later with *The Quilt Design Workbook*, written with her husband Jeffrey, an architect and quiltmaker. These books, and two others by the artist Michael James dated 1978 and 1981, were eagerly sought

after. The second Gutcheon book appealed to those who wanted to move beyond the basic pattern structure, by showing how that structure could be changed. It was important to artists such as Nancy Halpern, who had begun to make quilts out of love for the traditional designs. The Gutcheons helped her realize she could do something completely different. Halpern went on to make her own contribution by breaking free from traditional quilting motifs. In *Falls Island, Reversing Falls* she introduced what Michael James described as a "very fluid, freely drawn quilting design in combination with a crisply drawn geometric pieced surface . . . a vortex of curvilinear forms swirling and blending and crossing with total abandon."[35]

Some quiltmakers moved quickly from the traditional patterns to creating new designs, imagery, and structures. Molly Upton was among them; her intent was to create art, and she approached the medium freely, without prejudice toward the synthetic fabrics that the traditionalists rejected. Some of her geometric abstractions are "electrifying," wrote one reviewer.

Molly Upton, *Watchtower,* 1975,

110 × 90. Pieced, cotton and blends.

Courtesy of Barbara Upton

Artists Take Charge of the Medium The growing interest of textile artists at this time in exploring techniques of "surface design" was another encouraging development. The emphasis in textile arts until then was on construction, but many artists were also interested in dyeing and printing. A conference organized to discuss these topics and provide workshops for teaching them was overwhelmed with attendees. A newsletter, which eventually became the *Surface Design Journal,* was initiated, and in 1976 the Surface Design Association was founded.[36]

Surface design "encompasses the coloring, patterning and structuring of fiber and fabric. This involves the creative exploration of processes such as dyeing, painting, printing, stitching, embellishing, quilting, weaving, knitting, felting, and papermaking."[37] The most common form of surface design is hand dyeing of cloth—now safe to carry out in home studios because of the development of **fiber-reactive dyes** in the 1950s. In the same year that the association's first conference was held, the Museum of Contemporary Crafts was recognizing excellence in hand dyed textiles with an exhibit called *The Dyer's Art: Ikat, Batik, Plangi.*[38]

It was not long before artists and quiltmakers were learning techniques of surface design. In 1978 New England studio quilt artists Gayle Fraas and Duncan Slade began to teach workshops covering techniques for printing, air brushing, screen printing, and painting with fiber-reactive dyes. In 1984 and 1985 they were invited to teach dye painting on the West Coast, where quiltmakers Yvonne Porcella, Linda MacDonald, Miriam Nathan Roberts,

Nancy Halpern, *Falls Island, Reversing Falls,*
1979, 84 × 84. Pieced cotton quilt.
Photo: David Caras

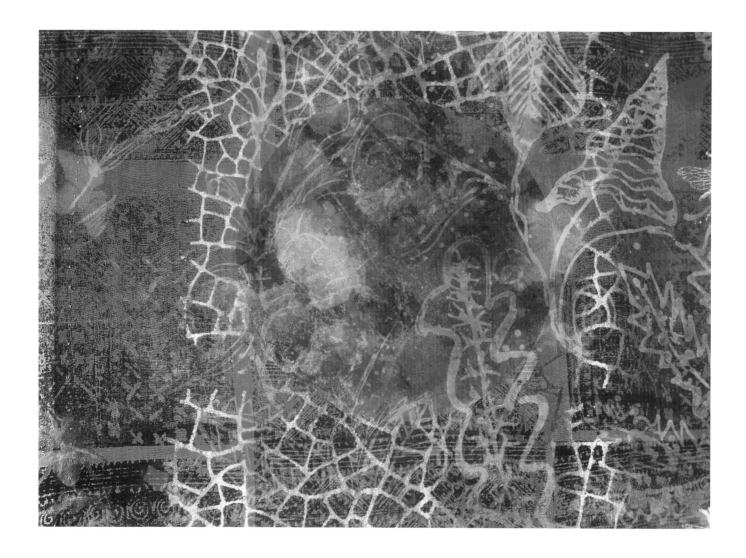

Jane Dunnewold, *Paradise II*, detail, 2005. Dunnewold has written extensively on techniques of surface design. This example of her work illustrates screen printing, hand painting, and the use of dyes and gold leaf on silk habotai and silk organza. *Paradise II* is also hand stitched and beaded.

and Ann Johnston were among their students. "As quiltmakers, 'what the work looks like . . . what it's communicating' has always been most important," say Fraas and Slade. "With fiber-reactive dyes we found a medium with which we could paint and screen print on whole cloth works in a studio setting, exploring all our visual interests. It was the easiest, most direct way we could get our ideas onto a fabric surface."[39] Their comments illustrate the creative potential that surface design has for artists, whom it continues to draw to quiltmaking.

Building a Support System With the exception of the Museum of Contemporary Crafts and the Newark Museum in New Jersey, few art institutions (museums, galleries, and schools) gave quilt artists support in the 1970s. Furthermore, their association with the traditional guilds was not a comfortable one, although it was through the guilds that these artists often found one another. Dissatisfied with guild exhibitions as venues for unconventional quilts and with the lack of other exhibition opportunities, in 1979 Ohio artists Nancy Crow, Françoise Barnes, and Virginia Randles organized the first competitive exhibition of non-traditional, contemporary quilts in

Gayle Fraas and Duncan Slade,
North Woods Suite: Waterfall,
2002, 76 × 76. Whole cloth
quilt, dye-painted and printed on
cotton, machine and hand stitched,
fused metal foil. Collection of
Nuveen Investments, Inc., Chicago

Below. *North Woods Suite:
Waterfall*, detail

Linda MacDonald,

Migration of the California Red-Legged Frog,

2002, 39 × 36. Cotton broadcloth; airbrushed,

hand painted and hand quilted.

Athens, Ohio. *Quilt National* soon became an international biennial event and now receives an average of 1,400 entries for approximately 65 selections for the juried show. It is considered to be the premier venue for exhibition of new work by many artists.

In the 1980s other venues were found in university galleries and art centers. More juried competitions were organized. On the West Coast, *Quilt Visions*, a second biennial national competition, was established in San Diego, California. Since its founding in 1986, *Quilt Visions*, which is slightly smaller than *Quilt National*, has become almost as prominent as its forerunner. Award-winning artists enter both competitions. Another development of the 1980s was the formation of formal and informal associations for the purpose of exchanging ideas, intellectual stimulation, and mutual support in New England, Ohio, New York, and the Northwest. One of the first was organized by quilt artists Linda Fowler and Nancy Crow in Ohio. Members of the Art Quilt Network were required to be "serious about their work and about exhibiting it."[40] Since then, similar networks have been organized in other parts of the country.[41]

Early in the 1980s, a few galleries devoted to "fine craft" began to represent quilt artists, notably the Works Gallery (now Snyderman-Works Gallery) in Philadelphia. As the decade progressed and the country's economy did well, corporations began to collect and commission textile art, including studio quilts, for their art collections and for the decoration of their headquarters and offices. Quilt artists were represented in the collections of the Federal Reserve, IBM, and AT&T. Medical centers such as Kaiser Permanente, countless hospitals, research centers, businesses, banks, industries, and hotel chains, working with art consultants, commissioned contemporary quilt art.

The New Quilts The broader public, however, was still largely unaware of the new quilts. To address this problem, in 1986 Michael Kile and Penny McMorris curated an exhibit for the Los Angeles Municipal Art Gallery which captured the breadth and the quality of studio quilts being made by the leading artists. With some notable exceptions, artistic explorations with the new medium in the early 1970s were fairly conservative, although they were still very different from traditional quilts. The artists experimented with geometric shapes, curves, the surface plane, spatial illusion, light, movement, and color. The twenty-eight quilts in the 1986 exhibit *The Art Quilt* represented a greater move away from the tradition. There were abstract, realist, surrealist, and narrative works. Still, the curators pointed out that the quiltmaking techniques were traditional. (Hand dyeing, stenciling, and painting had been used in the early nineteenth century; embroidery was used on bed coverings even earlier. Photo transfer could be found in Victorian crazy quilts.) "The difference between the works of these quilt artists and more traditional quilts is not in techniques," they wrote, "but in the application of those techniques and the choice of subject matter. . . . Today's quilt artists are proficient in the technical aspects of their craft and, being so, they are apply-

Terrie Hancock Mangat, *American Heritage Flea Market*, 1986, 84½ × 70. Cotton, cotton blends, and silk; pieced, appliquéd, embroidered; embellished with various ornaments. Hand quilted by Sue Rule. Exhibited in 1986 in *The Art Quilt,* curated by Penny McMorris and Michael Kile. Collection of John M. Walsh III

ing those techniques in new ways as they expand beyond subject matter once considered appropriate for quilts."[42] Artists represented in this exhibit, which toured the country after closing in Los Angeles, were Terese Agnew, Pauline Burbidge, Nancy Crow, Deborah J. Felix, Veronica Fitzgerald, Gayle Fraas and Duncan Slade, Jean Hewes, Michael James, M. Joan Lintault, Terrie Hancock Mangat, Therese May, Ruth McDowell, Risë Nagin, Yvonne Porcella, Joan Schulze, and Pamela Studstill.

An Important Question Is Raised   The same year that *The Art Quilt* began its tour, art critic Janet Koplos wrote an article for *Fiberarts* magazine in which she addressed a topic of increasing importance: "How do we decide whether a work of fiber is 'good'?" Now that quilts were being made by artists, it was important that this topic be addressed. How was this art to be judged? What criteria should be used? Koplos first noted that aesthetic creations range widely and, also, that definitions of art vary over time. She offered the following definition: "Among the factors that seem to define art today [1986], are originality, an ability to communicate an idea or emotion or some sort of message, a transcendence of the literal, and a quality of mystery or multivalence. Art involves some personal expression by the maker as well as expressive choices that are not simply arbitrary, but have some explainable meaning. Art is not just a concrete object; rather, it operates on a metaphoric level—the concrete object refers to other things, and the personal idea or image suggests a universal that can be shared. Art is never a simple or obvious statement; instead there is always a depth to it that holds our interest and allows the art work to be reinterpreted over time."[43]

Koplos went on to address problems which resonated in 1986, and which continue to resonate. "When fiber art fails as art, the explanation is usually too much reliance on material or technique to carry the work, banal content or no content (decorativeness or formalism), or too personal a content. There is nothing wrong," she continued, "with formalism or privateness—decorative works give visual pleasure and purely personal works can have psychological importance to the maker. Good art is broader."[44]

Koplos's commentary was especially timely because the number of traditional quiltmakers interested in designing their own quilts was increasing. Many were hobbyists who had little education in the arts and who did not approach their quiltmaking with the discipline required of professional artists. Adapting the title of the 1986 McMorris and Kile exhibit to their own use, these quiltmakers began to call themselves "art quilters."

Achieving Professional Status   By 1989, more studio quilts were being shown in craft and university galleries. Martha Stamm Connell, owner of the Great American Gallery in Atlanta, Georgia, urged some of the artists whom she knew to organize to promote their work to art publications, private galleries, and museums. Artist Yvonne Porcella took the lead, and in 1990 the Studio Art Quilt Associates (SAQA) was founded. Porcella was a

Anna Torma, *Jardin du Wiltz III*, 2006, 65 × 51. Hand embroidery on linen base, silk threads; quilted. Torma uses the traditionally decorative needlecraft of embroidery to create evocative contemporary studio quilts. Collection of the artist. Photo: Natalie Matutschovsky

prominent participant in the Artwear movement on the West Coast in the 1970s and had been making studio quilts since the early 1980s. SAQA's aims were to educate the public about the studio art quilt, serve as a forum for professional development of quilt artists, and act as a resource for curators, dealers, art consultants, teachers, students, and collectors.[45]

SAQA did not limit its membership to professional artists. However, it did establish a separate membership level for them and gave them an opportunity to have their work included in a portfolio to be used as a marketing tool with galleries, museums, and art consultants. In 1992 SAQA established an online registry of contemporary quilt art installed in public and private institutions throughout the country; the following year, another was established for quilts in museum collections. Its website is a valuable resource for artists and collectors alike. Both its regional chapters and national organization hold competitive exhibits of members' works. SAQA's national conferences and publications focus on professional development.

From the beginning, SAQA has been concerned with serving both beginning and professional artist members. It is not an easy task; the inter-

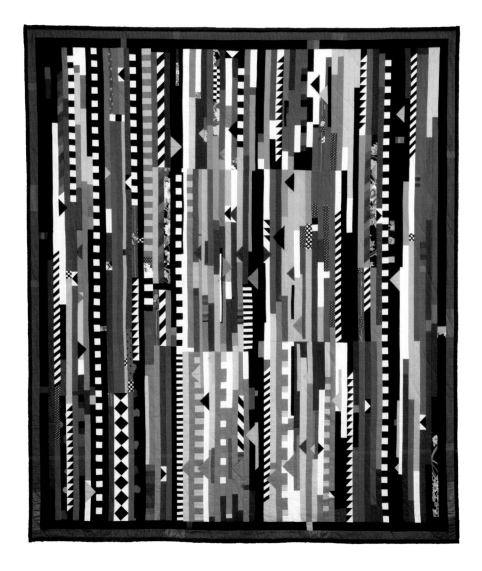

ests of hobbyists, beginning artists, and professional artists are not identical. As more people joined in the 1990s, the definition of "professional" became more important. Guidelines for the professional category are rigorous, but self-imposed. Between 1990 and 2006, membership grew from 50 to nearly 1,600 and now includes artists, teachers, collectors, gallery owners, museum curators, and corporate sponsors. By 2006, 320 of these were professional artists. It is worth noting that in comparison with the total number of people in the country involved in quiltmaking, these figures are minuscule.

Even before the founding of SAQA, the need for more and better professional education was becoming apparent. Without it, progress in developing standards of excellence would be slow and full acceptance of the art form delayed. Craft schools such as Haystack Mountain School in Maine and Arrowmont School of Arts and Crafts in Tennessee offered courses, but these classes and the workshops taught by such traveling artists as Nancy Crow and Michael James were not part of an organized program of study. "I realized that we desperately needed an intensive study program just for contemporary quiltmakers," said Nancy Crow.[46] In 1990 Crow and Linda Fowler co-founded the Quilt Surface Design Symposium to provide instruction in basic design and composition, and in techniques of surface design. Since then, the symposium has provided two-day and five-day classes each June for a two-week period.

Many other workshops, taught by accomplished studio artists, take place all over the country. They are sponsored by professional associations, quilt exhibit sponsors, and art centers and last from a few hours to a few weeks. Artist and teacher Katie Pasquini-Masopust, for example, established Alegre Retreat for quilt artists in 1991 and continued to hold this annual workshop for fourteen years in Santa Fe, New Mexico. In 2002, after relinquishing her share in the Quilt Surface Design Symposium, Crow turned a large barn, which she had moved onto her property, into classrooms and studios and established another educational program—the Timber Frame Workshops. There, she and several other teachers teach beginning, intermediate, and advanced instruction in quiltmaking and surface design. Crow's focus in the classroom has always been design and composition, which she sees as skills that can only be mastered by intensive involvement in the process over many years.

New Challenges The rapid progress made in establishing the validity of the quilt medium in art in the 1980s did not continue at the same rate in the next decade. The economic recession at the end of the decade affected corporate support for the arts, and fewer artists obtained commissions. The fine art galleries and museums, which many artists had expected to begin welcoming them, did so only slowly.

Their expectations, not unreasonably, were based on the fact that many American artists had been making art with non-traditional objects and craft materials since the early 1950s. Robert Rauschenberg's famous *Bed* (1955), a mixed media artwork in which part of a traditional quilt was incorporated directly into a painting, had long since demonstrated to the art world the metaphoric and symbolic value of the medium. His "assemblages" of found objects were exhibited in major museums. So too were the sculptures of Louise Nevelson, who collected wood scraps, arranged them as abstract forms in wooden boxes, assembled them in an upright, modular format, and then painted them. (The grid of Nevelson's work, with an abstract form set within each "block," as well as certain aspects of the assembly and overall visual image of these works, is reminiscent of both the process of quiltmaking and traditional quilt design.) Claes Oldenburg's gigantic soft sculptures of fast food made in the 1960s from stuffed and painted fabric had entered museum collections, as did the 1970s pieced fabric collages of Lucas Samaras, which bear a strong resemblance to Victorian quilt patterning. More recently, ceramic artists Robert Arneson and Betty Woodman have had exhibits of their work at the Museum of Modern Art and the Metropolitan Museum of Art in New York City.

Anna Williams, *LIX: Log Cabin,* 1993, 76 × 64½. Pieced; cotton blends. The improvisational methods of this quilt-maker from Baton Rouge, Louisiana, had a significant impact on many studio quiltmakers after an exhibit of her work was held in the early 1990s at the Quilt Surface Design Symposium, Columbus, Ohio. Ardis and Robert James Collection, International Quilt Study Center, University of Nebraska–Lincoln, 1997.007.1104. Courtesy of the artist

But quilt artists, in particular, are confronted with the commonly believed equation "quilts = bedcovers and grandmothers." They are not equated with museum-quality art. Some gallery directors, collectors, and curators, however, believe that this perception will not change unless the artists move beyond the support system of quilt-only exhibits they constructed for themselves. Most will enter their work into art quilt competitions. Fewer enter fine art competitions, even when the competitions are open to art in all media. This limits their audience in the art world and, consequently, prevents their work from getting critical review, both of which are necessary if studio quilts are to gain greater acceptance.

David J. Hornung, a painter who made studio quilts in the 1980s, and who now chairs the art and art history department at Adelphi University in New York, believes that the emergence of **Conceptual Art** in the late 1960s and **Postmodernist Art Theory** in the 1980s have also contributed to the slow pace of acceptance. The Conceptual Art movement challenged the "preciousness" of the art object, which became secondary to the idea or concept of the artist. Its proponents believed that the idea or concept *was* the art. "When an artist uses a conceptual form of art, it means that all of the planning and decisions are made beforehand and the execution is a perfunctory affair," wrote artist Sol LeWitt, in a now famous essay. "The idea becomes a machine that makes the art. . . . [This kind of art] is usually free from the dependence on the skill of the artist as a craftsman."[47] "With the emergence of Conceptual art in the late 1960s," Hornung writes, "it became obvious that art in craft media and 'fine art' were heading in different directions. It would be more difficult for craft art to communicate in the idioms of Postmodernism without disowning 'craftsman-like workmanship' in a self-conscious way." Today, Postmodernism continues to be influential among critics and art professors at the graduate level, says Hornung. "To those critics and professors, contemporary art must embrace [its] assumptions. It should display indifference to formal structure or craft skill. [Postmodernism] is skeptical about historical continuity [in art] and authenticity, even about the existence of self. It views personal expression as misguided, corny and potentially self-indulgent." Art is seen as "fundamentally informational."[48] Conceptual Art and Postmodernist Theory gained prominence just as many artists were recognizing the value of fiber and quilts as expressive media. Not all quilt artists were, or are, concerned with the expressive characteristics of their medium. Nonetheless, these new, constricting ideas about art seemed to dismiss much of its metaphoric value.

In recent years, the art world's interest in the concept of "materiality" has increased. Perhaps this will lead to renewed attention to studio quilts, the ultimate material art form. The success of the studio quilt as art, however, depends more on the artists than it does on acceptance by the academic art world. The full spectrum of American art is extraordinarily diverse. That diversity is seen in the background and training of contemporary quiltmakers. They come from painting, sculpture, graphic art, dance, architecture, textile

Ellen Oppenheimer, *Chiyogami Murasaki #1*, 2006, 68 × 55. Cotton; pieced, screenprinted, and machine quilted.

design, fiber art, weaving, and ceramics. While all their art is influenced by contemporary life in one way or another, these artists do not dance to the same tune.

Some Final Thoughts and Observations At the end of her essay in *Fiberarts*, Janet Koplos raised what she called the "inevitable challenge" for the fiber artist: Why use fiber? The artist who chooses to use the quilt as her medium faces a similar challenge: Why a quilt?

Several writers have thought about these questions. Artist Lois Martin, in a 1995 essay published in *American Craft*, wrote, "both the sensuous richness and the symbolic, metaphorical aspect of fabrics and fiber are compelling." She found a relationship between quilts and the idea of "text." "Geometric patterns in traditional folk textiles are often associated with words. Some patterns are said to confer a protective status." She referred also to the quilting stitches: "The tiny pulsing of the quilting thread has its own quiet insistence, in and out, in and out, marking time like breathing. Sometimes the quilting lines echo the design of a quilt top; at other times they counterpoint it; at still other times they act as hidden separate messages. . . . Another

Robin Schwalb, *Chinese Characters*, 2006, 67 × 93. Cotton, stenciled, photo silk-screened; hand and machine appliquéd, machine pieced; hand quilted. Photo: Karen Bell

reverberating psychological aspect of the art quilt is that it never severs its symbolic association to the bed quilt. . . . Viewed as an act of 'writing on the bed'—symbolic locus of birth, sex and death—quiltmaking has a subversive quality. . . . The quilt is also the cloak of the dreamer."[49]

Patricia Malarcher has observed the fields of fiber art and contemporary quiltmaking from a singular vantage point as the editor of *Surface Design Journal.* In the 1950s she was a student of Color Field painter Kenneth Noland. Some of her essays about quilts as art are insightful explorations of both their symbolism and aspects of their structure. "[T]he notion of 'quiltness' implies scraps of cloth sewn together," she writes. "Piecework is not confined to fabric, but to an approach that achieves pattern and complexity in any material . . . fabric provides the added nuance of 'patchwork' with its own associations. A patch can suggest wear, frugality, humility (as in the patched robes of Buddhist monks), fragmentation, random arrangement." From a structural perspective, patchwork allows for intrinsic freedom, she writes, "allowing leeway for incongruity or the chance emergence of unplanned relationships."[50]

The structure of craft forms and its importance to composition have also been written about by Stuart Reid. He comments on the difference between a stained glass panel and a drawing. "The difference . . . is less the difference of colour, line, and shape and much more the difference of emphasis on the physical structure and its design." Reid continues, "Their physicality and structural necessity have to be treated as important factors in the visual composition if they are to amplify and not diminish the aesthetic experience."[51]

Reid alludes to what Paul J. Smith, director emeritus of the Museum of Arts and Design, refers to as the "craft aesthetic"—the unique character which results from the artist's intense involvement with materials and process. "Nearly all of the really good pieces," says Smith, "reflect that intensity and the knowledge that comes from it."[52]

Observations and reflections like those of Martin, Malarcher, Reid, and Smith are in the thoughts of artists every day as they persevere in their work. To be good requires the integration of the idea, expression, or meaning with the intrinsic characteristics of the quilt.

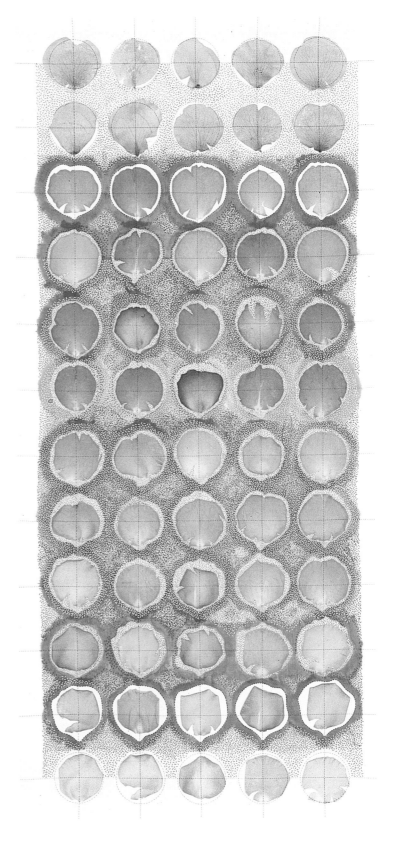

Ilze Aviks, *Improved Roses*, 2004, 80 × 38. Dyes and photo transfer on linen; painted, hand-stitched.

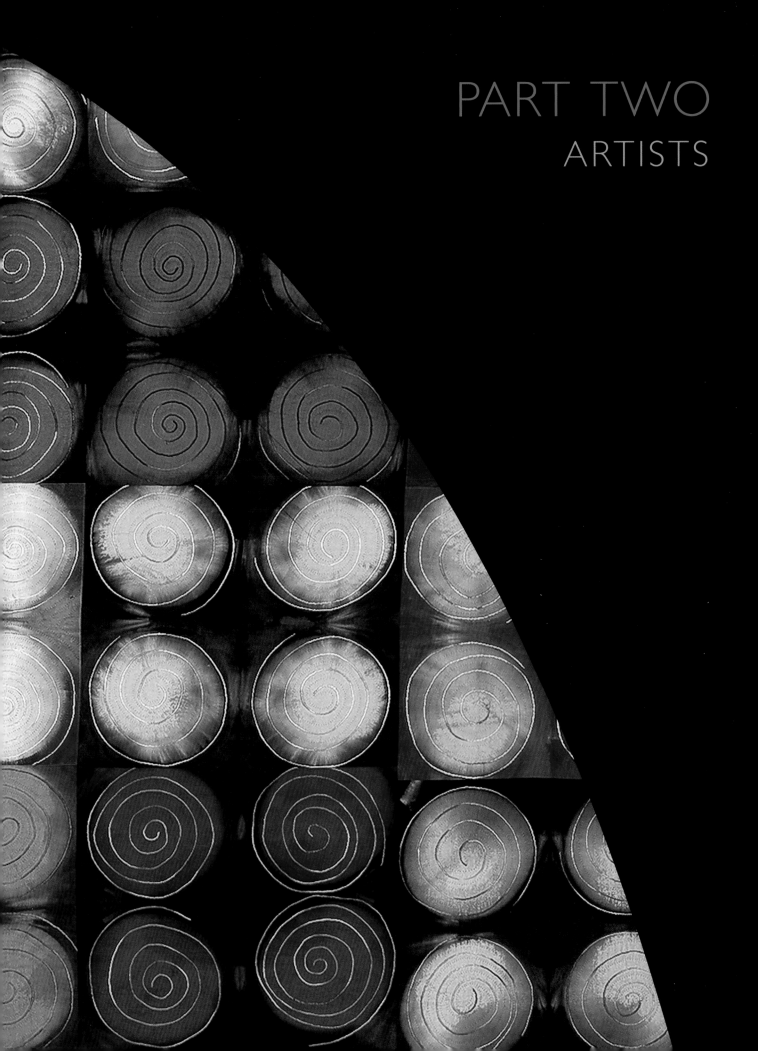

PART TWO
ARTISTS

Plate 1.
Emotions and Abstractions 4, 1997,
50 × 70. Pieced and stitched
cotton; arashi shibori patterning.
Photo: Hester + Hardaway

2

The architecture of the quilt comprises the design and making of the object and the encounters and conversations these processes sustain. . . . [It] opens ways of thinking about quilts in terms of tangible spaces defined and occupied by ideas and perceptions, not merely bodies.[1]

Liz Axford

Liz Axford is one of several artists—Jeffrey Gutcheon is another—who came to quiltmaking from architecture. After nine years of working as a professional architect, and of increasing disappointment with the difference between the imagined building and constructed one, she left full-time work, completed renovations on her own home, and began to quilt. "I could be drawing or painting, but the way this object comes together and can be manipulated . . . ," she begins, expressing her continued excitement about the art form and trying to explain what first drew her to it.[2] Organization and structure, attributes historically recognized and valued in quiltmaking,

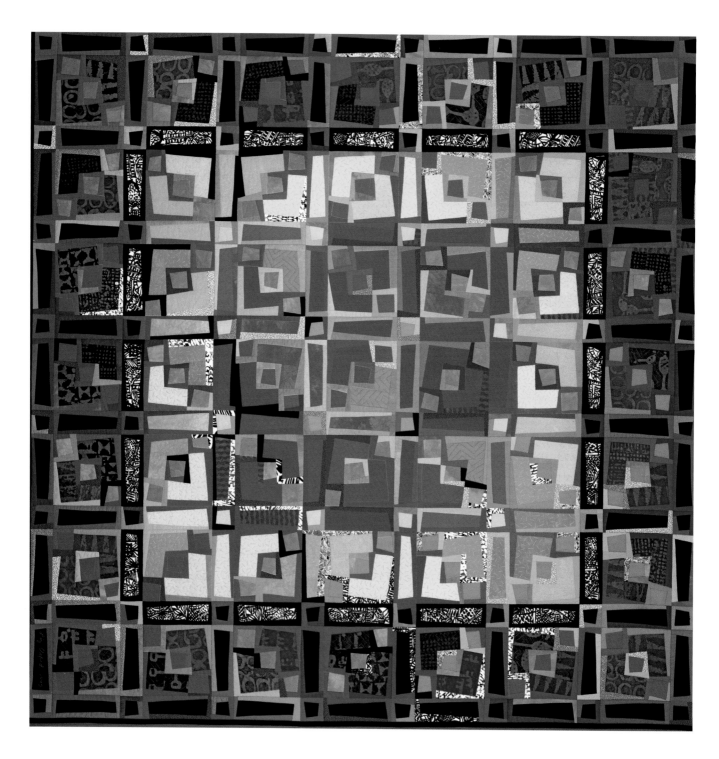

Plate 2.

Freehand 4, 1992, 70 × 70.

Pieced and stitched cotton.

Photo: Hester + Hardaway

are longstanding interests of this artist; she finds the "architecture" of the quilt replete with ideas and relationships to be investigated. Structure, in both its physical and visual aspects, is at the foundation of her art. Using layers, stitches, and patterning, Axford explores relationships between elements: front and back, within and without, obscure and revealing. At times, pattern becomes a metaphor for emotion. Throughout her twenty years as a studio artist in Houston, Texas, her quilts have been consistently engaging and intelligent.

Like many other artists in the 1980s, Axford had her first class in a quilt shop, although she was making quilts before then, guided by her training as an architect and her knowledge of garment construction. Her approach was never that of a hobbyist. In 1986 she took the first of several annual, three-day design workshops with artist Michael James; between 1988 and 1993 she took classes with Nancy Crow. A regular attendee at the Quilt Surface Design Symposium in the 1990s, Axford studied with Risë Nagin, Susan Brandeis, Mary Ann Jordan, and others. She now takes an active role in the professional community of studio quilt artists as lecturer, curator, judge, and teacher. Her art has been accepted into many of the major competitive quilt exhibits as well as into exhibits of mixed media art and fine craft.

Pattern is a prominent feature of Axford's quilts. "I think of pattern as a repetition of similar elements," she says. "They may be arranged evenly or predictably, but I usually use them in a looser way: similar elements, arranged with varying direction and spacing to create a sense of rhythm, movement, direction, for the eye to follow around the piece."

The formal characteristics of her compositions tend to subdue underlying emotion. In recent years she has begun to layer patterns, creating more complex work. "I veil the idea in such a way so the viewer can choose to engage with the concept or not." The water and wave imagery in her *Emotions and Abstractions* series, for example, represents the experience of grief. She writes, "I guess I hope that my ideas will insinuate themselves on the viewer's psyche without my having to spell them out."[3] But she would like the viewer to enjoy her work no matter what level he or she connects with.

Many of the artist's quilts are energetic fields of color and pattern in which a shift of value in the background is used to create a focal point. "The light bars in *Emotions and Abstractions 4* (Plate 1) organize the blocks," she explains. Her patterns engage viewers, pulling them into and around the work. In this quilt, she creates a sense of waves rolling over the surface through the repetition of colors, moving diagonally across the surface and counter-balanced by centralized whirlpools of activity. Sometimes Axford uses one dominant system of patterning such as in the *Boogie Woogie* pieces in which the alternating vertical and horizontal stalks of bamboo set up a rhythm. Other times, as in *Freehand 4* (Plate 2), one system of patterning is carried in the modified Log Cabin piecing and a second system in the quilting. "I enjoy the bit of tension that comes from the two competing systems."

Both the *Freehand* series and some of the *Emotion and Abstraction* quilts show the influence of the artist's exposure in the early 1990s to African American improvisational quilts, including those of Anna Williams. An exhibition of the work of this African American quiltmaker from Louisiana, at one of the first Quilt Surface Design Symposia in the early 1990s, astonished many of the participants. Both Nancy Crow and Liz Axford gave up their precise template method of cutting fabric for this freer approach. "It was fresh and lively," writes Axford. "Each new piece had to be considered in relationship to the whole—nothing became rote. It kept me fully engaged and in the moment."

The artist's approach continues to be primarily a formal one, however. "The bamboo pieces" (*Bamboo Boogie Woogie*, Plate 3), she says, "began as a sketch of a screen wall. I loved the relationship between the long thin elements: How much space between each two stalks? Do the stalks have breaks in them? How strongly is that break expressed? As I began to piece the blocks and manipulate the spacings, the relationship between foreground and background began to interest me as well. How much contrast between foreground and background? Could I create a cluster of stalks punctuated with a space that has as much visual presence as the stalks themselves? Could I create a sense of syncopation in the spacing of the stalks? Could the 'breaks' blend in with the background, abstracting the sense of the stalk? Could the stalks blend with the background, leaving the 'breaks' floating above the background? These are formal ideas. I was also dealing with density. How closely or distantly could I locate related elements: How does this affect the viewer's comfort level?"

Plate 3.

Bamboo Boogie Woogie, 2001,

43 × 60. Pieced and stitched cotton.

Photo: Hester + Hardaway

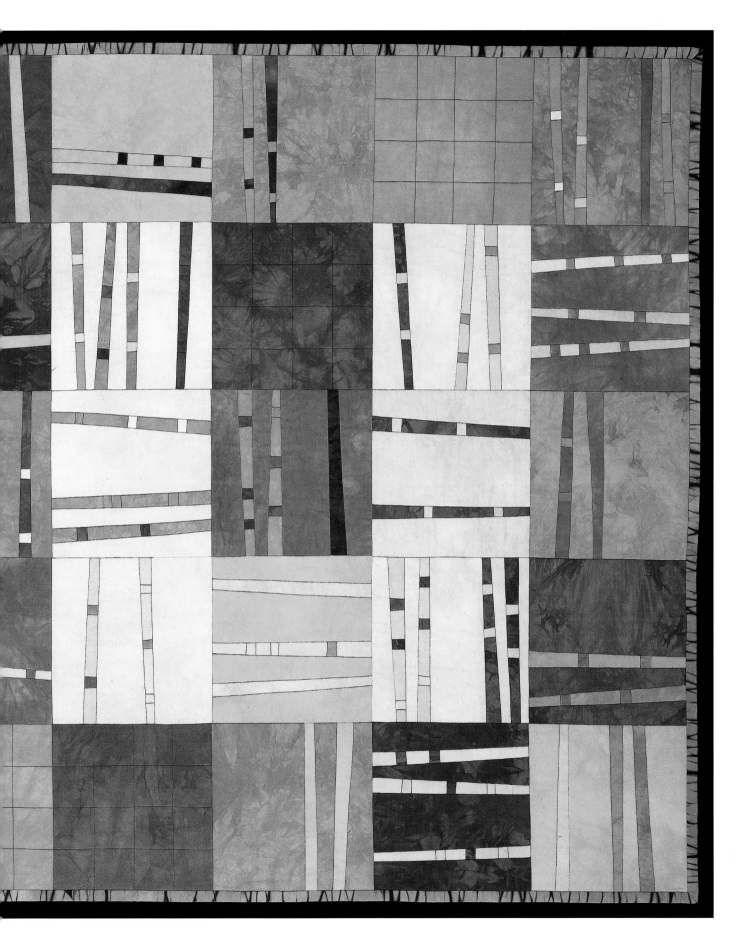

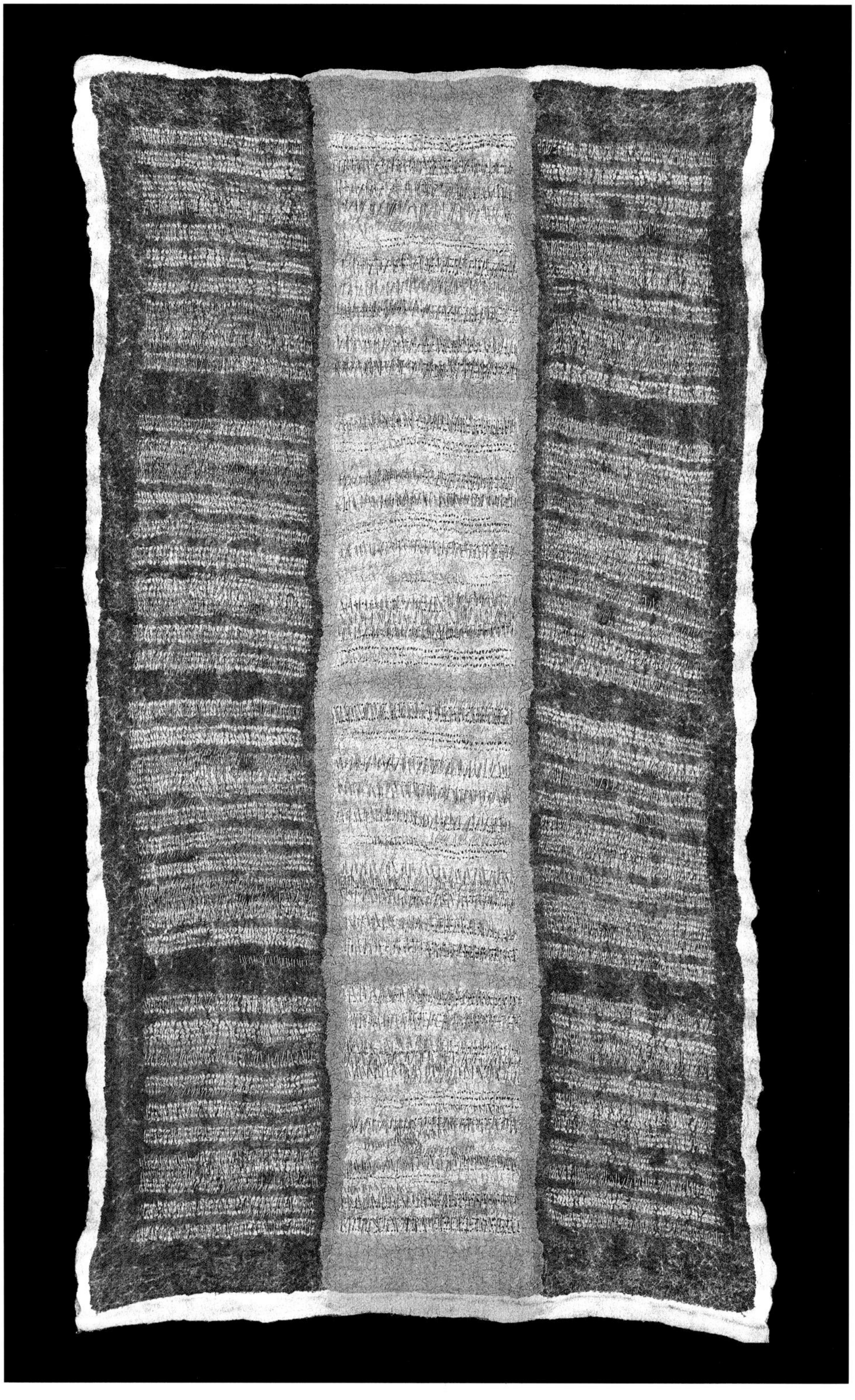

Plate 4.
Text/Subtext, 2004, 53 × 29.
Silk and wool, layered and felted;
stitched-resist shibori and hand
stitching. Photo: Hester + Hardaway

Still, it is the *processes* involved in making that Axford finds most pleasurable. And while engaged in those processes, she is able to dwell on the conceptual aspects of the work. Hand dyeing her own fabric and utilizing her knowledge of **shibori** allow her to achieve a range of color values and tones which give a painterly aspect to her quilts. In the early 2000s, collaboration with Houston artist Shelby Cefaratti took her in a different direction. Making use of a newly learned process for **felting** silk **organza** with wool roving, she has recently been exploring the possibilities of this new textile in her art.

Axford retains her belief that structure is fundamental. Using a markedly reduced color palette, she is now making complex surfaces, built from layers of pattern created by shibori and screen printing applied to both front and back surfaces. With hand stitching, she investigates the relationships of these patterns, which are otherwise invisible because of the opaque intervening layer of wool. While in a traditional quilt the stitches are used to hold the layers together, in *Log Jam* (Plate 5), she uses stitching as the means by which relationships are illuminated, in order to reveal what is obscure. The layers in this and other recent works are joined by the felting process. In *Reading between the Lines* and *Text/Subtext* (Plate 4), the artist introduces stitched shibori patterning reminiscent of text. Always, her intention is to achieve depth. "By depth," she writes, "I mean a deep space, but I mean depth in other ways as well. I typically work with simple classic geometric shapes, Platonic shapes. I want the viewer to enter a meditative state when viewing."

From time to time Axford struggles with the importance of three layers (the typical structure of the traditional quilt) to her work. "Could I do it with just 2 layers?" Her answer: "Yes, I think I could, and that is a direction I expect to take in the future. As I envision how I might make this shift, I will still likely work with patterning front and back and use stitching to emphasize the relationship. Perhaps the fabrics will be opaque, perhaps they will be transparent. . . . I'll probably try both," she says. It remains to be seen where her new work will lead, but undoubtedly her exploration of structure, experience, and aesthetics will continue to extend the visual language of quilts and lead to new ways of thinking about them.

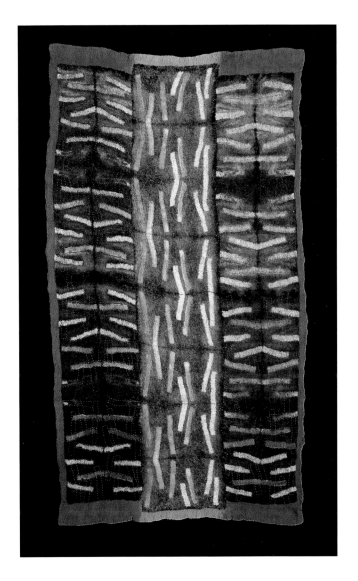

Plate 5.

Log Jam, 2004, 54 × 31.

Silk and wool, layered and felted;

clamped-resist shibori and hand

stitching. Photo: Hester + Hardaway

Plate 6.

Chanson du Bois, 1989, 60 × 90.

This work was included in the fourteenth

Biennial of Tapestry in Lausanne, Switzerland.

Photo: Marc Brandeis

3

Susan Brandeis

When I came back to doing large work in the late 1990's, I began a focused exploration of specific places in nature. I spent time at each place, photographing, sketching and making notes. I used the series of pieces that came from that research to try to describe the emotional and physical experience of being in that particular place. . . . In the works about the coast of Oregon, the colors focused on the lushness, wetness, quiet, intense, and even oppressive aspects of the coastal forest. In the works about the Southwest, the color hints at dry, hot air, dust, sand, rock, space, mysterious remnants, and human vulnerability in the landscape.[1]

Susan Brandeis's love of textiles and textile processes has been a constant presence throughout her twenty-five-year career as an artist and educator. She combines these interests with a fascination with nature, and with the ways humans view and experience the natural world. While her source of inspiration has shifted and her work has evolved, her focus is still much the same.

For many artists who began their careers in textile design or fiber art, their medium is intimately connected to their art. Brandeis writes, "I still hold dear the qualities that first attracted me to textiles: rhythm or repetition and pattern, complex color contrasts, textured relief surfaces, and the touch of the materials in my hand. I love and value the slowness of the making and the meditative quality of the process."

From the beginning, her approach to her work has been unique. In the late 1970s, when Susan Brandeis was a student there, Indiana University, Bloomington, was a community where textile art and artists flourished. Budd Stalnaker and Joan Sterrenberg were on the faculty; Diane Itter, Tom Lundberg, and Anne McKenzie Nickolson were students. Brandeis's primary interest

was weaving, but all students were required to learn the formal elements of art and to be familiar with other textile techniques, including spinning, knotting, braiding, felting, dyeing, screen-printing, piecing, appliqué, and other forms of embellishment. She still uses these processes and techniques in her mature work. After obtaining an MS at Indiana, Brandeis continued as an MFA student in textile design and fiber art at the University of Kansas, where she worked with faculty members Cynthia Schira, a well-known and innovative weaver, and Marna Goldstein Brauner.

As a young student, Brandeis was interested in African art, particularly the strip weavings of Ghana and Mali. By working with narrow woven strips and with double weaves, she created both dimension and rhythm in her work. A lecture by visiting artist Adele Akers stimulated her interest in aerial perspective, and she explored this approach. Two small embroideries she made at this time are in the collection of the Renwick Gallery of the Smithsonian American Art Museum.

Combining a growing interest in perspective with an ongoing effort to create both structural relief and fluid movement in her art, Brandeis experimented continually with her cloth. Her interest in weaving lessened as she manipulated cloth in her own way—stuffing it, layering it, and piecing small bits and torn strips of her own hand dyed fabric. She held these "constructions" together with hand and machine stitches. She also began a series of color studies to determine how to use color more expressively.

The artist was interested in the fact that from both a very close and a very distant perspective, shapes are perceived abstractly by the viewer. Some of her large pieces from the 1980s are similar in some visual respects to Abstract Expressionist art. They are Modernist, "all-over" pieces, without a focal point. Like the early twentieth-century painter Edouard Vuillard, one of the artists whose work she admires, Brandeis has sought to show both the detail of nature's shapes and their dissolution in distance and light; see *Chanson du Bois* (Plates 6 and 7).

Using color, she explored the effects of changing light and shadow at different times of day and in different places: dappled light in her *Forest Floor* series, reflected light in her *Sea Mantle* series, and broken light as it filtered

Plate 8.

Songs of Earth and Grass, 1998,

38 × 43. Mixed fabric content;

felted, appliquéd, stitched, printed.

Collection of Cindy Speicher.

Photo: Marc Brandeis

Below. Plate 9.

Songs of Earth and Grass, detail

through shuttered windows in her *Window* series. In these explorations she varied the kind of cloth she used (silk or metallic), changed the way she textured the cloth, and mixed various textile techniques. Her surfaces were alive with color and rhythm; opaque fabric became transparent and luminous.

By the late 1990s, Brandeis was becoming more interested in the emotional and physical experience of nature. (See *Songs of Earth and Grass,* Plates 8 and 9.) Her attraction to nature always had a spiritual basis, and she wanted to communicate that experience somehow through her art. She changed her

Plate 10.

Messages from the Past, 2001, 38 × 76.

Mixed fabric content; digitally printed,

hand dyed, screen printed, discharge

printed, felted, appliquéd, embroidered.

Photo: Marc Brandeis

fieldwork practice, settling at each site to absorb the atmosphere of place—the sights, sounds, light, colors, feel, and textures. On site she photographs, sketches, and keeps a diary of impressions, slowly letting a "visual vocabulary" of the place evolve. Her first field trip was to the Pacific Northwest and led to completely new work embodied in the *Perpetua* series. These pieces are less complex than previous work, but more evocative. By juxtaposing panels, she was still able to obtain multiple perspectives within each composition.

Around this time, pain and hand surgery necessitated a change in studio practice. Unable to continue some of the strenuous physical labor involved in screen printing, Brandeis familiarized herself with digital printing. But she was determined "to render the technology virtually invisible to the viewer—to use it as a means to expression, not an end in itself."[2] She now scans her photographs and sketches into her computer. While her photographs were always used to inspire her work, now the image itself can be printed on fabric by a digital printer. Brandeis thinks that the technology enables her to capture a more literal impression of a site—the textures, marks, and images—and to develop a more complex image and surface, as in *Messages from*

the Past (Plate 10). With the computer she is also able to change the size and scale of the images, adding and removing elements, and layering them.

Since 1982, the artist has been on the faculty of the College of Design at North Carolina State University. She is an active member of the fiber art community as a curator, juror, exhibitor, and participant in professional seminars and conferences. Her commissioned art is in numerous public and private collections. In 2002 contemporary textile curator Rebecca A. T. Stevens of the Textile Museum in Washington, D.C., included Brandeis's work in the exhibit *Technology as Catalyst: Textile Artists on the Cutting Edge*. In a catalog essay about the exhibit, author and noted weave technology expert Bhakti Ziek wrote: "For all these artists use of digital processes is an extension of former work which germinates fresh ideas from their understanding of previous modes of fabrications."[3] Through her understanding of textiles and textile processes, Brandeis has re-started her dialogue with the cloth that emerges from the printer. By texturing it with her own mark—her embroidery, weaving, screen printing, and quilting stitches—she brings to life the enormous expressive potential of cloth.

Plate 11.

To Stand, Move, and Hum, 1996, 60½ × 55.

Dyed cotton; Vandyck brown printed and

screenprinted; pieced, appliquéd, hand quilted.

Private collection. Photo: Mark Frey

4

One role of the artist is to focus attention on
ordinary things in an extraordinary way. In the
bright light of the artist's vision, we are compelled
to look more closely, examine deeper meanings.[1]

Seattle artist Rachel Brumer begins a lecture she gives about her art
by telling the audience that she grew up in Oakland, California, in a
family of displaced New York intellectual and political Jews. There is a
touch of humor in her observation that all three of her careers have been non-
verbal. As a young girl she trained in ballet but discovered in college that she
was better suited for modern dance. After graduation from Mills College in
Oakland, California, in 1978 with an interdisciplinary arts degree, Brumer
performed with dance companies in Seattle and New York City. In 1987, she
made a transition from dance to a career as a sign language interpreter. Two

Facing page. Plate 12.

Cover Them: Francoise—Kadosh, 1997, 70 × 69. Dyed cotton; Vandyck brown printed, screenprinted, stenciled; pieced, appliquéd, hand quilted. Collection of the artist. Photo: Mark Frey

years later, the death of a close friend from complications of AIDS prompted her to make her first quilt. It was the first time she translated a personal experience into a new art form and the first of many tributes she has offered through her quilts. *Marker VI* (1993), now in the collection of the Seattle Art Museum, is a commemoration of the life of dancer and close friend Heywood McGriff.

Brumer's art is influenced by her training, her life experiences, and her wide-ranging interests. It is compassionate, intelligent, and often humorous. While dance may seem an unlikely training ground for the studio artist, the formal elements of dance are similar to those in other forms of art. She explains: "Your arm is held in a certain way; that creates a line relating to your body and it creates a shape. If there is a person next to you, it creates tension. That shape has negative space on the stage which is changed by the other person's line or shape. That was my training. It certainly relates to every piece I make."[2] Many of her quilt compositions—*To Stand, Move, and Hum* (Plate 11), for example—have an air of expressive mobility. Patterns and rhythms of modern music also find their way into her compositions. She believes that Philip Glass's five-note compositions, with their repetitions, slight variations, and more repetitions, have their direct counterpart in traditional, pieced-block quilts.

Robert Wilson, the avant-garde theater director, has had the greatest influence on the way Brumer approaches her art. As a member of the Lucinda Child's dance company in the 1980s, she performed in Philip Glass's opera *Einstein on the Beach,* which was directed by Wilson.[3] "He talked a lot about how the opera was formulated as we were learning it. He shared with us the sources that prompted him to create, how he put his ideas together and worked from these sources. It opened my eyes," she says. "There is a long, huge process between the idea and the presentation."[4]

Cover Them (Plate 12), a quilt installation created in the late 1990s with a grant from the King County Arts Commission (Seattle), is evidence of how much she learned from Wilson. In 1996 Brumer purchased the newly published book *French Children of the Holocaust,* written by Serge Klarsfeld. In his seemingly endless list of murdered children, she found ten girls who shared her birthday and made a quilt for each, seeking, she wrote, "to create a link to these vanished children. Because no one can mourn at these children's graves, assembling the quilts has become a ritual of remembrance."[5] "The quilt images," observed one reviewer, "were so large (averaging 85 inches by 85 inches) and close, and had such a presence, that they themselves seemed to be the honored guests."[6] The colors chosen for the quilts were monochromatic, dirty browns; the symbols repeated throughout the series are fingerprints, identity cards, circular stamps, stones, and railroad car springs. Their batting is exposed and the stitches are large because "the young women being honored didn't have the time to do such work properly, if at all."[7] Thinking carefully about the materials and the presentation, Brumer went to as near a source as she could find. In Everett, Washington, "she stood there by the

tracks as if she were four feet tall as if she had to wait and wait. She focused on the train tracks, the rhythm of the tracks, on the car springs. . . . She photographed . . . what she saw, then photographed architectural drawings of railroad wheels, of trains with rocks in boxcars."[8] Some of the expressive power of these quilts comes from the artist's ability, as a dancer, to become the child, to see the world as though she were one of those ten children.

Quire: A Book of Findings (Plates 13 and 14), is a series of forty-nine folios, each held together with a steel hinge in the center. Because of their layered, pieced, and stitched construction, the folios can be loosely defined as quilts, but the artist was more interested in a book form. In this work, her concern that the importance of books would be lost to the new generations of technologically adept children and her interest in illuminated manuscripts came together. She began reading about *The Book of Hours* and the early religious manuscripts of Judaism, Christianity, and Islam, then went to the Getty Museum to see them firsthand. "Some were so precious. Lapis was ground for blue coloring and gold for gilt. I wanted to make something that could be just as precious but with humble materials." With bits of things found on the street during her daily walks and many hours of concentrated labor, Brumer created a visual language which became the text for her own *Book of Findings*. It is not the preciousness of the materials that makes books

Facing page. Plate 13.

Quire: A Book of Findings, 2001.

Mixed media including metal hinge; brown printed, dyed cotton. Photo taken during exhibition at the Seattle Art Museum, Seattle, Washington

Above. Plate 14.

Quire: A Book of Findings, Folio, detail, 23 × 30 × 3. Photo: Mark Frey

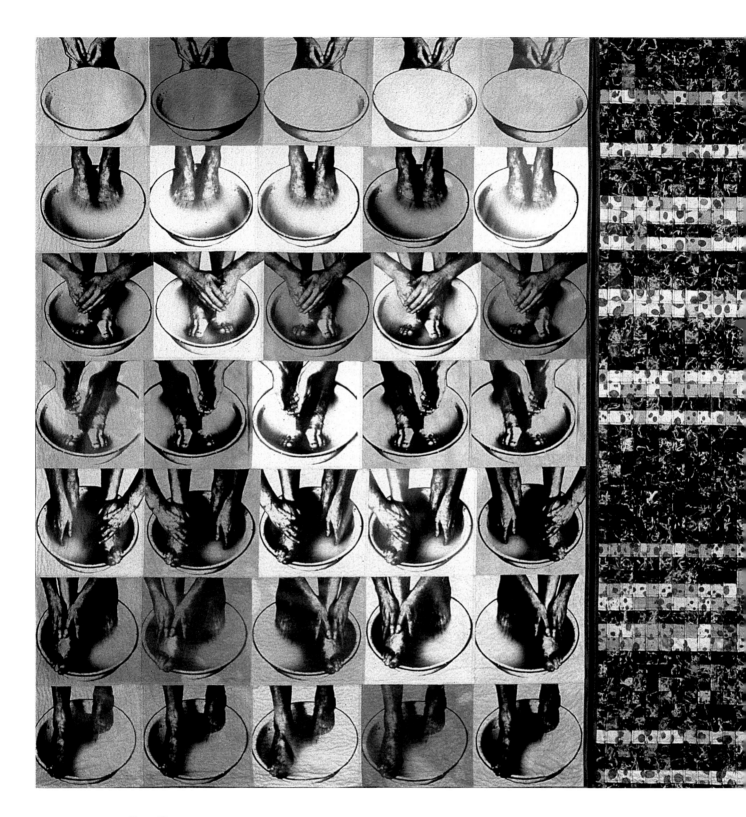

Plate 15.

Describing Rain, 2004, 84 × 120.

Dyed cotton; printed, pieced, hand quilted.

Collection of John M. Walsh III.

Photo: Mark Frey

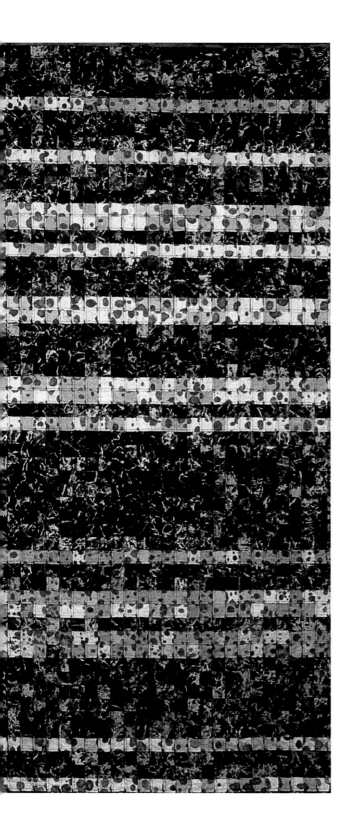

valuable. The hours of labor and what this labor signifies make them precious. Her manuscript is not without its own decoration—it contains thousands of embroidered **French knots.**

The backgrounds of Brumer's quilted compositions are hand dyed or painted, and pieced together in a traditional manner. Imagery is sometimes appliquéd by hand, but the artist also uses **Vandyck printing**, screen printing, rubbings, stamping, and stenciling. She prints photographic images, such as those used to create the text for *Quire: A Book of Findings* and those in *Describing Rain* (Plate 15), in her studio.

Describing Rain is a quiet, almost humble diptych. When quilt art collector John M. Walsh III commissioned it, his only suggestion to the artist was that it have something to do with water. Brumer used the biblical story about Christ washing the feet of the poor as the starting point for her research. She learned that the act of foot washing is a symbol of humility in several religious traditions. The left panel of this work takes the eye of the viewer through row after row of repeated washings, with subtle variations in value or direction. Even more quiet and meditative is the right panel. Covered with images of water droplets and seaweed, its rhythms can be viewed as text awaiting interpretation.

Sandra Kroupa's thoughtful commentary about artists, cited at the beginning of this essay, is especially true of Brumer. She compels us to look more closely and does so in an extraordinary way.

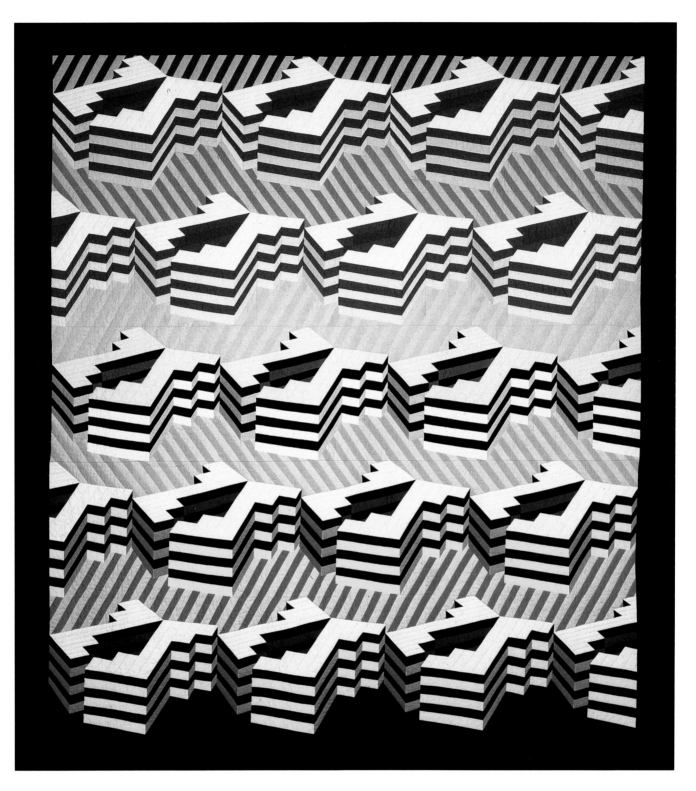

Plate 16.

Licorice Allsorts, 1983, 95 × 88.

Pieced cotton. Private collection in

the United States. Photo: John Coles

5

I need to immerse myself in colours and shapes. I spend a great deal of time creating a connection with the world around me. I observe details in my surroundings—the countryside, the flora and fauna, plant forms, and the changing seasons. All this helps me feel that my work is emotionally connected to the celebration of life.[1]

Pauline Burbidge is one of Britain's most acclaimed studio quiltmakers. Her art is in the Victoria and Albert Museum and numerous other British museums. The International Quilt Study Center in Lincoln, Nebraska, has four of her quilts in its collections, several of which were donated by Ardis and Robert James, important collectors of both traditional and contemporary quilts. In 1994, with support from a commission by another American collector, John M. Walsh III, she was able to continue the explorations that began in the late 1980s and that were leading her away from traditional quilt structure.

This was not the direction Burbidge expected to take when she left St. Martin's School of Art in London in 1973 with a diploma in fashion and textiles. After the small garment design business that she founded with a partner was dissolved in three years, she took a stall in Portobello Market in West London, selling secondhand clothes and textiles. It was in this context that she spotted her first quilt and found a copy of Ruth Finley's 1929 book, *Old Patchwork Quilts and the Women Who Made Them.* With the book as her guide, Burbidge made her first quilt; it was a turning point in her life. She was soon making quilts full-time. "My love of colour, texture, and fabric drew me to quilts, but it was my earlier training in art and design that first helped me to appreciate the beauty of traditional patchwork."[2] She was soon creating her own designs and developing the techniques to carry them out. In 1982 Burbidge received the John Ruskin Craft Award from the Crafts Council of London and began to establish connections with American artists who were making quilts. In 1983 she was invited by artist Michael James to exhibit her work in Massachusetts. In 1985 her work was accepted in the fourth *Quilt National* exhibition of contemporary quilts in Ohio.

In the introduction to *Quilt Studio,* Burbidge's book, artist and author Michele Walker traces the development of her work. It is a story of continual self-challenge, of an artist who determines what she wants to do, then develops the techniques to accomplish her goal. Early hallmarks of her work were strong graphics and an interest in stripes. She worked with a limited palette but used color, including black, boldly. In 1980 Burbidge dispensed with the symmetry of traditional quilts and began to work in an optical style. The colors, the positioning of her blocks, and careful craftsmanship characterized these works. *Licorice Allsorts,* 1983 (Plate 16), represents work done during this period.

By 1985, however, Burbidge's interests were changing. She lived in Nottingham, a town filled with canals, docks, and warehouses, and these outdoor scenes, particularly the water, interested her. At the same time, like many American artists, she had finished her "apprenticeship" with traditional quiltmaking and was ready to move on. Until then, Burbidge had been using a commercial sewing machine to piece and quilt. In Nottingham she began to sketch and photograph her surroundings. She adopted a collage format and began to cut freely and directly into her fabrics, using her sketches and photographs as a reference. She **fused** fabrics and machine-stitched over them. Later compositions such as *Boatday/Contemplation* would have been impossible using traditional methods of quilt construction. Walker notes that although the artist continued to use a repeat block format for her quilts, the grid became less regular and the images within the blocks showed movement. Block designs were simplified as the eye followed them across the surface of the quilts.

In the early 1990s a new series was begun following a move to the rural area of the Scottish Borders. With a commission in hand from John M. Walsh III, Burbidge now had time and resources for research and experimen-

Plate 17.

Tweed Reflections II, 1995, 48 × 48.

Fabric collage. Collection of John M. Walsh III.

Photo: Keith Tidball

Plate 18.
Colour Study I, detail, 1997, 68 × 68.
Cotton, found natural objects, laminating plastic; stitched. Collection of the artist. Photo: Keith Tidball

tation. She described her new interest in *Quilt Studio:* "An ongoing project in recent years is a series of quilts that arose from my observations of reflections in water. I am fascinated with the ways water moves and dances, changing from one moment to the next. A clear image of a tree reflects in calm water; a moment later the wind blows and the entire image is broken up."[3] She began her commission by taking photographs of water reflections along the canal banks and abstracting a design from these images. Working with a limited but still bold palette, she created a number of major new pieces, including *Tweed Reflections II* for the Walsh Collection (Plate 17), *Whiteadder* (1995), and *Paxton Studies I* and *II* (1997). These pieces are consistently graphic, but the series has a reflective character. Burbidge's "reflections" refer as much to an inner state as to surface qualities. Like the American textile artist Susan Brandeis, Burbidge was seeking to recreate her own experience of nature in her art.

Toward the end of the 1990s, while still working on the *Reflection* quilts, the artist initiated her *Colour Studies* (see Plate 18). Working first with black and white feathers, and later with other natural objects, she carefully grouped the objects on pieces of fabric and then covered them with laminating plastic. These were cut into blocks, put together like quilts, and hand stitched on their surfaces. The merging of colors between the background and the objects makes possible the detection of subtle variations in tone and value. Burbidge also used laminating plastic on her water quilt *Whiteadder*, 1995, adding to the reflective quality of its surface.

Since 2000 there has been a definitive change in her art. Water continues to be an important theme, but Burbidge has turned her attention to the texture of the quilt surface and is using only subtly valued blacks and whites. She has dispensed with the block format altogether, and her images are no longer contained within borders. Experiments with a hand pleating machine

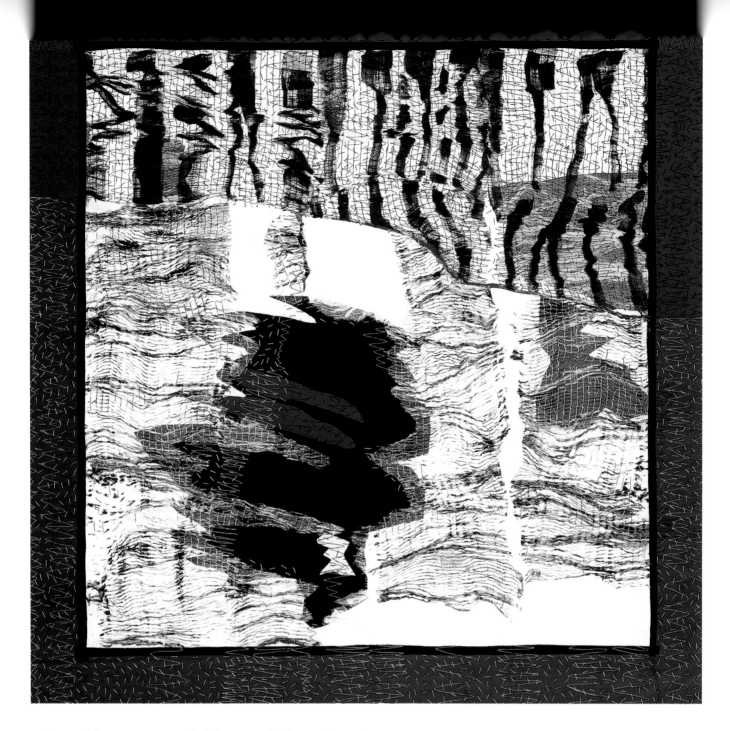

Plate 19.

Boatday/Contemplation, 2004, 43 × 43.

Fine cottons and silks. Private collection,

United Kingdom. Photo: Keith Tidball

and use of fine transparent cloth have resulted in surfaces that seem to merge image with technique, as in *Boatday/Contemplation* (Plate 19). Hand and machine stitches hold gently distorted pleats in place, giving the surface an almost sculptured character even while their shaping gives the impression of movement. "The gentle, reflective surface of a quiet stream gives way to the powerful crash of falling water, finally dissolving in white mist," writes art historian Judith Duffey Harding.[4]

Burbidge's interests have been clear since 1973. "Intellectual ideas do not rule my work," she says. "I am concerned with the making, the textiles, observation, my 'gut' reaction to color, and the elements of line and form."[5] She does not mention the beauty or evocative power of her studio quilts, qualities which she consistently achieves even as her work continues to evolve.

Plate 20.

Schoodic Storm, 1983, 32 × 30.

Painted and pieced canvas.

Collection of the artist

6

As more and more "art quilts" find their way into galleries and museums, it is apparent that numerous artists have reached beyond the traditional quiltmakers' idiom in search of a contemporary visual language. Still, it seems that relatively few have tapped the creative intuition that gives rise to poetry, myths, and visual art with deeply personal as well as universal meaning. When a work emerges from that creative source, every element resonates with import: color sparks an emotional response; shapes are evocative gestalts; structure enhances, rather than restricts or distorts, imagery.[1]

As a young graduate with a degree in painting and art education from the Rhode Island School of Design (RISD), Elizabeth Busch began her career in the high school art classroom. Within a few years she moved on, and from 1966 to 1984 she worked full-time in architecture while also caring for her family and managing chores at her old house and farm in Maine. During these years, painting was "squeezed in" before the household awoke.[2] Meanwhile, her understanding of three-dimensional space deepened as she gained experience in architectural design. It now suffuses her studio quilts and kinetic sculptures.

Early in the 1980s, Busch began making studio quilts. "It seemed a natural next step for me not to use stretcher bars with my paintings." After all, she says, "*canvas* is fabric." She knew how to sew because she sewed for her family. Using Michael James's book *The Quilter's Handbook* (1978) as a guide, she made her first quilts, using her own designs but constructing them in the traditional manner. But the piecing process was disenchanting. Not until Busch "serendipitously" cut up one of her painted abstract landscapes and combined it with commercial fabric did she find a way to integrate her art with the quilt form. *Schoodic Storm* (Plate 20), the quilt constructed from the cut-up painting, was very different from other work and she was excited. Working with *this* quilt form presented new possibilities.

Busch remembers her years at RISD most for her introduction to color study. "It opened a world for me that had previously not existed. Josef Albers's book, *The Interaction of Color,* offered me a powerful and beautiful understanding of color." That she has become a skilled colorist is not surprising. "Learning that color needed to relate across the flat surface of the canvas made sense to me," she writes, "and I work that way still, even in my sculpture. It is true in nature as well that a color relates across the plane of our vision even in its three-dimensional form." Eager to take on a challenge, Busch wanted to have color relate not only across the surface but also into an illusional space; quilts became the vehicle. "Quilts automatically allowed me to think in that 'layered' manner. As soon as I painted a canvas and added a colored pencil grid to the surface, I had a dimensionally visible second layer. Airbrushing another color on top created yet another layer. Color was relating across the surface and in 'depth' as well. By adding pieces of fabric, some embroidered stitching, batting and backing, the spatial illusions became even more complex."

Many of the artist's first quilts were made with torn or freely cut strips and pieces of fabric and exposed batting. At times, she fractured the grid and recomposed it abstractly. For an invitational exhibit at the Portland Museum of Art, she made a series of five large quilts about the bed that were visually related to the functional purpose of traditional quilts. In *When We Were Young* (Plate 21), now in the collection of the Museum of Arts and Design in New York, the red hot colors of the formal triangular center and "pillows" are counterbalanced by the neutrally colored, abstract landscape seen in the distance and by the patterning of the stitches and the black-and-white fabrics pieced to the quilt at its base. It is an engaging and provocative work of art. Patricia Malarcher, in an essay entitled "In Search of Quiltness," wrote about this work: "The spatial tension between the dominant frontal triangle and the illusion of deep landscape space suggests the tension between the moment and the broad sweep of life. Beyond that, the piece elicits questions: Is the bed a shield against the world in the window? Or, is the bed itself part of the window? Although Busch's theme might suggest saccharine clichés, the strength of her composition and compressed imagery give the work a power that soars above sentimentality."[3] Later, recalling her years at RISD, the art-

ist commented: "Abstract Expressionism was the 'ism' of the day in the early 60s. In studying composition, I recall how much more energized and dynamic asymmetry was than symmetry. Wouldn't it be a great challenge to make a symmetrical composition just as energized and dynamic?" She later wrote: "*When We Were Young* does that: It provides enough interesting content to cause the viewer to see the illusion of symmetry and asymmetry at the same time."

Plate 21.

When We Were Young, 1989, 80 × 68. Painted and pieced canvas. Collection of the Museum of Arts and Design, New York. Photo: Brian Blauser

Plate 22.

Morning, 1995, 16 × 42. Painted and pieced canvas. Collection of the Nortel Corporation, Calgary, Alberta, Canada.

Photo: Dennis Griggs

In the late 1980s the artist received a request for proposals for a project at the Maine State Cultural Building in Augusta. Knowing that quilts were not appropriate for the forty-foot-high, light-filled atrium, she began using theater gels to create kinetic sculpture. Within ten years, Busch completed fifteen commissions using this new process. The illusion of space in her quilts becomes physical reality with her sculpture as each medium feeds new ideas to the other. Her sculpture now hangs in public buildings throughout Maine and elsewhere in the United States.

Her studio quilts, meanwhile, have continued to evolve. In the 1990s she produced a series in which pristine land and seascapes are seen in the distance, removed from the viewer by layers of architectural structure. *Morning* (Plate 22), which references both architecture and the sea, is an internal landscape, however. Busch's interpretation of three-dimensional space goes beyond the architectural construct. "The concept is important on many levels,"

she writes. "I/we exist in a multi-dimensional way. My quilts are about me: my physical and spiritual presence in my environment; my emotional presence, past and present; and my intellectual presence in the events of the world." Yet there are parts of her art-making that remain a mystery to her. "How I choose to make a quilt has more to do with where I am when the 'call to work' arises. I respond to whatever that is, not knowing why, and not having a clue what the result will be. For example, the pieces on my studio wall now make absolutely no sense . . . for whatever reason, several days this past week 'I needed to paint.' I did. Now I look, move pieces around with others I have pulled out. It's like a jig saw puzzle without a picture to follow. Will it come together this time? Will I ever understand what this work is about? Today, I still don't, but I usually learn after the fact. Then, it always makes sense!"

Busch speaks of her work as leading her rather than the reverse. "I never

Right. Plate 23.

Transition, detail, 2004.

(Quilt is 42½ × 57.) Painted, whole cloth. Collection of the artist

Facing page. Plate 24.

Imbalance, 2006, 48 × 42.

Canvas and purchased fabric; airbrushed, hand painted, hand and machine quilted by the artist.

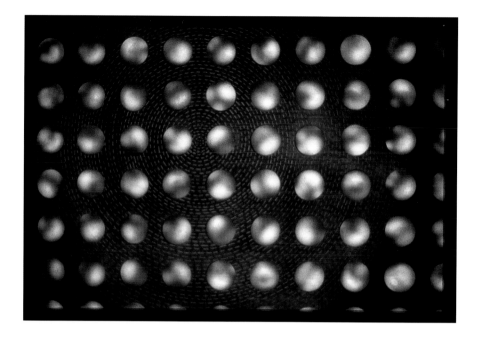

know how many pieces it will take to finish a particular group, series, or process, to no longer feel the need to do what I've been doing. The process leads me to what I need to do next. Some of what happens has real significance as a transition, as the title of *Transition* (Plate 23) signifies. It was while working on this piece that I began to sense that something else was to happen. The last quilts in the series were building within for four years. These quilts, the *Odyssey* series, are very personal and multi-dimensional."

The *Odyssey* series is another example of Busch's skill at relating color across illusional space (see Plate 24). The painted spheres on black draw the viewer directly into the unending blackness of the cosmos. Yet the presence of the spheres seems welcome and reassuring. The architectural divide in her earlier landscape quilts has been replaced with dense curtains, but they are drawn curtains, open to these spherical neighbors from the cosmos.

Many of the artist's studio quilts are large in scale. The recent series has been smaller. "I like the stretch it takes to create small works that have big impact," she writes. "A big piece automatically has impact with size which is not automatically a good thing. . . . The size of my pieces is, once again, not something I chose. As strange as that may sound, the work does build itself without indicating size to me." Busch has a way of making her art seem simplistic, as if it all stems from her unconscious self. Yet, she brings to her work a great deal of practical skill and experience and successfully stretches architectural constructs beyond the physical into art.

Plate 25. *For Sandra,*
1997, 54 × 24.
Pieced and felted wool.
Collection of the artist

7

Regardless of the form that my work may take, the thinking, the influences, the rapture with materials and techniques . . . all of these aspects are part of the process, in each and every piece. Whether I create a wearable, a sculpture or a piece for the wall, the journey is down a path where the concepts influence the forms, then it's one step at a time expressing ideas along the way.[1]

Jean Williams Cacicedo is a distinguished textile artist and a prominent participant in the Artwear movement. Originating in California and New York, Artwear became "a parallel, alternative art practice that is avant-garde in its own way, encompassing women's art, body sculpture, narrative content, and unexpected materials."[2] While Cacicedo is known primarily for her vibrant and graphic work in this genre, her wall pieces and sculpture make up at least half of her creative output.

Educated at Pratt Institute in Brooklyn, New York, in the late 1960s, the young student relished the art life of the city and her access to the city's great museums. "I loved the Matisse room at the Museum of Modern Art. The sculpture of Eva Hesse and Claes Oldenburg, painting constructions with fabric and collage by Rauschenberg and Jasper Johns were all a big influence," she says. "Abstract Expressionism gave me permission to do something different with my art." At Pratt, Cacicedo was required to study the formal elements of design but was free to explore media that were not taught. "All my final projects ended up incorporating yarn crochet because ordinary mediums did not interest me."

In the 1970s Cacicedo's interest in fiber art deepened. A year in the San Francisco Bay area's active textile arts community was followed by a move to Wyoming, where she experimented with techniques for dyeing yarn and created textile forms that combined knitting and fabric with crochet. "Wyoming provided the physical and visual space for me to continue on my own." In 1980 she returned to California, where she has lived and worked for the last twenty-five years. Dyed and **felted** wool replaced the crochet as her main material. Her prominence grew as Artwear was exhibited in galleries and museums in California, New York, and other parts of the country. In 1986 Cacicedo's *Celebration Buffalo Coat* was included in *Craft Today: Poetry of the Physical,* an important exhibit at the Museum of Contemporary Crafts.

Cacicedo's art is narrative, no matter what form she uses. "Storytelling is the way I bring images, color, and textures into my work. They [her art pieces] are often quite simply, a personal statement about someone or some place or some time and include journeys, both physical and spiritual." *For Sandra* (Plate 25) and *My Father's House* (1999) are about loss. Both of these pieces are "about rebirth through images and memory," she says. *Bed of Roses* (Plate 26) is "a celebration about the give and take in marriage." The artist's imagery is rich and varied; it includes archetypes, such as the human hand and eye, motifs associated with various forms of nature, and personally significant places. *Raincoat: San Francisco Bay* (1998) is a commissioned piece that includes views of Marin County of personal importance to the owner. Cacicedo's art can be humorous, too, as Melissa Leventon has noted. Her raincoat is full of holes.[3]

"Drawing is an important step in making my art," says Cacicedo, who credits her strong academic background in the arts for providing her with the foundation for the way she thinks and acts upon her work. "Drawings communicate ideas without necessarily revealing the form they will take. As I draw a series of ideas, these images may manifest into coats, sculpture or wall pieces, depending on what inspires me to create at the time. The form from which these drawings manifest can also be influenced by need. I remember the time I fashioned a garment from an almost completed wall piece because of a deadline. I was in need of a garment for an exhibition."

Cacicedo never diminishes the craft in her art. She celebrates it. "Our textile world is rich in process and history," she says. "When working with cloth, it is always interesting to understand where the cloth was made and to discover the nature of its physical properties. I honor the integrity of my cloth and the process and craft from which my work gets developed. Without my craft and love of process there would be no art to create. Spinning wool,

Bed of Roses

natural dyeing, felt making, sewing, and manipulating cloth are the traditions that continue to be an important aspect to the work I create."

"Wool is unique to all fibers in that it shrinks and dyes beautifully. The transformative shrinking process of working with wool is still very exciting to me after thirty years and there continues to be an element of surprise with each exploration." Because each wool fiber actually has microscopic "hooks" on it, the shrinking process causes these fibers to tangle. Transformations also occur with the dye process. "The alchemy that occurs during immersion dyeing is quite irresistible. There is always excitement as the colors of saturated cloth emerge from the steaming dye pot."[4] Other art processes Cacicedo uses are reverse appliqué, slashing, **resist** shrinking paste, and occasionally a burn-out technique to mark the cloth. Of the textile traditions that inspire her, she says, "I have always been drawn to the beauty of handmade ethnic textiles. It was my study of molas and their colorful technique of reverse appliqué that created a foundation for my sewn cloth."

Plate 26.
Bed of Roses, 1998, 75 × 53.
Pieced and felted wool.
Photo: Barry Shapiro

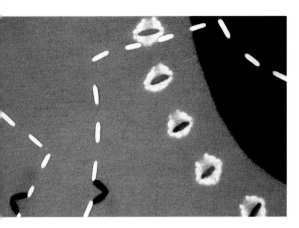

Above. Plate 27.
Markers II, detail

Right. Plate 28.
Markers II, 2005, 64 × 40.
Pieced and felted wool.

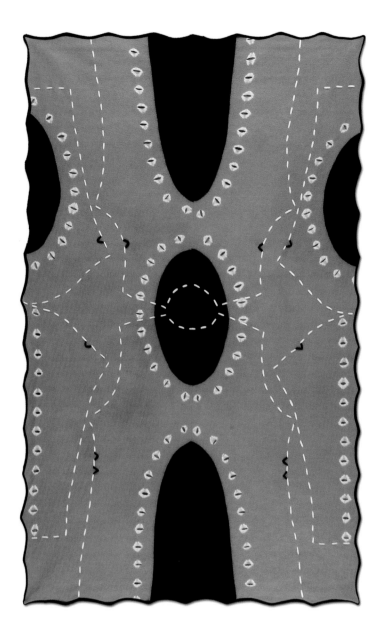

In 2004 Cacicedo traveled to Australia. Impressed by the vastness and scale of the Australian landscape, she wanted to enlarge and simplify all of her images to that scale. She was also inspired by the "dots" in Aboriginal paintings which reminded her of her stitched lines in cloth and the quality of the light. Wanting "to make the memory of these images visible in my own art, I created a new body of work called *Markers*." *Markers: Style 2-504* was accepted into the 2005 *Quilt National* exhibit. For *Markers II* (Plates 27 and 28) Cacicedo hand dyed her wool in the deep reddish-brown hues of the Australian landscape.

Quilts are a new vocabulary for Cacicedo, but not a new art form. She finds that the structure of the quilt has practical benefits for her wall pieces because the quilting of the layers holds the face fabric in place without its sagging over time. "With regards to the actual construction of my quilts, I find the design possibilities of actually piecing elements of cloth and then

felting the finished piece most exciting. The stitching through the layers of cloth creates yet another dimension, depending on the approach." Her large, intentionally visible running stitches made with cording enhance the surface tension of her quilts. "I see many possibilities to my quilt making," she says. "My love of collage and mixing up of different types of materials could very easily direct me towards a quilt that is totally non-functional. Combined with the need to tell a story, I know there will also be the need to define and redefine what quilt making ultimately means to me. When is a quilt a quilt . . . and when is it not?" In *Layers of Meaning* (Plate 29), a recent commission from an architect friend, she continues her explorations.

As she moves into a new genre of art, Cacicedo's inventive work with cloth, her love of storytelling, and her commitment to the fine craftsman-ship of materials continues. Whatever form her work takes, her ingenuity and creativity and the intelligent beauty of her art are impressive.

Plate 29.

Layers of Meaning, 2006.

Two panels, 87 × 36. Felted and layered wool. Collection of George Dedekian, architect

Plate 30.

Thaw, 2001, 105 × 118¾.

Cotton, with stitching.

Collection of the Museum of

Arts and Design, New York

8

The universe is in these pieces. We are enveloped by the physicality of the cloth, their surfaces scarred by repeated abrasion, punctured by oversized embroidery thread and marked by accidental hot wax drips.[1]

There was no textile art taught at Tyler School of Art in Philadelphia when Dorothy Caldwell was a student there in the late 1960s. She studied painting and sculpture. But she recalls watching her mother dye wool to make rugs and remembers her great grandmother's pieced quilt. "It has been a slow journey back to retrieve and acknowledge those important early experiences with cloth," she wrote in 1993. Caldwell recalls being convinced by the Whitney exhibit *Abstract Design in American Quilts* (1971) that fine art could be made from cloth; her previous exposure had been only to the hard-edged art of the 1960s. It was a hand painted pillow made by Lenore Davis which the artist saw in a 1974 craft show that "formed the bridge for me between painting and textiles."[2]

Over the last twenty-five years, Caldwell has developed a unique visual vocabulary that is centered in both the land and worldwide textile traditions, two areas which she continually explores and which are fundamental to her art. Commissioned in 1986 for a large work in Red Deer, Alberta, she set off on her bicycle to gather visual information and to experience the local landscape. Caldwell had located black-and-white aerial photographs during her research and was intrigued to find the patterns in these images in the land through which she was traveling—"the grid of the land survey, the diagonal movement of natural land forms across the grid, the circular man made ponds and farming patterns etched into the surface of the earth." These were all incorporated into her art, and abstract imagery of land has been a feature of most of her art since then. *Landstat*, 1988, the commissioned work for which the research was done, was her first quilt. The art form offered the structure and stability she needed for this monumental work.

Caldwell's art, however, is not landscape art. "I have always felt that landscape, which implies a view, was not the right term to describe my work," says the artist. "My intent is more to examine how the land is patterned and marked by humans and by natural geological phenomena and how these marks form the 'stage' on which we live." But this intellectual framework does not convey completely the essence of her art either. Working abstractly and without affectation, Caldwell presents her maps to the onlooker. She marks them with patterns—"their surfaces scarred with repeated abrasions." These maps, with their patterns imposed by both humans and nature, are imbued with the rhythms of time, past and present, and graced with beauty. In *Thaw* (Plate 30) and other works, with cloth as her medium, Caldwell leaves the imprint of her own presence on the stage in the expressive and intimate gestures of her stitches, dots, and lines.

Caldwell has received several grants from the Ontario Arts Council and the Canadian Council for the Arts, which she has used for textile research. Her study has taken her not only into museum archives and collections but also to Australia, Japan, and India, where she has observed textile artisans at work. **Kantha** has influenced the way she uses stitching and alerted her to the narrative voice in textile art.[3] And she has adopted an African artisanal practice of integrating spots and irregularities into her design. Studying at the Museum of Civilization in Gatineau, Quebec, Caldwell discovered that the quilts to which she was drawn were rough and utilitarian. "These everyday quilts were made from fabrics that came with a previous history. New fabric was not purchased to make these quilts. It brought home the idea of how a textile can encode a sense of time and history and a feeling of lives lived."

In 2004 Caldwell had an exhibit at the Textile Museum of Canada which was based on her study of artifacts in the museum's historic collection. Contemporary textile curator Sarah Quinton, writing in the exhibit catalog, noted that the exhibit was an exploration of "how the act of mending or repairing cloth creates new meaning and renewal, marking time and build-

Plate 31.

A Hill/A Lake #1, 2002, 19 × 59.

Cotton; appliquéd and stitched.

Collection of Ron Fitzgerald

Plate 32.

An Island/A Pond #1, 2002, 19 × 59.

Cotton; appliquéd and stitched.

Collection of Ron Fitzgerald

Plate 33.

A Lake/A Bowl #1, 2001–2003,

19 × 59. Cotton; appliquéd and stitched.

Collection of the Museum of Civilization,

Gatineau, Quebec, Canada. Courtesy

of the artist

ing history." "While examining the marks made by construction and repair," says Caldwell, "I became much more conscious of the way cloth continuously wears out and breaks down and is then reconstructed into a new whole." The artist selected mended garments and textiles from her own and the museum's collections, which were installed throughout the exhibition. "These old and carefully repaired pieces, of cloth," noted the curator, "harmonized with Caldwell's own language of mark making." Caldwell made a lengthy sampler of marks, *Day by Day* (2003), using ordinary stitching—a patch, a mend, a seam, the most basic and functional stitches. Quinton cogently wrote: "With this vocabulary, the artist is restating the materiality of her work as she claims a context for it. She works in deference to domestically prescribed utilitarian skills, and yet pulls them away from their private arena and symbolically places them into the exterior world of the land."[4]

In this same exhibition, three of the artist's studio quilts—*A Hill/A Lake #1* (Plate 31), *An Island/A Pond #1* (Plate 32), and *A Lake/A Bowl #1* (Plate 33)—were also displayed. Quinton, who assisted the artist during her residency at the museum and interviewed her extensively, commented on the harmony of Caldwell's visual vocabulary. "The recurring elliptical forms are examples of Caldwell's allusive formal vocabulary: the ellipses suggest both land formations and geometrically precise and spatially complex abstract elements—they also mimic the uneven, circular patched areas in a threadbare utility blanket."

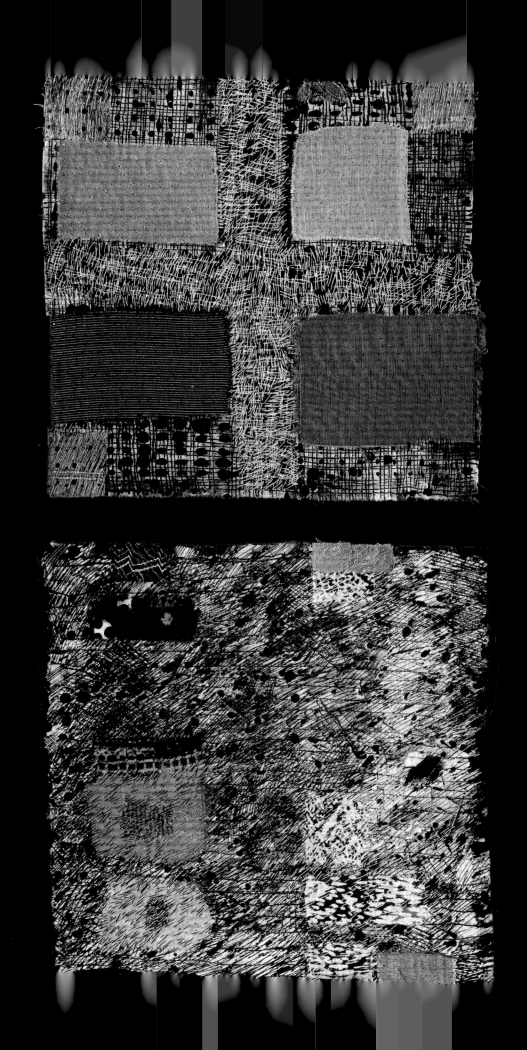

The grid of the land survey which Caldwell first discovered in 1986 underlies the patterned surface of many of her quilts. Additional pattern is sometimes applied by printing with blocks that have been gouged and scraped. Despite the patterning, however, her work has a spare and minimalist character. She likes the graphic quality of black and white and captures the idea of a particular place with additional layers of pattern and texture. Simple swatches of color sometimes depict the color of the land or "denote the melody or the specific atmosphere of a time and place," she says. "I think about the energy created on a black and white field in winter by a patch of red dogwood bushes or how a bright green field of winter wheat energizes the bland color of the landscape at that time of the year."

Drawing and expressive gesture are very important to this artist. She speaks of her need for drawing, and she meets it by marking with wax, using the **tjanting** tools of the Indonesian batik artisan. The process allows for the emergence of drawn "line" through the **discharge of dye** from the cloth. To this, she may add **running** or random **stitches:** "I want my stitches to be free and expressive and unique to the moment."

Caldwell's studio quilts capture her personal landmarks as well as her studies of other geographical sites. A trip to Newfoundland led to a series of small and intimate quilts, *Ground Cover* (Plates 34 and 35). The quilt *Fourpatch: Hay, Wheat, Rye, Barley* reflects the land configuration of the farm where she lives and its relationship to the "fourpatch" quilt block. The lake seen from the front window, the hill on which the studio sits, and the fields surrounding the house are all daily markers that appear as abstracted forms in her work. John E. Vollmer has commented on the "wealth of interactions and relationships between field and border" in some of her pieces.[5] Evidence of the continual nourishment of her art from textile study is found in these borders. "Borders are an integral part of textiles, not a frame or container," she says. "In some textiles the border is where most of the activity occurs while the central area of the piece may be a large plain field. I have worked with this idea in a number of my pieces." She compares it to fields of wheat where trees and scrub, fences, piled stones, and vines in time grow over the survey lines and delineate the underlying grid. Border activity in her quilts marks the patterns of human settlement.

"[T]he centre of Caldwell's studio practice," wrote Quinton, "is poetic invention: she draws out innate qualities from her subject matter and her materials." Caldwell understands the unique information contained within both. She demonstrates it not only in her work but in her admiration for the skill of the local, traditional quilters who finish her pieces with their "tiny perfect stitches."

Facing above. Plate 34.
Ground Cover: Walking on Moss,
2000, 12 × 12. Textile construction.
Private collection

Facing below. Plate 35.
Ground Cover: Moss, 2000,
12 × 12. Textile construction.
Collection of Sue Rankin

Plate 36.

Aura V, 2003, three frames,
11½ × 9½. Corn leaves, grass,
silk organza, thread, frame.

9

My work is collaboration between Nature and myself. I always think of nature having a personality, just like we do, with its own language to communicate; whether it is expressed by shape, pattern, color, texture, form, scale, sound or temperature and its changes. My works have been made while searching for and exploring that common language I could share with nature.[1]

When Kyoung Ae Cho came to the United States from South Korea in 1988 to pursue graduate studies in fiber art, she already possessed an undergraduate education in traditional textile skills and had taken additional courses in virtually all the visual arts, including architectural drafting. But it was in childhood, from watching her grandmother sew, turning small scraps of cloth into precious gifts, that she learned the respect for materials and craftsmanship that are the leitmotifs of her art: "If you make anything from the depths of your heart, even with the humblest of materials, it can become something very special."[2]

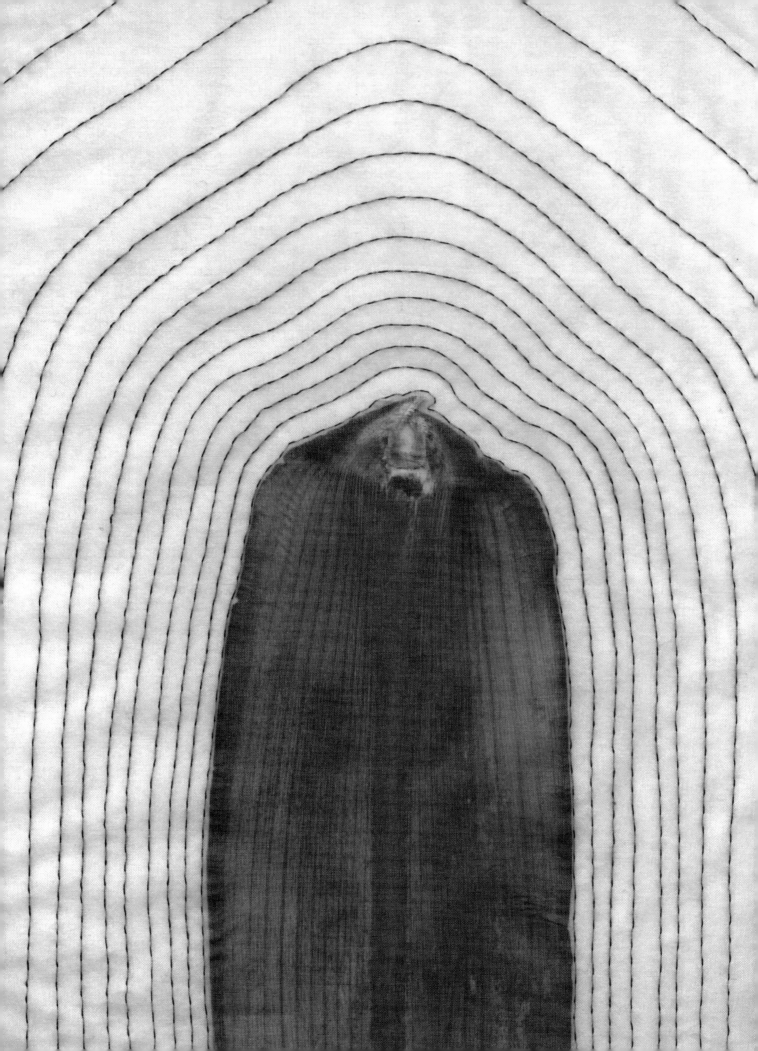

After spending a year as a fiber student at California State University at Northridge, living with her extended family while becoming acclimated to her new country, Cho was accepted as an MFA student at Cranbrook Academy of Art in Michigan. Arriving there without her luggage, which was misplaced for a month in the moving process, and having nothing to remind her of her art in the new studio, the artist turned her attention to the beautiful natural setting surrounding the school.

Nature became her new medium. The process of making art became one of discovery as she sought to identify and learn from nature's sometimes hidden cycles and rhythms of growth, adaptation to change, and death, or metamorphosis. She believes that humans, too, are part of that rhythm, despite the tragedies we endure and the sometimes chaotic nature of our lives. In her effort to understand and collaborate with nature, the artist begins with the smallest, often overlooked, elements: pine needles, twigs, or the grain lines in trees. Through her art, she celebrates the life and history of these overlooked natural objects. Using such elements, as well as shells, moss, stone, wood, silk, and even hair, her art has taken the form of installations, sculpture, weavings, and quilts. Like nature, it often has an air of impermanence. Its aesthetic, as seen in *Aura* (Plates 36 and 37), is minimalist, elegant, and beautiful.

In the late 1990s Kyoung Ae Cho returned to her sewing. Her quilt *AGED, covered by wisdom* (Plates 38 and 39), was accepted into the 1997 *Quilt National* exhibit and won the Award of Excellence. She exhibited new works in a series called *Quilts?!* Of these combined wood and fiber works, she wrote: "In autumn a tree sheds its leaves, which cover the ground nurturing the earth for the next generation. Useless rags meanwhile have been gathered and assembled to create a beautiful quilt or blanket that is handed down to the next generation with love and care. I chose instead to use lumber, crosscut and put together to create my quilt pieces *AGED, covered by wisdom* and the *Quilt?!* series. Through this process, I have been able to combine my love of wood and my love of sewing as well."[3]

In *Veil* (Plate 40) another series constructed in the manner of a quilt, Cho sandwiches maple veneer, marked with burns to highlight the grain, between layers of silk organza. "I was thinking of the gentle, delicate side of nature," she says. But by marking the grain lines—the mark of a tree's life and experience—she seeks to recall that past life to our minds.

In these series, as well as in her *Landscape* and *Inner-Scape* series (2000), Cho's format is typical of traditional quilts. The wood grains are cut and arranged geometrically, allowing the viewer to easily trace them. Her collaboration with these elements offers us a chance to recognize that we, too, are part of the natural order.

From her training in textiles, Kyoung Ae Cho has learned to be sensitive to material, to pay attention to the detail, and to respect the process. This means being patient with time-consuming monotonous processes at times. In describing Cho, independent curator Catherine S. Amidon wrote: "She

Plate 37.

Aura V, detail

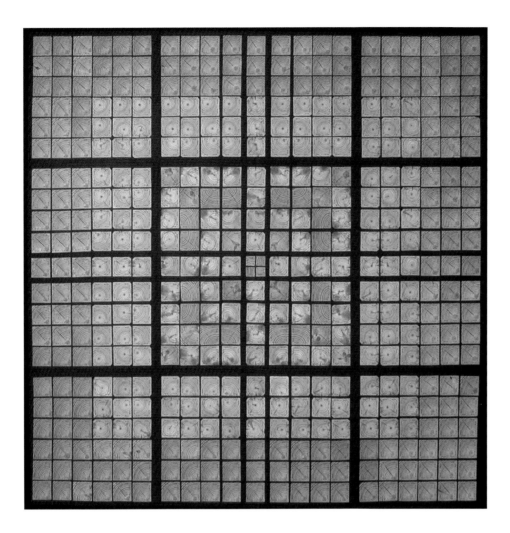

Plate 38.
AGED, covered by wisdom,
1996, 108 × 108. Wood,
fabric, waxed cord, thread.

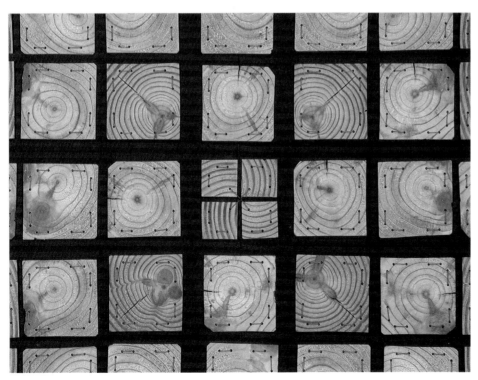

Plate 39.
AGED, covered by
wisdom, detail

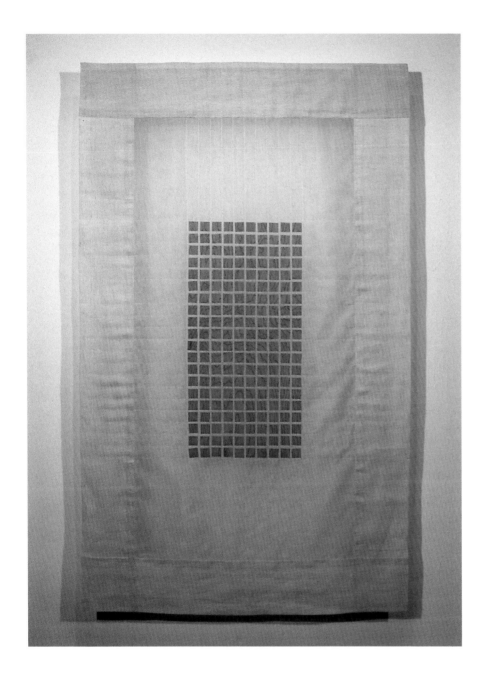

sees her material as a partner rather than a substance to force by her will. It bends, she bends, as they collaborate and change together through a working process."[4] As a student at Cranbrook, Cho studied under Gerhardt Knodel, the school's director and a highly regarded fiber artist, who writes of her as "consistently generous and life affirming . . . in awe of conditions that are beyond her knowing."[5]

Cho expects to continue working with both wood and fabric; they are both necessary to her art. But she remains open to other methods and media "for wherever my idea leads me," she says. Whatever form her art takes in the future, it will undoubtedly leave its imprint on viewers, causing them to pause, meditate, and admire the quiet beauty and celebration in her art.

Plate 40.

Veil I, 2001, 60 × 36.

Burn marks, maple veneer,

silk organza, ramie, thread.

Plate 41.

Lady of Guadalupe II, 1987, 80 × 64. Pieced, cotton.

Ardis and Robert James Collection, International Quilt Study

Center, University of Nebraska–Lincoln, 1997.007.1089.

Courtesy of the artist

One of my goals is that by the end of my life, I will have done the best I can to hone my eyes to the most exquisitely beautiful and dynamic spatial relationships. These will be in geometric forms because these are what I love; and these relationships, among lines, shapes, colors, values, will be the best I can do fitting them all together.[1]

Nancy Crow is one of the foremost studio quiltmakers in the country. A master colorist, her work portrays a lively inner world and an active engagement with the outer one. For Crow, beauty is the perfect proportion of all the elements of art to one another. Yet there is nothing static about her art. It is dynamic, tense, and beautifully resolved. This was just as true of her early work, when she was constructing her quilts with an elaborate and laborious **template** method, as it is now, when the templates have been abandoned and replaced with free-form cutting and piecing.

The path the artist chose—to focus solely on studio quilts—has not been easy. Despite a career filled with accomplishments, she still receives only scant attention from the art world. The craft world has not been so reticent.

Her work was noticed early on by Paul J. Smith, the director of the Museum of Contemporary Crafts. In 1980, four years after she decided to devote her career to quiltmaking, *March Study* beckoned onlookers through the glass windows and doors of the museum. For Crow, it was very important that Smith, whose "eye" she already respected, was encouraging her in this way. Six years later, *Yellow Crosses IV* was included in the 1986 inaugural exhibit of *Craft Today: Poetry of the Physical* at the MCC. In 1993 she was given a solo exhibit there, and in 1995 another solo exhibit at the Renwick Gallery of the Smithsonian American Art Museum. In 2002 Crow's work was exhibited at the Museum of Fine Arts, Boston, in *Eloquent Threads: The Daphne Farago Fiber Collection.* In her thirty-year career, she has exhibited work in countless solo and invitational exhibits in this country and overseas. Her quilts are in the permanent collections of the Museum of Art & Design in New York, the Indianapolis Museum of Art, the Museum of American Folk Art in New York, the Miami University Art Museum in Ohio, and the International Quilt Study Center in Lincoln, Nebraska. In 1999 she became the first quiltmaker to be made a fellow of the American Craft Council.

Crow began her art education as an undergraduate in ceramics and later obtained an MFA in weaving and ceramics. In 2002 she told an interviewer: "By 1976, I realized I loved quiltmaking. I love line and shape. It was just the beginning of my being able to identify how important those are to me."[2] Later, she added, "I made quiltmaking my chosen medium when I realized how closely allied it was to painting; how easily I could move compositional forms around; how I could use color and make color."[3]

The passion that Nancy Crow has about her art extends to her work habits, which explains why she is so productive. In the beginning, she took traditional patterns such as the Double Wedding Ring and the New York Beauty and made quilt after quilt until she became so familiar with the shapes that she could intuitively and spontaneously break them down. This is why working in a series is so important, she says. Only after that understanding of shape has become intuitive do breakthroughs occur. "That's when the excitement begins," she says. "The first quilt isn't necessarily the best."

Although spatial relationships and geometric form are of great importance in her art, all of Crow's work has an emotional underpinning. Her *Bittersweet* series (1980–1981) was about "coming to terms with the fact that I had to accept responsibility for making myself happy and fulfilling my own life." The *Yellow Crosses* series (1983–1986) was about the burdens one has to bear in life.[4] In 1985, she had a strong need to make quilts that reflected a sense of goodness; the result was the *Lady of Guadalupe* series (see Plate 41).

This series was inspired by Van Gogh's painting *Portrait of Woman with Carnations.* "I saw log cabin patterning in the shirt and a yellow halo in the background," she wrote in her 1990 book, *Quilts and Influences.*[5] The quilts demonstrate the artist's attraction to indigenous folk art and ethnic textiles. Since the 1990s, Crow has led annual textile tours to Latin America and South Africa. She is constantly alert to color, texture, and pattern during

these trips and returns home with sketches, photographs, and artifacts, particularly textiles. Collections of baskets and ethnic textiles line her studio walls and fill her closets; all of them, along with elements in her natural environment and the many art books she owns, provide continual nourishment for her art.

By 1988 Crow's work was defined by increasing complexity. But she was growing dissatisfied with the process. "I was trying to introduce more freedom into my work," she told art historian Jean Robertson. Folk art and the quilts and improvisational style of the African American quiltmaker Anna Williams attracted her. That same year she began her *Color Blocks* series (see Plate 42). The first three quilts were as visually complex as her preceding work, but she stopped working with templates and used only a ruler. In 1990 she simplified further by working with only one motif, a square, and she avoided printed fabric. "I hoped I would be able to make a breakthrough to some sort of freedom." In 1991, when she reached the fifteenth quilt in the series, Crow allowed her squares for the first time to be different sizes. It became an engineering challenge to construct the quilts, but she enjoyed it. She was achieving the longed-for breakthrough. The next step was to dye her own fabric, which gave her both the deeply saturated colors and the range of values (light to dark) she needed.

Plate 42.

Color Blocks 33, 1993, 48 × 66.

Pieced, cotton; hand dyed; hand quilted by Marla Hattabaugh.

Photo: J. Kevin Fitzsimons

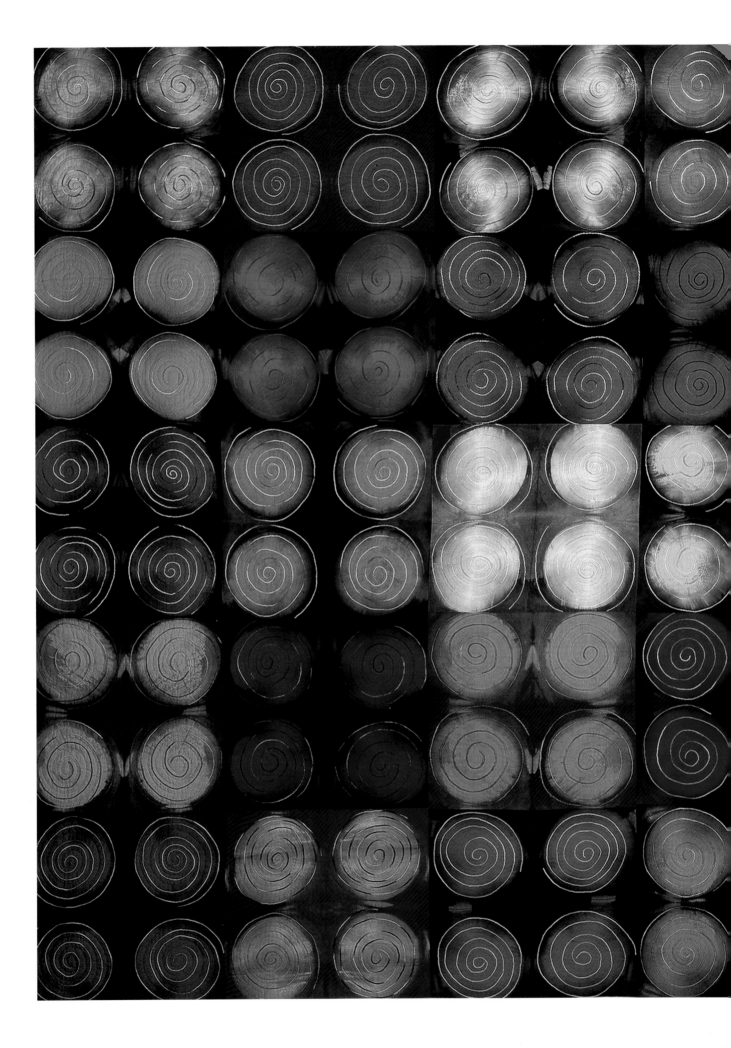

Plate 43.

Chinese Souls # 2, 1992, 81 × 89.

Pieced, cotton; embroidered, hand dyed;

resist-dyed by Lunn Fabrics; hand quilted by

Marla Hattabaugh. Collection: Indianapolis

Museum of Art, Mary V. Black Art

Endowment Fund. Courtesy of the artist

The passion that underlies Crow's approach to art is, per-haps, most evident in a series she began during a trip to Chi-na. An award from the Ohio Arts Council took her and fel-low artist and quiltmaker Susan Shie to Shaanxi Province in 1990. While there, she was witness to a cruel form of justice being carried out on young men who had been arrested for minor crimes. With ropes around their bodies and packed in a cattle truck, they were being driven around the city be-fore being executed to warn would-be offenders. Horrified, Crow returned to her room, took out some small pieces of dyed cloth, and began "embroidering ropes around the souls of the young men."[6] On returning home, she made a series of ten quilts. *Chinese Souls #2* (Plate 43) is in the collection of the Indianapolis Museum of Art.

By 1993 Crow was cutting freely into her fabrics and work-ing improvisationally. In her recently published book, *Nancy Crow*, she writes: "I approached each composition with no planning, no idea of what might happen. I embraced the idea that ART WAS A PROCESS OF DISCOVERY, that for me the freshest ideas, the most interesting ideas, came about by observing shapes and lines that had been cut, then pinned to the wall. With practice, I came to believe that shapes and their spatial relationships would lead the way if I could relax enough to let it happen."[7] She began to cut freely into the fab-ric with her **rotary cutter** and spent the next two years making quilts this way until she felt she had trained her hand, wrist, arm, and shoulder muscles to draw lines across the cloth.

In 1995 she began new work. *Constructions* (see Plate 44) is a large, ongoing explorative series containing several subsets, each representing an investigation of ideas that arose in pre-ceding work. The artist strives to make these pieces both dy-namic and lyrical. Her well-honed skills of cutting the fabric

Facing page. Plate 44.

Constructions #17, 1998, 82 × 41.

Pieced, cotton; hand dyed; hand quilted
by Marla Hattabaugh. Photo: J. Kevin
Fitzsimons

and choosing colors, and her careful attention to every element in these pieces, result in visual symphonies of color and shape, mood and emotion that range from somber to lighthearted.

Crow no longer allows the art world's disinterest to preoccupy her. She concentrates on art and teaching. She has always been a force for change in quiltmaking—as a founder of *Quilt National* in 1979, of the Art Quilt Network in 1986, and of the Quilt Surface Design Symposium in 1990. Now, teaching in a course of study that she devised for her Timber Frame Barn Workshops in Ohio, as well as in workshops around the world, she continues to push herself and her students to work harder. Her concern is that quiltmaking be taken seriously as art. She can convey what that means to her students, if not to museum directors. "It takes years to learn to use fabrics before you can express yourself with them. There is this conception that anyone can make quilts anytime they want. . . . It's taken so long for quiltmaking to be considered an art form because people dismiss it. They don't realize what it takes to be able to do one."[8]

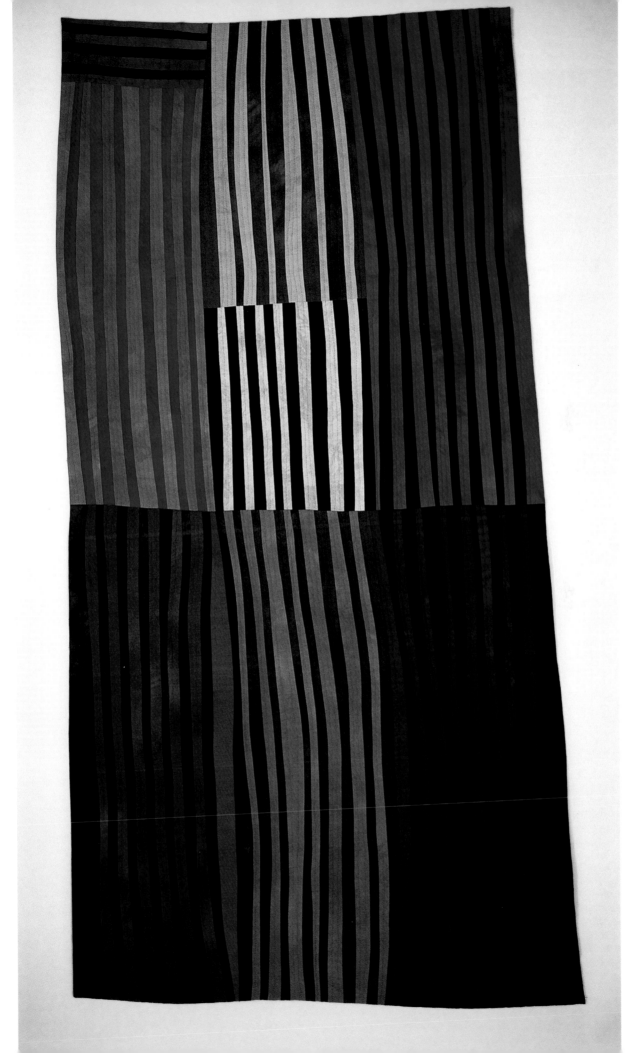

Plate 45.

Hall of Memory #7: The Wondrous Green Room,
1998, 59¾ × 59. Whole cloth; appliquéd, machine
stitched, painted.

In all my works, the capybaras, ravens, lions, cheetahs
and bears are acknowledged powerful elements in my
life; they act as familiars, or spiritual guides in the lives
of humans, and it is they who re-establish communities
and retell the old myths.[1]

Nancy Erickson has lived most of her life in Montana. Her home
and studio are located in the Pattee Canyon, near Missoula but
away from urban development and city lights that obscure the
night sky. Sometimes the animals who inhabit her paintings, drawings, and
quilts stroll across her yard as she works. She has experienced the destruction
wrought by forest fires firsthand and has been a committed pacifist since the
1960s. The constancy of her hope and her unique vision of a different kind of
world have nourished her creative output for more than thirty years.

Erickson obtained her college degree in zoology and was in graduate
school before finally submitting to her love of art. After several years of
extension classes in painting, she returned to graduate school in the mid-

nancy erickson

Facing page. Plate 46.

Interiors: Summer Solstice, 1985,

114¾ × 58. Whole cloth, cotton;

painted on black background.

Collection of the Museum of

Arts and Design, New York

Left. Plate 47.

Interiors: Summer Solstice, detail

1960s to acquire an MA and MFA in painting and drawing. While there, she experimented with fabric sculpture. Her first quilt, made in 1975, was a combination of fabric sculpture and quilting. Technical difficulties with the construction eventually led her to drop the sculptured aspect and to focus on variations of the quilt form.

Erickson works from her drawings, first enlarging them, then tracing them with paint onto fabric, and cutting them out. She paints the surface of these images with fabric paint and oil paintsticks and then lightly glues and stitches them to the cloth background. Fabric offers her great versatility and numerous options for enhancing the texture of her work. Cotton, satin, and velvet, for example, reflect and absorb light differently, enabling her to make use of these varying effects. Machine appliqué and **satin stitching** also enrich the texture of her quilts. Her fabric pieces, such as her *Interiors* series (Plates 46 and 47), tend to be large. "Large works move you out of the ordinary," she says. "I love to be surrounded by someone's huge painting or huge environment. I merge with it."[2] She also works in smaller sizes, however. Many of her drawings (oil paintsticks on archival paper) are half the size of her fabric art.

Whether she is drawing, painting, or making quilts, Erickson's art is a visual narrative; she is a storyteller. She has been consistently concerned with humans' use of their environment in ways which she believes show profound disrespect for the dignity of animals, and with their ignorance of the history and importance of the "bond between humans and other animals." While ominous signs of destruction resulting from both war and natural causes are often visible in the "landscape," these catastrophes do not dominate her work. Instead, the viewer sees tenacity and even humor in the spirit of human and animal figures as they cope with the chaos about them. The titles of some of these pieces, observes Margaret Kingsland, curator and former executive director of the Montana Committee for the Humanities, suggest that things are not as they seem.[3]

Erickson's art conveys her belief that the world humans have built and the way they order their life cannot ultimately succeed. In work dating from the 1980s and 1990s, fragments of human structures—stairways, televisions, and light bulbs—are strewn about. These are not peaceful landscapes; the dangers are apparent. But the artist also offers us a vision of what life might be like after the apocalypse. In *her* community, humans and the higher mammals share their space. Capybaras, cougars, bears, and female nudes live in harmony. Erickson's animals, even within their species, are individuals. She gives them human expressions. In this new world, they seem completely relaxed in each other's company. They survey their surroundings or gaze out toward the viewer with expressions of puzzlement, annoyance, reproach, and wariness.

Quilts made in the 1980s and 1990s—for example, the *Interiors* series, *Restless Mountain,* and *The Clear and Present Danger*—have a compressed intensity and tension which come from the power of her convictions, but which are conveyed through strong, dignified drawings and juxtapositions of pure colors. Her colors—striking reds, blues, purples, and oranges—bear no relation to reality; they outline shapes, evoke menace or warmth, and at times create an illusion of distance. Sharp diagonal lines and the large scale of the images often add to the power of her work, in both large and smaller pieces. At times, figures are cut off at the borders, leaving the viewer eye to eye with an animal. Many of her animals, even with their familiar expressions, have gleaming red eyes set in gold. In some of her quilts, both humans and animals are inhabitants of man-made spaces that are clearly ill-suited to their size or nature. "The grandeur of the wild animal contrasts with the pedestrian domesticity of the small stool and rug," writes Kingsland, making note of two elements that appear in many of the quilts.[4] In others, the structures seem to provide shelter, but cataclysmic events are visible through open doors and windows.

In the late 1990s Erickson began a series she called *Hall of Memory*. Recalling childhood stories of polar bears and interested in recently published
books about the prehistoric cave drawings in France, she wrote: "I wanted
to think of a future time in which the bears returned to deserted habitations
and taught their families about the past: the owls, the hyenas, the huge and
wonderful dish-nosed cave bear, the cave lions."[5] In these pieces the intensity
of color is somewhat diminished. In *Hall of Memory #7: The Wondrous Green
Room* (Plate 45), the bears have come upon a room built by humans—we can
tell by the floor boards—and are engaged in a museum visit of their own,
exclaiming, peering, and deep in concentration as they examine evidence of
their own history drawn on the walls. But the floors are skewed, leaving us
feeling somewhat disoriented, and the cougar's expression is wary.

In a newer series of cougar quilts, one of which was awarded "Best of
Show" in the 2003 *Quilt National* competition (*Felis Forever I*, Plate 48),
Erickson frees the animals entirely from her strange landscapes. They exist

Plate 48.

Felis Forever I, 2000, 39 × 69.

Cotton, velvet, satin; paint and

charcoal; appliquéd, embroidered,

machine stitched.

as free beings, but still bear their history imprinted on their skins. These cougars are not fearsome; their skins are battered and bruised. They gaze at us with one red eye and one blue. These are disconcerting works, but they do not allow us to ignore them or to turn away unmoved. Since 2003 the artist has been at work on another series telling the story of the Toklat wolves of Denali Park, Alaska. She has also begun work on a group of women at campfires; now they are the tellers of tales (Plate 49).

Nancy Erickson's quilted paintings inhabit their own ambiguous environment. They have been rejected from quilt exhibits because they are paintings and from art galleries because they are quilts. Nonetheless, she has persisted for decades on the strength of her passion for both the natural world and for art.

Plate 49.

Pleistocene Memory, 2005, 78 × 74. Whole cloth, satin and velvet; appliquéd, painted, quilted. Three shaped pieces on a black background. Photo by the artist

Plate 50.

At the Crossroads, 1993,

75 ⅝ × 54 ⅜. Pieced, cotton.

12

I strongly believe that all art is autobiographical and my art reflects my life and everything that I encounter. My quilts are filled with the color, rhythm, patterns and the music of every day. I see and feel the color and rhythms around me all day, every day: the way the shadows from a wrought iron fence fall across the sidewalk, the way the windows punctuate the brickwork in the building across the street, the color combinations of that group of teenagers making their way down the street and how the colors and patterns interact as they walk, skip and strut along.[1]

Carole Harris's rich and vibrant art invites interpretation. This is why she works abstractly, to allow all viewers to bring something different to their viewing and to interpret it in their own way. But through color, rhythm, pattern, and music, she also reaches back toward her own childhood and to a lost past she has tried to understand, reclaim, and celebrate. Her quilts tell stories and reference the African way of making non-literal art.

Harris describes her art education as being in the "classical Euro-American tradition." The painter Richard Diebenkorn has been an influence, but so have the African American artists Jacob Lawrence and Raymond Saunders.

After studying painting, drawing, and art history, she obtained her BFA in 1966. But she was more interested in design than painting and worked for several architectural firms in Detroit before founding and serving as the president of her own design firm for the past thirty years. Like many studio quiltmakers with training in the arts, Harris was drawn to fabric because she loves the way it feels. She began making quilts in the late 1960s and since 1977 has extensively exhibited her work in solo and group exhibitions in the United States, Canada, and France. Her work was included in the *Spirits of the Cloth* exhibition organized by Carolyn Mazloomi and exhibited at the American Craft Museum in New York,[2] the Mint Museum in Charlotte, North Carolina, and the Renwick Gallery of the Smithsonian American Art Museum. Her studio quilts have been seen in numerous university galleries and are in the collections of corporations, non-profit institutions, and private individuals.

Harris's work is grounded in the traditional craft, but the expressive visual language she has developed is distinctive and personal. "It wasn't until I began finding my own vocabulary from a mixture of traditional quilt patterns, forged with some of my own imagery, impressions, and experimentations that another aesthetic started to emerge which bore an uncanny resemblance to African textile and art traditions," she writes. Harris studied these traditions and found some similarities between her own art and the art of the Congo and also the Yoruba in Nigeria. Their textiles were densely layered with pattern—patterns that repeated and materials that overlapped. Harris's spontaneous way of working is also very similar to that of the Congolese and Yoruba artisans.

When the artist describes her art-making process, she is describing the improvisational quiltmaking used by some African American quiltmakers. This process has enriched the genre of American quilt art immeasurably and has been a significant influence on many studio artists. "It may be a little more difficult to explain, since I rarely explain it, I just do it. . . . I rarely have a specific theme in mind when I begin a new piece. The colors are usually the result of combinations I've seen and found interesting. I love the feel of fabric, so I begin each piece by just gathering, touching, sorting, moving and looking at groups of fabrics until I find a combination that pleases me. I particularly like the combination of saffron and burgundy or red and hot pink, very saturated colors that I use frequently. I start by assembling the fabrics, being aware of colors and patterns, moving them around, placing them against each other; testing to see what kind of energy they create. Then I begin to 'play.' I say play, because this is the most enjoyable part for me. Cutting strips and pieces and sewing them together, manipulating the cloth as it directs me. Once I get into the process, one thing usually leads to another. The work generates ideas and direction. Then I cut and sew and cut and sew again and again until I have created enough new pieces, or blocks—you see I still use some of the traditional vocabulary—to begin the composition. The composition is very important to all of my quilts and is probably due to my

training and work as a designer. The composition must have proper balance, in color, shape, patterns and value, according to the combined European and African aesthetics."

At the Crossroads (Plate 50) shows the importance of color to all of Harris's compositions. This 1993 quilt began as a personal challenge to work only in black and white. But it was not as expressive as she wanted it; small accents of terra cotta were added. These "began to assert themselves" as she assembled the pieces, finally leading to a composition in which large, earth colored areas are punctuated by rust and black divided squares. The title, she says, is an appropriate metaphor for both quiltmaking and for life.

The composition of *Something Like a Jitterbug* (Plate 51) was the result of her study and interpretation of the Yoruba "Egungun" ceremonial dance dress. "I had been trying to develop a technique that would allow me to move my quiltmaking out of the flat two dimensional plane," she writes. "This was my second attempt, and took over a year to complete. The composition began as a vertical totem-like column, but was too static for the high energy piece that I was trying to create. After many revisions, the panels emerged and the varying sizes and colors of the divided square along with the multiple printed fabrics helped create the energy I was seeking, while the solid areas of color helped to moderate that energy. The title was an acknowledgement of the dance element of the African celebration, but also a tribute to a celebratory aspect of African American dance."

Often an understanding and appreciation of one art form enriches one's understanding of another art form. In an essay written for *African American Quiltmaking in Michigan,* the artist's husband, author Bill Harris, compares Carole's art to American jazz. "The parallels between Harris's techniques and those of jazz music are obvious. While experimental, it is never unconsciously haphazard." He continues: "It is as with a Charles Mingus or Ornette Coleman composition, with their various elements: tempos, textures, rhythms, tones coming together, intersecting, interdependent, and yet free to change from moment to moment within a moment."[3] This is exactly the feeling one has when viewing Carole Harris's work.

Yet quilts, such as *The Appropriateness of Yellow* (Plate 52), have an architectural quality that exudes strength. Forms may overlap but are not transparent. Sometimes they intersect; at other times they take over or just run into each other. But they are all connected. Large black and other solid-colored areas "are not just background," she says, "they play a significant role in creating the proper balance. They give the eye a rest or punctuate the high energy, super saturated colors and heavily patterned areas. The solid or black areas provide respite, but on closer examination, you will find, they are almost always very heavily quilted, creating a different, more subtle kind of energy."

View from the Kitchen on Preston Street is a cityscape (Plate 53). It is Harris's interpretation of "the joyous amalgam of life in the city with its multitude of colors and textures. To some it may seem chaotic," she writes. "To me, there is a definite sense of order from the warmth of the color pallet to the vertical placement and balance of the pieced blocks with all manner of things going on within each block. The title comes from when I was a young girl. From the kitchen of our second floor flat, I looked out of the window across the alley to see the rhythm of the angled tops of houses and garages."

Down the Road a Piece (Plate 54) from her landscape series, while highlighted with brilliant fuscia, red, and gold, is far quieter than earlier work. Her blacks and grays relate more to highways than to fields, yet the warmth of her color at this new crossroads establishes the human presence. The little bits of colorful string quilting and the few small but brilliant patterned quilt

Plate 52.

The Appropriateness of Yellow, 1990, 77 × 60.

Pieced, cotton. Collection of the Michigan State

University Museum of Folk Art

Below. Plate 53.

View from the Kitchen on
Preston Street, 1999, 36 × 65½.
Pieced, mixed fabrics.

Facing page. Plate 54.
Down the Road a Piece (*Landscape*
Series), 2003, 77 × 60. Pieced,
cotton. Collection of the Michigan
Council for the Arts and Culture.
Photo: Jim Thayer

blocks tell us there is still joy in that presence. There is mystery in this work, too. Harris would invite our interpretations. Is the sliver of yellow letting the viewer in on a secret? Is someone peeking out into the night? What's going on in this direction? In that direction? The quilt's evolution from earlier work is evident. Its rhythm, textures, and tones sometimes intersect, sometimes take over or just run into each other. But they are all, as her husband has noted, interdependent.

Plate 55.

Roundelay, 2000, 69 × 45.

Pieced silk; hand dyed. Collection

of the artist. Photo: Don Tuttle

13

Piecing fabric together is like composing. There is a musical quality
to how patterns and color come together and how my hands go
over the cut pieces arranging, turning, observing, going back to a
refrain. It is the process, rather than the finished piece that brings
me back to the studio.[1]

In 1972, following post-graduate study of ceramics in Japan, artist Ana
Lisa Hedstrom traveled to Southeast Asia and India. It was an epiphany
for her to see magnificent textiles in their cultural context, and she returned to Oakland, California, determined to study textiles. She enrolled
in a workshop at Fiberworks in Berkeley taught by Yoshiko Wada. "There
was an investigative quality to this early workshop as we tried to decipher
the techniques of these obscure and labor intensive processes. It was a little
like reading a code." Hedstrom returned to Japan in 1982 and spent several
months in Arimatsu, the center of traditional shibori artisan production.

It was the inventive and deceptively simple concepts and intricate patterns of arashi shibori that captured her imagination (see a sample illustrated in the introduction), and she turned her attention to it full-time. In a catalog essay for an exhibition of her work at the Robert Hillestad Textiles Gallery at the University of Nebraska in Lincoln, artist Michael James states that Hedstrom's "longstanding reputation as one of the leading creative forces in the exploration of arashi shibori and other surface design processes was built on years of experimentation with those techniques."[2] Her mastery of the traditional Japanese processes, her contemporary adaptations of those processes, and her artistry led to her designation in 2003 as an American Craft Council Fellow, an award signifying an outstanding artist. Hedstrom's art is in the collections of the Cooper Hewitt Museum of Design of the Smithsonian; the Museum of Art and Design in New York; the M. H. de Young Museum in San Francisco; the Oakland Museum, in Oakland, California; Takeda Kahei Shoten in Arimatsu, Japan; and the Aichi Shibori Archive in Nagoya, Japan.

For Hedstrom, it has always been the nature of the process which held her interest in shibori. She describes arashi shibori as a "collaborative process in which the material, the manipulation process, and the dye application all play a part in the result." "The options are so great that an inventive approach to the process will yield endless variations of pattern and texture." But there are also constraints, having to do "with scale and what the fabric and dyes will or will not do. You are always working with these elements and you are never completely in control," she says. This means there are often surprises when the cloth is unfolded. "You have to respond to the materials you are working with. This is what I mean by collaboration."

The artist's use of her patterned and hand dyed cloth as a medium for creative expression has taken several forms over the years. Early efforts to use it for pieced wall hangings were set aside in the 1980s as the Artwear movement burgeoned. She found the intimate scale of shibori patterning and the fine textures and pleats conducive to designing clothing. Her considerable achievements with this expressive form are due not only to her mastery of the processes and the artistry of her cloth, but also to her view of the human body as a kind of moving sculptural form. Working improvisationally and intuitively with color and pattern, her visually stunning coats and vests are regarded as an art form in their own right.

Early in 2000 Hedstrom returned to the two-dimensional form and began to work on several series of studio quilts. Freed from the business considerations and technical constraints of pieced clothing, she feels that the experience has been liberating for her. She describes her new work as abstract and painterly, her imagery as larger and graphic. Pattern is a constant presence, as in *Roundelay* (Plate 55), but "with my wall pieces, I control the pattern, so it is really more about shape, line, volume, color, and depth." Still, she differentiates her work from that of the painter: "A painter really begins with a blank canvas, although there is a material element in the type of paint,

brushes, etc. I think that when a fine artist begins to paint, he is in his mind more than in his hand and eye. Craft is different because the materials and the characteristics of the materials are so central to the experience, both in creating and viewing."

Hedstrom's intentions for her work, however, extend beyond the boundaries of traditional craft. In the *Lexicon* series (see Plate 56), she returns to the concept of shibori as a language. "I respond to pattern," she says. "I believe we all do. We follow pattern almost as a script. Once this capacity was used to follow subtle changes on a forest floor, but we still have satisfaction in detecting subtle variations in color and pattern. A hand-dyed fabric requires the eye to travel, unlike a printed cloth where the idea is usually grasped all at once. People tend to 'peruse' the surface patterns of hand-dyed fabric. They find it engaging. *Lexicon* refers to this idea of reading fabric, pattern, or hand-dyed fabric. . . . In my community of dyers . . . we can read a textile from Japan or China, because we can recognize what happens when you pleat and stitch, or wrap around a core. . . . We share a particular lexicon. The large abstract shapes allude to open books. . . . It is a very bold piece and reads from a distance, but it invites the reader to come up and peruse the surface."

Plate 56.
Lexicon, 2000, 46 × 82.
Pieced silk; hand dyed.
Photo: Don Tuttle

Plate 57.

Riff, 2003, 74 × 50. Pieced silk;

hand dyed. Private collection.

Photo: Don Tuttle

The improvisational method to which Hedstrom alludes at the beginning of this essay is used in her construction of wearable art, as well as for some of her quilts. An avid listener of the blues, jazz, and blue grass music, she observes parallels with American patchwork and quilt traditions. She finds models to emulate among the artist-quiltmakers of Gee's Bend, Alabama, who utilize a structure while freely playing with the elements of their compositions.[3] "I hope to work similarly with my fabrics. Yet I don't see my work as having a strong folk quality to it." Michael James has described her pieces as "the quirky geometries and unpredictable asymmetries of a confident artist."[4] *Riff* (Plate 57) and *Syncopation* are good examples.

Plate 58.

Geometry II, 2003, 69 × 49.

Pieced silk; hand dyed. Private

collection. Photo: Don Tuttle

Her wall panels, he continues, are "intelligent, austere, without being minimalist." In *Geometry I* and *II* (see Plate 58), as in her *Lexicon* quilts, Hedstrom has been particularly interested in layering dye and using dye discharge to create the illusion of dimension. In 2003 a brief residency at the University of Nebraska enabled her to use a large-format digital printer to do just that. Using the computer software program Photoshop to adjust and rework scans of her own hand dyed cloth and the computer's Sophis CAD programs to further develop the imagery, Hedstrom "played" with transparencies, layers, and illusionary piecing. *Geometry Weave* (Plate 59) was produced this way.

She does not, however, seem to be planning a major shift in the direction of technology-aided art. "During a creative career," Hedstrom writes, in a manner both explanatory and instructive to younger artists, "a map emerges, with exciting industrious times and slower reflective times. After working on a series it is necessary for me to change my terrain. I often do this by experimenting with new fabrics or techniques. I think it is essential for an artist to intuitively know when an idea is exhausted. I know I am on the right track when there are questions to pursue, not the rehashing of old ideas and visual answers. The digital printing was exciting by allowing me to change scale and composition . . . and I can see how it could interface with my studio work again. But at the moment I have been working with needle punching layers together. My husband, a metalsmith, calls this welding!"

Plate 59.

Geometry Weave, 2003, 69 × 64.
Hand dyed silk. The layout of this quilt is based on a repeat pattern created in Photoshop from a scanned square of dyed fabric.

Plate 60.

A Vivid Air, 2001, 35 × 52.

Pieced silks, hand quilted. Collection:

United States State Department,

Cambodia. Photo: Karen Bell

14

The forms found in the vaulting of a cathedral seemed more valid and instructive and a more voluptuous experience than either geometric or action painting.[1]

When asked about artists who have influenced her work, Marilyn Henrion mentions the painter and sculptor Ellsworth Kelly, whose observation and reflections are quoted above. Although she works with fabric, not paint or metal, Kelly's influence is discernible. Like his, her art is hard-edged and voluptuous. But while his painted, opaque forms are spare and one-dimensional, Henrion's are neither. Her art is about the beauty of form and color; her quilts are located in a place more dreamlike than real. Using the rich and sensual texture of jewel-toned silk, at times combined with floral cotton prints, she draws the viewer into her world, sharing literary references that resonate with her while she works. *A Vivid Air* (Plate 60) from her *Fragments* series, begun in the aftermath of the attack on the World Trade Towers, is a striking portrayal of the artist's interpretation of the poetry of Percy Bysshe Shelley: "Life, like a dome of many-colored glass, / Stains the white radiance of eternity, / Until death tramples it to fragments."

Henrion has lived her whole life in New York City. She was an art student concentrating in graphic design at Cooper Union College of Art and Science when Abstract Expressionism dominated the New York art world. After rearing her children and working for many years as a career counselor at the Fashion Institute of Technology, she was finally able to turn her full attention to her own art. For the last twenty years, she has been making studio quilts. She is also a director of the Noho Gallery in Chelsea, the only cooperative gallery in New York City which consistently shows art quilts along with other fine art media. Henrion has had numerous solo and group exhibitions all over the country. Her art is represented in the collections of the Museum of Art and Design in New York, the Museum of the American Quilter's Society in Paducah, Kentucky, the U.S. Embassy in Cambodia, and of numerous corporations and private individuals. She has received six grants and fellowships, including a New York Foundation for the Arts Fellowship Award in 2005.

Long exposure to the art world in New York City has affirmed Henrion's conviction that the "art scene" is often more about fashion than art. "I stay attuned, but it is important to me to do my own work. . . . Beauty has been out of fashion for a while now, but I still believe in creating beautiful works."[2] Confident about the value of her medium and her work, the artist has not hesitated to take on the New York art establishment for its continuing dismissal of studio quilts as a valid form of fine art.

Henrion was drawn to work with fabric, particularly silk, by the pure pleasure of handling it. Her use of printed fabrics is inspired by the use of pattern in Matisse's work. Like other fiber artists, she finds that the process of construction enhances her creativity. She is not a surface designer in the sense that she dyes, prints, or embellishes the cloth herself. Her materials come from shops that serve New York's garment and theater districts with textiles from all over the world. She cuts, pieces, and quilts them by hand; it is labor-intensive and old-fashioned work. "But art is not about processing," says the artist. "It is about intent and expression. . . . Sometimes I begin without an idea; the idea develops as I proceed. All of my work reflects what I am thinking and experiencing at the time. . . . The viewer is invited to interpret it in his or her own way."[3]

The large format in which Henrion usually works—her quilts range from 18 inches square to rectangles with dimensions as large as 15 feet high—suits the graphic character of her work. Her love of color and interest in geometric form have been apparent in her quilts since 1989 when she made *167 and Counting* in anticipation of leaving her job and beginning her artistic career. In subsequent years, Henrion stopped using traditional block design and borders to frame her art and began to extend her forms past the edges on all

Plate 61.

Innerspace 1, 1998, 36 × 47.

Mixed fabric content; pieced, hand

quilted. Collection of Emily Leff.

Photo: Karen Bell

four sides. But she never stopped hand quilting, and her skill in using the line of the quilting stitch as an element of composition is exceptional.

Since the middle of the 1990s, the artist has mostly worked in series—some inspired by her travels in Russia, Spain, and Japan. Many of her pieces have a distinctly urban feel. Her geometric forms allude to architectural space, but the two- and three-dimensional forms that appear and disappear within them are more suggestive of the "architecture of one's inner life." Of the works in the first *Innerspace* series (see Plate 61), writer and artist Lois Martin notes: "All four present a cubed space, a squared-off world . . . and yet they seem open and expansive—perhaps because of the movement of color off the plane of the wall."[4] Color and pattern, which sharply define both her curved and angular forms, often soften the formality of this art, as does the line of her hand quilting.

Arches and circles are elements in several series, as are the rectangles that give viewers the impression of windows, doorways, or some beguiling inte-

rior space. Her motifs intermingle and are repeated. The archway was first used following a 1996 trip Henrion made to Russia, which was funded by ArtLinks Partnership.[5] It is prominent in her *Byzantium* series (see Plates 62 and 63) and in *Etudes* and *Nocturnes* (1999–2000). In the former series, the archways symbolize passageways and interconnections. In the latter group, the motifs are much larger and are mostly two dimensional; here, one experiences Kelly's voluptuousness in the form alone. The seemingly transparent circles that float across the surface of the quilts are symbolic of "fragility and evanescence in human life." In Henrion's quilts, the structural necessities of her medium are not only integrated with the art but are an essential component of it. Her forms are firmly defined by seam lines and the juxtaposition of

Plate 64.

Innerspace 12, 2004, 40 × 40.

Pieced silks, hand quilted.

Photo: Karen Bell

contrasting fabrics, justifying the choice of fabric and quilts as her medium. Martin characterizes Henrion's frequent juxtaposition of hot and cool colors as her signature, as demonstrated in the *Innerspace* series (see Plate 64).

Following the horrific events of September 11, 2001, Henrion worked on two series. *Fragments* contains only four quilts, but her experience using color and geometric form to convey mood and emotion resulted in dynamic and impressive artworks. In *Disturbances* (see Plate 65), the sharpness of the re-

action is gone, but her geometry has become unmoored, as Ed McCormack observed in his catalog essay.[6] The viewer is left trying to maintain balance.

Henrion's association of her work with literary references adds to the viewer's understanding and discourages a purely decorative view of her accomplishments. But recognizing her literary allusions is not essential to appreciate it. The evocative beauty and geometry of her forms and colors shine through.

Plate 65.

Disturbances 4, 2005, 48 × 48.

Pieced silks, hand quilted.

Photo: Karen Bell

Plate 66.

A Fine Romance, 1966, 59 × 57½.

Pieced cotton and silk; machine quilted.

Photo: David Caras

15

No other material is so closely connected to the human body. And I think that essential quality is what gave me a rationale for adopting it as an expressive medium. . . . I felt that anything that was so closely connected, so necessary for human functioning, had value, a kind of essential value that to me legitimized it as an artist's material, as a material with potential creative value.[1]

Since the mid 1970s, Michael James has played an important, ongoing role in the development of the studio quilt. His accomplishments are impressive. He has received fellowships from the National Endowment for the Arts and awards in national and international competitive exhibits. He has private and corporate collectors in this country and Europe. His quilts are in the collections of the Museum of Art & Design in New York, the Renwick Gallery of the Smithsonian American Art Museum, the Mint Museum of Craft and Design in Charlotte, North Carolina, the Indianapolis Museum of Art, the Newark Museum in New Jersey, the International Quilt Study Center in Lincoln, Nebraska, and others. James is the first and only studio quilt artist to hold an academic position in quilt studies.

In his 1998 book, *Michael James: Art and Inspiration*, he wrote: "When I made my first quilt twenty years ago the popular idea of what a quilt should be was defined by centuries of what we think of as 'tradition.' I've tried over the years to broaden that popular definition to suggest what a quilt can be."[2] This is a modest statement for an artist who has turned the constraints imposed by tradition into personal challenges and met them head-on.

Throughout his undergraduate and graduate education, James concentrated on painting. Abstract art was the predominant visual idiom of the time. He loved color and was drawn to Color Field painting, often staining unprimed canvases. "But as I developed my work . . . I started leaving more surface unpainted . . . the textile became a critical component of the composition. . . . I started to recognize that the textile area that was visible had its own sort of inherent beauty—the weave itself, the directional aspect of that weave and the texture that resulted. . . . I [began] to appreciate textiles as beautiful materials in and of themselves."[3]

There were other influences. The School for American Crafts was part of the art college at the Rochester Institute of Technology where James earned his MFA. As a student, he worked part-time in the ceramics department. By 1973, the year of his graduation, he seriously questioned the prevailing view that painting and sculpture were superior disciplines to "the humble work of hands." Within three months of graduation, he gave up painting. Several years earlier the Whitney Museum's exhibition *Abstract Design in American Quilts* had attracted the attention of the art world. In 1974 James saw Amish quilts for the first time and heard Jonathan Holstein, the co-curator of the Whitney exhibit, lecture at the University of Rochester's Memorial Art Gallery. He was particularly impressed with how the colors and geometric forms of these quilts created powerful abstract surfaces.

At the same time, the media was giving significant press to traditional American handcrafts and folk art because of the upcoming bicentennial. "I was very much carried on the wave of interest in American traditional arts that the American bicentennial had prompted. . . . [It was] an opening into a whole realm of creative activity that I didn't know a whole lot about." It also helped that his wife, Judy, who had a BFA in graphic arts, was an avid sewer.

It was not sentimentality that influenced James's decision to make quilts. In a review of a recent series titled *Interference Effect*, art historian and critic Glenn Brown observed that James "continues the project that he began in the 1970s: the labor of demonstrating that the contemporary quilt need not derive its primary conceptual value from its symbolization of the past, its role as holdout for the redeeming properties of manual production." He continues: "The momentum of James's innovation within the art quilt movement has always been maintained through the ability to achieve interference without sacrificing consummate craftsmanship."[4]

Consummate craftsmanship is one of James's hallmarks. He first mastered the fine points of the traditional construction and then set out to determine step by step how to use fabric to achieve color transitions, transitions from light and dark, shading, and illusions of space and transparency.[5] Because the seam lines in a pieced quilt appear as line drawings in a composition, it was critical to master these transitions if he was to be able to control color and movement across the surface of his compositions. Quilts such as *Aurora* and *Moonshadow*, made in the late 1970s, demonstrate the success of his efforts.

In 1979 James began to create his own cloth by piecing colored strips together. He then constructed the quilt tops by first cutting curves through the pieced cloth. "The curved seam as a design form offers literal fluidity and an organic flexibility that cannot be achieved with the straight seam," he writes. "Curved seam images have the capacity to pull us more actively into and around the quilt surface. They become more sensual designs."[6] Many of the quilts made during the 1980s have titles alluding to or directly based on music (*Rhythm/Color: Bacchanal*, 1986). He often listens to music while working and observed that the rhythms "by some sort of osmosis, worked their way into the quilts."

The seam lines and the problems of transitions were not the only constraints he encountered in the traditional quilt form. The greatest challenge was its grid structure, and he constantly sought ways to overcome it. By combining stripes, curves, and color, James was able to obtain a fluid movement that succeeded in burying it. An overriding characteristic of his work in the 1980s, though, was "a kind of formal resolution." Both his curved and sharply angled forms in quilts of this period have a feeling of solidity and order.

Taking care to point out that these did not represent the conclusion of James's career, the author and interviewer David Lyon writes: "The quilts of 1992–94 capture the artist at the height of his form." In 1990 James was awarded a fellowship for a three-month residency in France. Feeling that he had reached the limits of strip piecing, he decided to use the time only for drawing. The quilts he made following this period were based in part on these drawings. He was finally able to dispense altogether with the grid. They were strip-pieced, but James describes them as a kind of "last hurrah" for this cloth.

It is these quilts for which the artist is best known. Quilt Number 150 (*Rehoboth Meander*, 1993) is in the Renwick Collection. They are about tension, he writes: "the tension between the stripes . . . and the surface imagery; the tension between the impulse toward order and the potential for chaos; the tension inherent in metamorphosing forms that were neither fully geometric nor biomorphic. Out of a system of parallel stripes I attempted to create a world of forms and movements and interactions that were as many and varied as those systems in nature, in physics, and in music for which they functioned as visual analogues."[7] While extraordinarily energizing, they are satisfying and well-balanced compositions, such as *A Fine Romance* (Plate 66).

In 1996 the artist began working in a style that was radically different from previous work. He stopped strip piecing, reduced his color palette, and began experimenting with the juxtaposition of colors and diversely patterned panels. Pattern had been a constant presence in his quilts, but it now took on a different significance. His interest in formal abstraction was lessening. In *Wall I* (Plate 67) his interest in introducing a different kind of content and meaning into his art is apparent.

In 2000 James assumed an academic position as a senior lecturer in the Department of Textiles, Clothing and Design at the University of Nebraska–Lincoln. In 2003 he was named the Ardis James Professor of Textiles, Clothing and Design. Not long before, the department obtained a Mimaki textile printer, and James took on the challenge of mastering the manipulation of imagery and color through digital technology. He has created hundreds of unique fabrics from scanned images, some from his own photogra-

phy and others appropriated from other sources. Of *A Strange Riddle*, now in the collection of John M. Walsh III, the artist has written, "I adapted imagery from a family photograph to explore my own relationship to pattern and to memory."[8]

A subsequent series explored "notions of concealment and revelation, order and chaos, beauty and ugliness and the unnerving contrasts and visual paradoxes" he has encountered while traveling. "Our human capacity to synthesize and to negotiate physical and emotional terrain representing great opposites holds deep fascination for me," he wrote in an article about his use of computer-manipulated imagery and quiltmaking.[9] "Most of my work is now conceptually driven," he said in an interview in 2005.[10]

In a recent quilt, *Interference Effect: (Betrayed) Lover's Knot #2*, James conveys dissonance through abrupt changes in style, imagery, and color, notes Glenn Brown. The viewer's eye "flits" about trying to make sense of and

Plate 68.

Interference Effect: (Betrayed)
Lover's Knot #3, 2005, 52 × 80½.

Digitally developed and digitally printed cotton; pieced.

Photo: Larry Gawel

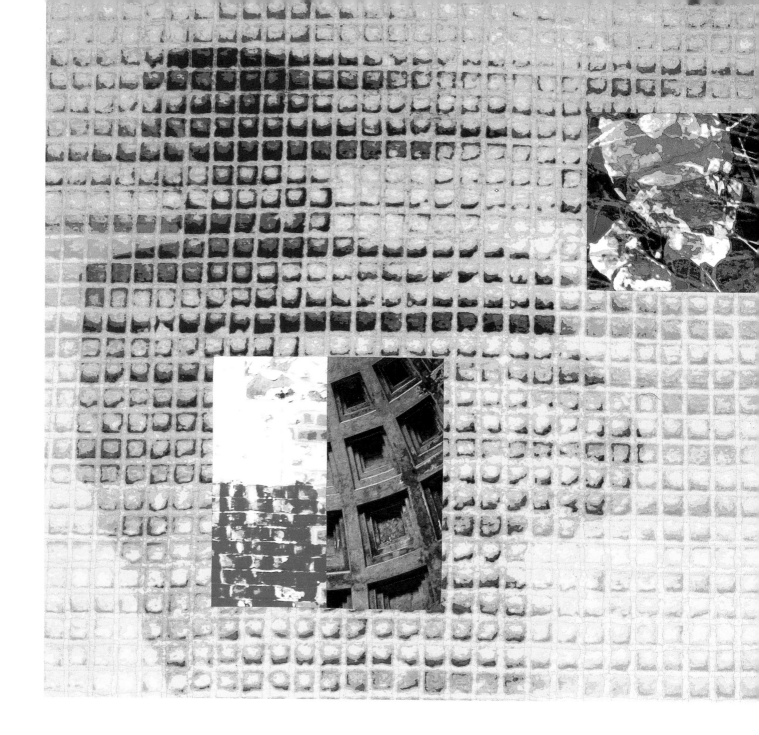

Plate 69.

Ghost Figure, 2005, 36½ × 78½.

Digitally developed and digitally printed

cotton; pieced. Photo: Larry Gawel

assimilate what he sees. It is, he writes, like trying to view numerous television screens at once.[11] The monumental work combines hard-edged grids and sections, made even sharper by the color contrast, with the soft, limp curves of a nude partially obscured by another grid, this one appearing to be deconstructing, and finally the potentially restful image of a stem of leaves, except that it is colored red. Not only dissonance but discontinuity and fracture are dominant aspects of this work. The images one carries away from it are disconcerting. Another quilt in this series, *# 3* (Plate 68), has similar sharp contrasts and breaks in pattern and color. This one, however, has no place for the eye to rest, even momentarily. "A basic goal," he says, "is to provoke some thinking on the part of the viewer, to reach into that person's

head and make contact in one form or another. If that can be done with some sense of poetry, all the better."

James has begun to turn his attention toward environmental and social issues, although not in a polemical way; he hopes that his quilts will stimulate thought and discussion in these areas.

In his thirty years as a studio artist, Michael James has broadened the definition of what a quilt can be many times over. Now, in works like *Interference Effect* and *Ghost Figure* (Plate 69), through the technology of the printer and computer he is doing it again, integrating his craft-based art with the visual culture of modern life.

Above. Plate 70.

Ophelia's Dream, 1994, 68 × 76.

Pieced, cotton; shibori patterning.

Collection of the International

Quilt Study Center, University of

Nebraska–Lincoln

16

I intuitively put the fabrics together, and find to my surprise
that they often speak to other people in some spiritual way.
It is not, I hope, just the technical accomplishment of a well-
designed work. This is not a conscious thing for me—but
I can't help but think that one's spiritual life enters into all
aspects of endeavor.[1]

Jan Myers-Newbury's superb design skills and many years of experience
working with color and shibori underlie and strengthen her intuitive approach. Her abstract quilts have the strength and power of classic Lancaster County Amish quilts. The contemplative spirit they evoke is comparable to that of Mark Rothko's color field paintings.

Myers-Newbury began her education as a music student but in college
discovered that she had a talent for drawing. This led her to study print-
making in graduate school; while there, she changed course again, before
finding the structure she sought in design. She and fellow graduate student

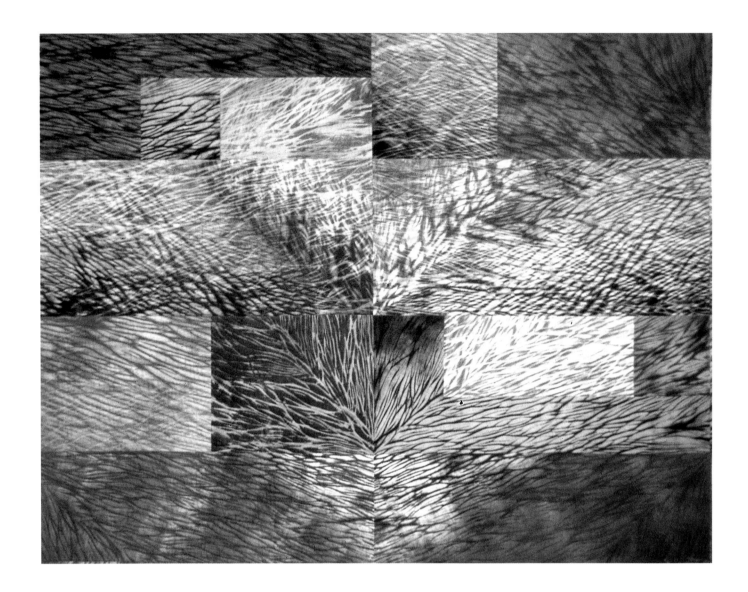

Plate 71.

The Trysting Tree, 1996, 58 × 76.

Pieced, cotton; shibori patterning.

Alpern Rosenthal, Pittsburgh.

Photo: Sam Newbury

Debra (Millard) Lunn submitted the first ever MFA thesis topics in pieced quilts in the design department at the University of Minnesota. "I had had a needle in my hand since I was a very little girl, so it seemed only natural to construct a final class project in the fabric, and BIG, since fabric allowed one to do that."

It was color that attracted her interest most, and Josef Albers's *Interaction of Color* was "pivotal," she says, to her understanding. "The first body of quilts were entirely about Albers—gradations light-to-dark moving across the grid of the pieced quilt in methodical ways, creating a sense of luminosity and depth." These quilts were made with her hand dyed fabric, an essential process if she was to have the gradated color necessary to achieving her purpose. Myers-Newbury's work during this period was not unlike that of other artist quiltmakers and painters, who were interested in optical effects.

In the late 1980s, however, her method, if not her intention, changed. Working on her own, she discovered and began to use "a kind of rudimentary shibori."[2] *Precipice* (1989), now in the collection of the Museum of the

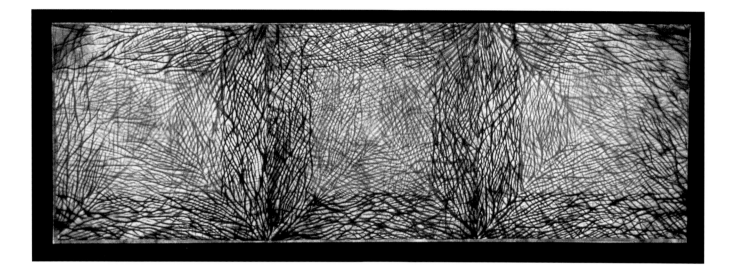

Plate 72.

The Three Graces, 1998, 18 × 54.

Pieced, cotton; shibori patterning.

Private collection. Photo: Jan

Myers-Newbury

American Quilter's Society, was a "threshold piece" for her new way of working. She experimented with creating a linear design in fabric and discovered she could do this by folding and binding it.[3] In their classic book on the subject, Wada, Kellogg, and Barton describe this form of Japanese shaped resist dyeing. Shibori "encompasses a variety of ways of creating design in cloth by shaping and securing it before dyeing . . . cloth treated in this way is given a three-dimensional form by folding, crumpling, stitching, plaiting, or plucking and twisting." The process allows for infinite variation in patterned design, but, says Wada, its strongest appeal to both artists and artisans is that the outcome is not completely under their control. There is an element of chance or accident in the process.[4] Myers-Newbury was drawn to shibori by an "openness to and a need for change that would challenge me in new ways. I am intrigued by what can happen in a dyebath. . . . As the fabrics themselves have more character, they have taken on much of the design task."

She has used shibori since 1989 to dye all the cloth from which her studio quilts are made, and her unique techniques and skill have enabled her to obtain the luminosity and depth she sought at the beginning of her career. But, as Vicky A. Clark, the former curator at the Pittsburgh Center for the Arts, has noted, instead of manipulating small pieces of cloth, she is now able to do so with larger ones, achieving a surface that is "sensuous, rich, and intricate," yet still true to the simplicity she values.[5] *Amishibori* demonstrates this rich surface (Plates 73 and 74).

Myers-Newbury sees her role as orchestrating the interplay between the patterned fabrics she has created. She is not interested in symbolism, although at times the interplay between color and the arashi shibori patterning results in compositions that are palpably dramatic. Other times, there is a loose and rhythmic wave in the gently curved, interwoven lines which flow across the surface of the quilt. Although her work is consistently abstract, the layering of color hues and values produced by the distinctive methods for dyeing and

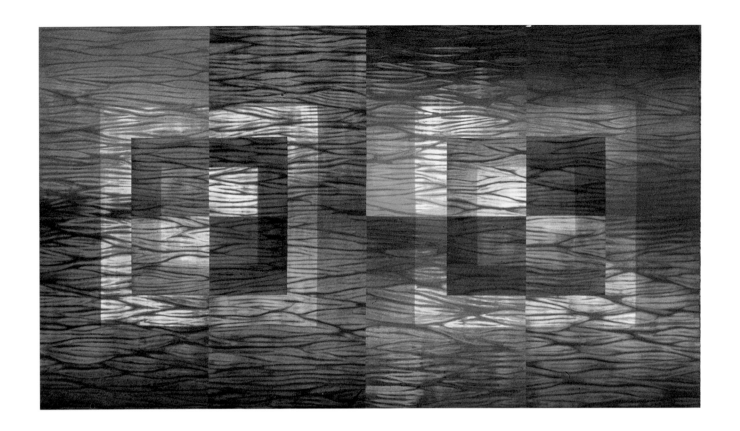

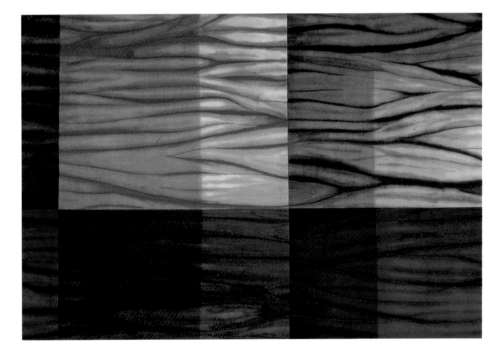

Above. Plate 73.
Amishibori, 2005, 39 × 69.
Pieced, cotton; shibori patterning.
Private collection

Left. Plate 74.
Amishibori, detail

discharge dyeing enable her to produce both depth and glow—on the forest floor at midday in *Ophelia's Dream* (Plate 70) or at *The Trysting Tree* (Plate 71). The contemplative character of these quilts is enhanced by their almost overpowering size.

While color study and the principles of design have always been important to her work, Myers-Newbury says that the main influence on any particular quilt is the one that preceded it. "The evolution has been very slow if you look at the body of work as a whole, and has come from within the work." Her compositions have moved from geometric to organic and back. In *The Three Graces* (Plate 72), as in all of her work, she has allowed the character of her dyed cloth to guide her. "I don't see the grid as a limitation. Sometimes it is the absolute best way for me to deal with the fabric I've created, and I feel that I am, at heart, a very traditional quiltmaker." Nor does she shy away from expressing her love of beauty. "My work is an oasis," she writes.

Myers-Newbury's studio quilts have been accepted into thirteen *Quilt National* exhibitions and have won several awards. She exhibits her work frequently in Pittsburgh, where she is a member of the Fiber Arts Guild, and in invitational exhibits in the United States and overseas (Japan, Germany, and Great Britain). Her quilts are in the collections of the Museum of Arts and Design, the Minneapolis Institute of the Arts, and the International Quilt Study Center in Lincoln, Nebraska, among others. She is also an active member of the fiber art community, teaching workshops at the Surface Design Association conferences and the Quilt Surface Design Symposium and at several craft schools.

Plate 75.

Sights in Transit (kimono back view), 1984,
60½ × 51½. Mixed fabrics; pieced, appliquéd,
embroidered; hand sewn. Collection of the
artist. Photo: Sam Newbury

17

Risë Nagin

Because I think of myself as a painter, my textile pieces reference painting as much or more than they do fiber. This is increasingly the case as my current work develops. That being said, the qualities of various fabrics combine to create intensely rich and satisfying surfaces. Through staining and layering sheer fabric, I am able to build translucent layers that give the work a spatial quality. Fabric conducts light in ways that paint cannot. In a sense I am manipulating light.[1]

Risë Nagin's remarks offer keen insight into the rich possibilities for artists who work with fabric. But they also suggest that her textile art is about the imagery, not the fabrics. She uses cloth because "it's the way to say that thing."[2] Balancing the content and the form of her art is essential. "The two should become indistinguishable, so that they become completely necessary to each other."[3] Her work has evolved from sewn "studio art quilts" to "assembled/layered paintings."

Nagin obtained her BFA in 1972. She has not only worked with fabric but has also drawn and painted for thirty years. Evident in all of her work is a strong belief in the importance of design, formal composition, and color. Imagery in early quilts and artwear in the collections of the Museum of Art & Design in New York and the Philadelphia Museum of Art in Pennsylvania shows the influence of James Rosenquist and other Pop artists of the 1960s, whom she admires for expanding the subject matter considered acceptable for fine art. Her *Turnpike* series, 1982–1985 (*Sights in Transit,* Plate 75) is a record of her fleeting impressions while driving on the Pennsylvania Turnpike. These constantly changing impressions of reflectors, tire treads, dividing lines, and road signs were transformed into patterned designs that show the artist's admiration for Japanese design. Writer and artist Patricia Malarcher notes that these robes of soft silks associated with a leisurely pace and the "feminine" present innate contradictions with highway imagery typically linked with commerce and high speed.[4]

From the beginning of her art-making, Nagin has been interested in light and the changing conditions of light. In school, she had a brief exposure to textiles, which she began to incorporate into her paintings. Textural variations that fabric afforded became increasingly important. "After a while I began to play with transparent fabric like organza and organdy," she says. "I was staining a lot of things with paint to get the colors I wanted. When you allow the light to pass through some sections of the quilt and make it very opaque and dense in others, this is actually a way of manipulating light."[5] By using various fabrics, along with metallic glitter and cellophane, "Nagin is able to achieve visual effects beyond the scope of oil and acrylic paints. . . . In her layered compositions, she can create the transparency and luminescence that painters seek with glazes."[6] Over the years, she has developed a whole repertoire of ways of thinking about and using layers, color, fabric, and transparencies.

The artist's interest in light has merged with other considerations. During the 1970s she began to experiment with ideas about perspective, not one perspective or the other—looking in or looking out—but the commingling of the two. The quilt *Night Swarm* (1979), now in the collection of the Renwick Gallery of the Smithsonian American Art Museum, is one of a series of window quilts. "In this quilt," she says, "the inside and outside merge. This is something I think about a lot in my work."

These explorations eventually coincided with a radical change of focus. By the mid-1980s she had turned from an outer to an inner landscape. Quilts such as *Illustrated Passage* (Plate 76) and *Gate* (Plate 77) are the visual expression of "anxiety about dark things," which she believes all people experience in their lives.[7] In the first of these, extended hands and biomorphic forms float both inside and outside of a window-like frame.

The ideas and imagery in this series are more closely related to Surrealism and Abstract Expressionism than to Pop art. Nagin studied images from religious and folk art for this work. It is populated with symbols and shapes—snakes, fish, disembodied figures, skulls, hands, and zigzag forms.

Plate 76.

Illustrated Passage, 1988, 64 × 50.

Mixed fabrics, cellophane; appliquéd, quilted.

Collection of the Renwick Gallery of the

Smithsonian American Art Museum,

Washington, D.C.; gift of KPMG Peat Marwick

Plate 77.

Gate, 1989, 70 × 70. Mixed fabrics, cellophane; pieced, appliquéd; stained, layered, quilted. Private collection

These symbols, called archetypes, have power to arouse emotion and to signify meaning across cultures and are believed, therefore, to have roots in the unconscious. Nagin made them part of her visual vocabulary. The rich surface textures of these quilts increase their power to engage the reluctant viewer. "The intention," Nagin says, "was to convey the seductive nature of evil." Her quilt *Drop Cloth* (Plate 78) particularly conveys this idea.

Interest in the capacity of archetypal forms to evoke emotion has led to a move toward abstraction. In recent works, her vocabulary of symbols has included circles, crosses, and squares. Many of these take the form of mandalas in which she employs limited elements to generate complexity. Nagin draws continually, allowing forms to evolve from spontaneous doodles—"funny organic shapes," she calls them—somewhat familiar but not really. "I am a very intuitive artist. I am interested in talking about different aspects of human experience and the human condition. . . . I don't usually know when I begin a series what the work will be about. I start making drawings and then the drawings evolve into a group of images that are talking to each other. I just follow where the images want me to go. As I work, the content becomes apparent to me and then I have a clear direction. It sounds passive, but it is not, nor is it without intention. I am always moving toward what seems right to

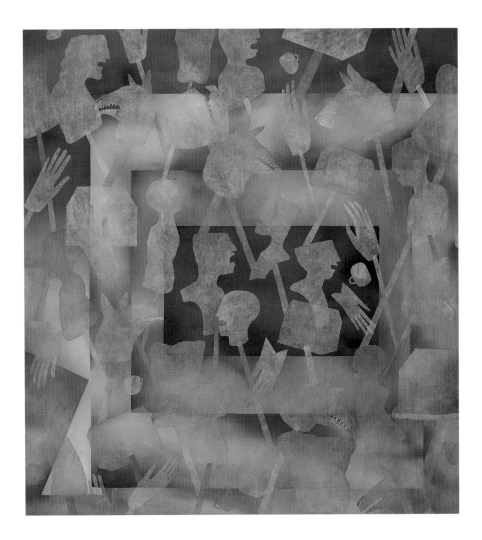

me, but I must make a balance between what is very intuitive and the intellectual order I impose on it as the designer and artist."

During the 1990s Nagin reduced the time she spent in her studio to take care of her family and to work as exhibition project director for *Fiberart International* 1997 and 2001. Her decision to return to her art full-time was made in Cambridge, England, where the family had moved for six months in 2003. While there, she began painting more. "Cambridge is a very beautiful place. I think that the color, the taste of the air, the smell, the whole landscape and the light of that part of England really soaked in." In response to this experience, Nagin began work on a series of experimental gouache paintings. "I was playing with gestural marks . . . all generated out of a sense of what it is like to be in nature. When I came back to Pittsburgh, I continued to work this way. Pittsburgh is a very green, beautiful place—a combination of woods and water and the ruins of what used to be heavy industry. The light is beautiful and liquid. . . . All those things inform the drawings. They are abstract reflections on the landscape that may convey a sense of the color or the energy of a place. It is very subtle. You wouldn't say 'Oh, that's Pittsburgh' or 'that's Cambridge.' You would not necessarily be able to trace the images back to a specific place."

Plate 78.

Drop Cloth, 1993, 78 × 84. Mixed fabrics; pieced, stained, appliquéd; hand sewn. Collection of the artist. Photo: Sam Newbury

Nagin's most recent work includes the 2006 installation entitled *heliotaxis* (Plates 79 and 80). Conceived as part of a solo exhibition, held at the Three Rivers Arts Festival Gallery in Pittsburgh, *heliotaxis* (the response of organisms to sunlight) consists of thirteen translucent scrims sewn, painted, and fused with abstract shapes. Designed to hang in front of a thirty-five-foot wall of windows, the piece plays on the way light changes over the course of the day. Floating images are obscured and revealed as the light filters through a succession of overlapping veils suspended in various configurations. Of this work, Nagin says: "As visitors walk through the installation, they become part of a transitional environment, a private world, bridging interior gallery space and the city outside. Viewed from the street, it presents a different aspect. The windows become a second point of entry. I wanted to establish an atmosphere, to evoke emotions associated with the experience of beauty."

heliotaxis, like all of her work in the last few years, is two sided. It represents her continuing exploration of light, perception, movement, space, and form. Nagin hopes the beauty of these pieces will draw the viewer in deeper and deeper, where, as in Japanese screens and the natural world, there is more and more to see. "There is an elegant simplicity inherent in using a few materials and very simple techniques," she states. "As I grow in the work, less is more."

Facing above. Plate 79. *heliotaxis,* 2006, two full views of the installation, overall size approximately 11' × 35' × 12'; variously sized fabric panels. Fabric; painted, bonded, hand sewn. Lighting by Stephanie Mayer-Staley. Three Rivers Arts Festival Gallery, Pittsburgh. Photo: Larry Rippel

Facing below. Plate 80. *heliotaxis,* detail

Plate 81.

Canyon Falls, 1998, 85 × 48. Pieced,

cotton, linen, silk. Collection of John M.

Walsh III. Photo: William Taylor

18

The colors of dogwoods in bloom, the turning of
autumn leaves, the breathlessness you feel when
a landscape appears as you come up over a hill
or around a bend—these are moments that
inform my work.[1]

The viewer's experience of any work of art varies greatly depending
not least on the expectations, knowledge, and willingness to engage
which he or she brings to the encounter. The experience is also defined by the artist's skill, purpose, and the content of the artwork. Sometimes
the artist's intent is to convey a message or to raise a philosophical issue for
the viewer to ponder. The art experience is more of an intellectual endeavor
than an aesthetic experience.

For many viewers, however, the art which holds their attention is that
which arouses their sense of wonder, joy, or mystery—art which has the
power, again and again, to make them forget other pressing concerns. For

Facing page. Plate 82.

Seminole Study III: Gravity and Grace,

1982, 92 × 68. Pieced, cotton.

Collection of the Museum of Arts and

Design, New York. Photo: William Taylor

more than twenty years, Joy Saville has been making studio quilts that have this effect. Her work is her attempt to capture and convey abstractly and through color the sensations evoked by encounters with nature. The surfaces of quilts such as *Canyon Falls* (Plate 81) are made from a multitude of tiny patches of silk, cotton, and linen that "shimmer like brushstrokes in an Impressionist painting."[2]

Saville's early quilts are significantly different from later work when the natural world became her primary focus. Early explorations with the interplay of pattern and color gave way over time to a concentrated focus on color alone. Taken together, her experiments with techniques of piecing and color have greatly expanded the expressive language of pieced cloth. "In Joy Saville's panels," wrote Patricia Malarcher in 1993, "color yields light; geometric piecework breaks up into fluid surfaces; sensuousness is permeated with intelligence."[3] Her works are painterly, yet their structural framework is inseparable from the traditions of pieced cloth. They are not substitutes for paintings. The piecing and the cloth are as inseparable from her art as the color. Together they make possible the shimmering movement in her work.

Saville is a self-taught artist, but her accomplishments are considerable. Her studio quilts are in the collections of public and private museums, major corporations, and many private individuals. Surprisingly, she attributes her decision to become an artist in part to her experience as a nurse in an earlier career. She once gave serious thought to becoming a physician but concluded that medicine was no longer practiced as an art. It was the creative process that interested her.

Choosing fabric as a medium was not a difficult decision. In Nebraska where she grew up, sewing, stitchery, and quiltmaking were part of her heritage. As a young woman living in Princeton, New Jersey, in the 1970s, Saville was well aware that contemporary quilts were being shown in museums and galleries in New York City. "I don't remember wanting to make anything like what I saw in those shows in the 1970s," she says, "but those quilts confirmed and bolstered my own vision."

Her approach to art has always been experimental. She constantly, but systematically, varies pattern, color, and shape as she sews. The quilts she exhibited in the early 1980s were dynamic, patterned, and completely untraditional. She had already abandoned symmetry, which was too static for her, and discovered the dynamic movement that diagonal lines produce. *Time Warp* (1980) was described by one reviewer as "a torrent of energy."

Early in the 1980s, Saville began to concentrate exclusively on a form of diagonal strip piecing used by the Seminole Indians. In her artist's statement for a solo exhibit at the Newark Museum in 1983, she wrote: "My focus was on the design created by the interplay of patterns of colors and patchwork lines and its influence on form." During those years, some contemporary artists were using garments as a surface for imagery and pattern, but the contours of Saville's *Seminole Studies* (see Plate 82) were formed by "the natural extension of their internal structure."[4] By intensively exploring the

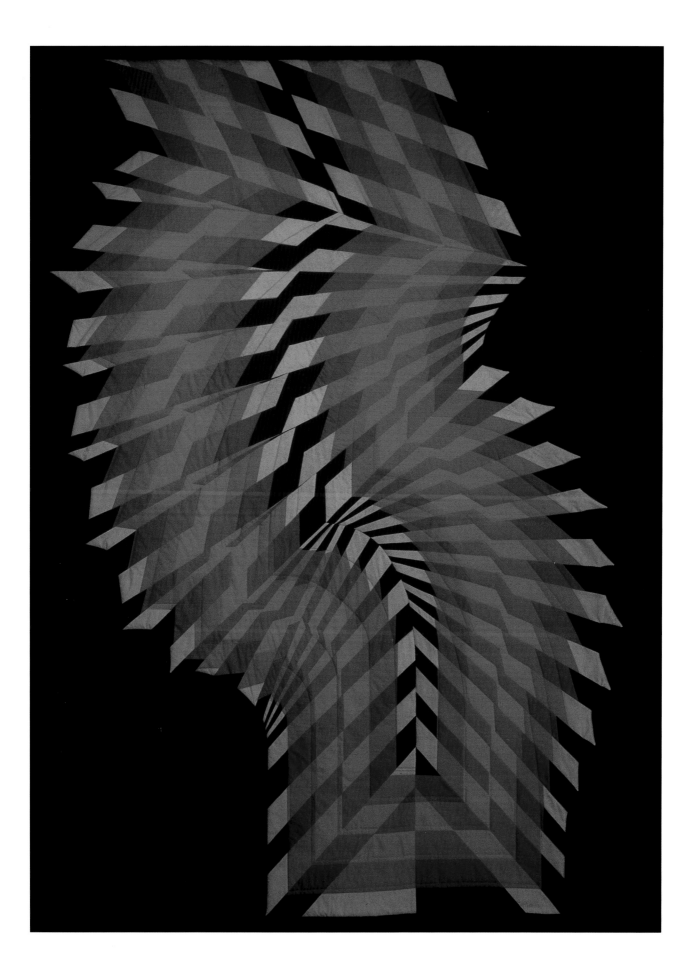

design possibilities of **Seminole patchwork** in these studies, she made discoveries that were to be important to later work.

In 1987, with the assistance of an arts fellowship from the New Jersey State Council on the Arts, Saville again changed direction. Work on a church commission in the mid-1980s led to a shift in focus from pattern and design to color. Aided by the abundance of major museums near her home, she immersed herself in the study of Monet, Seurat, Picasso, Matisse, Van Gogh, and O'Keeffe, paying careful attention to the way these artists put color together. But the energy she felt radiating from the paintings of Van Gogh was compelling.

Limiting her color palette and confining herself to the pattern in Seminole patchwork, she began new work. Explorations aimed at understanding the process and development of this pattern eventually led to a process of her own that allowed the manipulation of color. This was a breakthrough; blending color is much more difficult with solid-colored cloth than it is with paint. "From there I was able to develop a process that is completely intuitive and continues to hold my interest today."[5] The results of those first "breakthrough" pieces, as she describes them, were "a Cubist-like fragmentation of lines, planes and tones. . . . Rich reds from burgundy to crimson resonate, crash, and blend like the brass section in an orchestra. There are chords of dark purple and molten orange."[6]

Saville's earlier works were a prelude to the symphony that followed. Recent work, such as *Les Fleurs de Babylone* (Plate 83), shows the continuing importance of this breakthrough to her work. Slowly, she introduced more color. Her interest in the natural world increased as her subject matter grew. Saville has never been interested in reproducing the exact colors of a natural setting, or even the fleeting impression of reality, as were the Impressionists. She chooses colors to communicate either a visceral reaction or an implied concept, as exemplified in *Silent Scream* (Plates 84 and 85). Her quilts are composed of hundreds of hues, values, and shades. They envelop the viewer in an atmosphere—not the meditative one of the Color Field painters, but a crystal clear, often joyful and exuberant one, radiating, as in *Turbulent Rhythm* (Plate 86), with energy.

Plate 83.

Les Fleurs de Babylone, 50 × 70, 2004.

Pieced, silk. Collection of the Southfield

Public Library, Southfield, Michigan.

Photo: William Taylor

Above. Plate 86.
Turbulent Rhythm, 1999, 48 × 63.
Pieced cotton, linen, silk. Collection of
GoodSmith Gregg & Unruh LLP,
Chicago. Photo: William Taylor

Facing above. Plate 84.
Silent Scream, 2000, 48 × 30.
Pieced, cotton, linen, silk.
Collection of the artist.
Photo: William Taylor

Facing below. Plate 85.
Silent Scream, detail

Plate 87.

Steve Martin's Brain, 2004, 55 × 86½.

Pieced quilt; cotton, silk, paper; transfer

processes, printed, machine pieced and quilted.

Collection of John M. Walsh III

19

you can dance through life shoeless
but baby it's all about shoes—
. . . .
make your footprint
think of a dance
not set pieces perfectly performed
but improvised while stepping
lightly in great shoes[1]

I n her many poems, quilts, collages, and handmade books, Joan Schulze
records the images and impressions of a lifetime. She could be called a
landscape artist, but her landscapes are not about place so much as they
are about the rhythms of life and the passage of time.

Her accomplishments are a testament not only to her talent but also to her
determination to be an artist. Knowing she needed an income immediately
after college, Schulze majored in elementary education. As a result, her art
education—echoing her poem—has been an improvised dance. And she has
made a footprint. She began exhibiting in the late 1970s, and in 1986, two
of her quilts were included in *The Art Quilt,* the important exhibit curated

by McMorris and Kile. Since then, her work has been in countless exhibits, national and international. A noted book and collage artist as well, Schulze finds that explorations in each medium provide nourishment for her work in others.

In the 1960s Schulze moved from Illinois to the Bay Area near San Francisco with her husband. Fueled by faculty and students at the University of California, Berkeley, the California College of Arts and Crafts, and other schools, activity in the textile arts was rapidly increasing. She was initially drawn to stitchery, which combines embroidery with fabric collage, and took several workshops with Constance Howard, an internationally known expert in contemporary embroidery and the former director of the textiles degree program at Goldsmith's School of Art in London. After retirement, Howard traveled, teaching workshops in the United States. She recognized the young mother's talent, determination, and productivity and became her mentor. Although Schulze eventually changed her medium to fabric and quiltmaking, Howard taught her design and gave her confidence by sharing samples of her student's work with her English colleagues.

Schulze had neither interest nor knowledge of quilts in the 1970s. She thought traditional design was not challenging and quiltmaking was too rule-bound. But when the opportunity arose to teach this newly popular craft, she accepted it, learning enough to stay just one step ahead of her students and improvising considerably along the way. She came to love the "suppleness" and appearance of the quilt. Its possibilities as an art medium for someone who loved to experiment were enormous, and she quickly recognized this.

The artist calls herself a collage thinker. "Collage is its own world and the compositions are more open ended as I pursue an idea." She taught herself photography and takes pictures wherever she goes. She also collects old manuscripts, pictures from magazines, and bits of text from newspapers, poems, and books. Describing how she pieces her quilts, she compares the process to poetry: "I create poems the way you piece a quilt together. I write random thoughts. Then I recombine the words to get a sense of what I've written. It's the same way that I gather my fabric pieces together for making quilts or collages. I happily rearrange the pieces and put it together. I find the theme over a period of a couple of days."[2]

It sounds like a simple process. But Schulze has spent years struggling to transfer imagery from her "collections" onto cloth. Allergic reactions to fabric dyes and other chemicals interfered, and she switched to acrylic paints. Her image transfers were limited to photocopying, an older technology which she still uses. In the 1980s Schulze successfully developed a process of image transfer using archival bookbinder's glue as a medium. After many years of experimenting with it, she is now able to control the character of the image produced—to distort it, to give it a rough or polished appearance, to collage it onto other images, and to produce just parts of it. The results are a mixed-media surface texture. "Erasures, fragments, and layering" characterize a significant portion of her work and symbolize the passage of time. "My glue transfer methods are slow, which encourages discovery of complex rhythms and stories." The process becomes part of the art's meaning. Schulze thinks of her quilts in a literary way, equating large works such as *Step Lightly*, 2001, to the novel form. "My Haiku . . . series of small works in paper and fabric are visual poems, reduced in size, rely on severe editing, and are more meditative in feeling."[3]

Step Lightly (Plate 88) captures the rhythms and vistas of modern life. This large quilt calls to mind the fences erected on city streets around construction sites. Over time, they are plastered with layers of notices, posters, and advertisements. Schulze's "fence" bears the effects of time and weather. A briskly moving leg with a walking shoe, partnered with a shapelier one in a stiletto heel, focus our attention, but only for a brief moment. We are quickly drawn to other partially faded, half obscured, or peeling images—fashion models, a city bus, a tangled audio tape. Dancers, clock faces—motifs the artist uses in several of her quilts—are here, too. Graffiti-like grass pokes through the fence below and above, and luminous blue squares float above the surface, reminding us of patches of sky.

Schulze's art is patterned and rhythmic. In *Step Lightly*, the blue squares and faded gold circles provide patterned counterpoints to surface complexity, affording the viewer a moment's rest. She associates her use of pattern and repetition of line, color, and elements (circles, squares, calligraphy, and swirls) with "musical thinking." The pattern in *Late Rain* (Plate 89) moves across the pieced surface of the quilt like the flow of water down a city street. Text, too, becomes pattern, as it does in *Steve Martin's Brain* (Plate 87). "People expect to be able to read it," she says. "I like perverting its normal use by using it layered, upside down, inside out and mirrored."[4]

In recent work, such as *Butterfly Logic* (Plate 90), Schulze has been experimenting with a new process for making quilts. Although these pieces look very different from previous work, they have clearly evolved from it, and the artist still thinks of them as landscape. In her view, the line made by quilting stitches is a drawn line, serving not only to hold the layers together but to reinforce the meaning of the quilt. By transferring the images of these lines from older works onto a new surface, she is creating new landscapes from the fragments of old ones, a process which carries its own meaning. The work is done with black stitches and toner ink on layers of transparent silk organza. These pieces seem quieter and more meditative, but there are traces of dancing steps and butterfly wings. They read like the text of a visual poem, drawing the viewer into the work.

Painters who share the building where her studio is located have asked Schulze why she doesn't "just paint." She responds: "You can't do in painting what I can do in quilting. I use the same materials, paint, digital imagery technology, and I am painting my fabrics, but the effect I produce cannot be done with paint."[5] With her "effects," she continues to contribute in significant ways to our understanding of the value and possibilities of quilts as an art form.

Plate 88.

Step Lightly, 2001, 48 × 120.

Cotton, silk, paper, metal leaf; photo
transfer, printing, appliqué; machine
pieced and quilted. Collection of Faith
and Jonathan Cookler

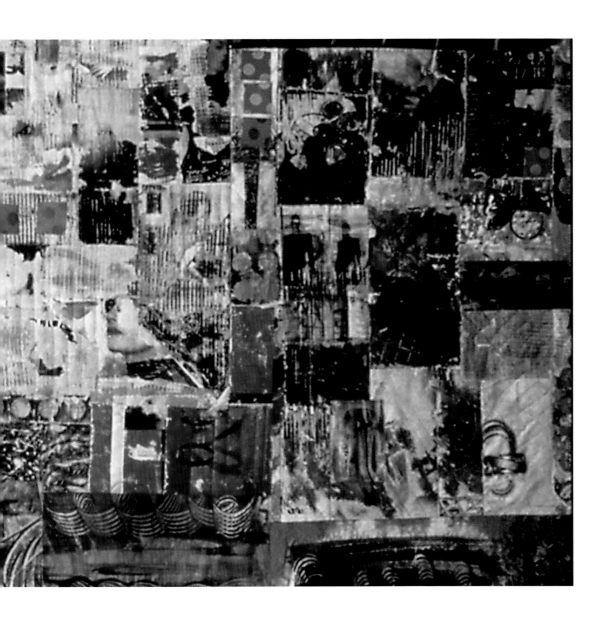

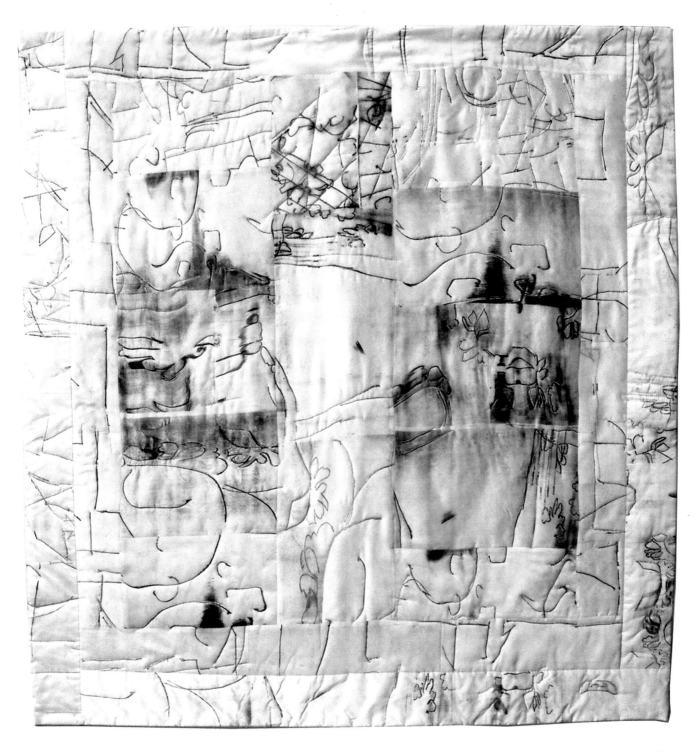

Facing page. Plate 89.
Late Rain, 2003–2005, 67½ × 43.
Silk, paper, cotton, metal leaf; photocopy
and glue processes; machine quilted.

Plate 90.
Butterfly Logic, 2006, 45½ × 44.
Silk; toner drawing, photocopy
processes, machine quilted and
stitched.

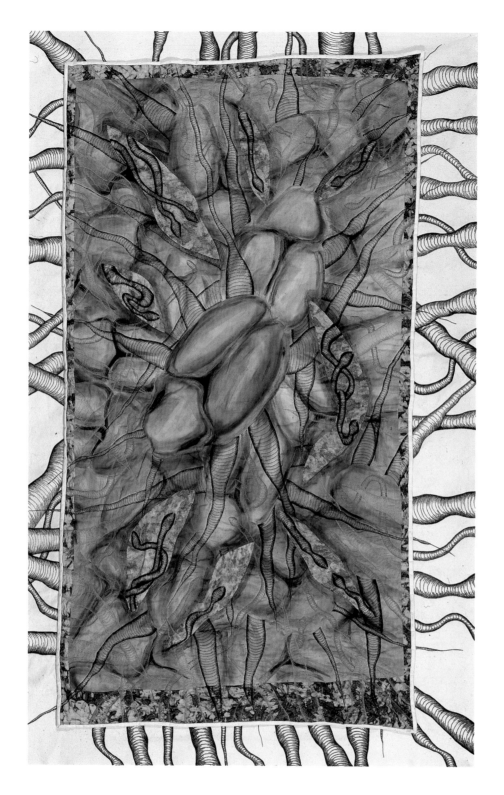

Plate 91.

Infestation: A Floor Cloth, 2002, 83 × 54 × 3.

Painted canvas, thread-drawn line, ink drawing.

Collection of John M. Walsh III.

Photo: John Lanning

20

Julie John Upshaw

Whatever form or definition the work takes, the bottom line is the content of my work is motivated by conflict, ambiguity, and discomfort. Sometimes it is small and personal like juggling all of the roles and titles I have in life: artist, teacher, graduate student, mother, and wife. Other times it is about larger incongruities found in human interactions and human systems.[1]

J ulie John Upshaw first came to the public's attention when *Human Nature* (Plates 92 and 93) was awarded first place in the Art Division of the 2002 Husqvarna Viking Masterpieces exhibit at the *International Quilt Festival* in Houston, Texas. Four years later, her installation *Insecurity* was exhibited at the San Jose Museum of Quilts and Textiles. These works of art are indicative of a new approach to art taken by many young artists. Specializing in a particular medium, like painting, sculpture, or fiber, is less important to them than communicating their ideas. Their medium depends

Above. Plate 92.
Human Nature, 2002, 57 × 71.
Cotton and organza; painted and
thread-drawn line. Collection of the
Husqvarna Viking Gallery, Sweden

Plate 93.
Human Nature, detail

on their message. What connects Upshaw's work is its capacity to evoke discomforting emotions and her frequent use of thread-drawn figures. "I draw with thread. Sometimes my fiber pieces can be identified as quilts because they are made of layers of fabric, or similar substances that are held together with stitches. Sometimes my work fits into categories of fiber art, textiles, or mixed media pieces."[2] Unlike some young artists, however, she does not take craftsmanship lightly.

Upshaw had no exposure to fiber art while studying for her BFA at the University of Texas in Austin. Her interest was stirred by a television series she saw in the early 1990s about American quilts. "I wanted a family and I didn't want to use toxic art chemicals during that process. [Art quilts] looked like painting with fabric which seemed perfect."

Upshaw recognized that stitches are the equivalent of drawn line, but she saw greater possibilities: "It is the only medium I know in which you can draw on both sides of the surface at the same time. When I realized that, I wanted to figure out how to use that property to its best advantage. I used holes, sheer fabric, and eventually clear vinyl. It makes no sense to me to have the backs of quilts against a wall."[3] She experimented with the visual aesthetics of transparent materials for five years before completing *Insecu-*

rity.[4] Her quilts may be composed of as many as seven layers. And like many younger artists, Upshaw is comfortable using **ready-mades** from daily life in her art if their use facilitates the transmission of her ideas.

Human Nature was made in the months following the World Trade Center bombing in New York. "The colors, pictures, and ideas from newscasts on television from Afghanistan influenced the images on the quilt. I could not stop thinking about humans living and hiding underground. And that these caves would become graves." Although she had done many thread-drawn studies of the human form, Upshaw did not use them in her work until she made this piece.

While her work with human forms is "more intense, personal, and usually out of frustration and conflict," she gives them insect, animal, and plant qualities. The organic forms in works such as *Infestation: A Floor Cloth* (Plates 91 and 94), now in the collection of John M. Walsh III, and *Viral Impressions* (2003) are part of Upshaw's evolving visual vocabulary. They are derived from impressionable experiences in her childhood. "I wouldn't know what other image to use to express these thoughts and feelings I have about life," she says. "We had a lake place in East Texas that we went to every weekend when I was a kid. I played with cups of earthworms, and made houses for them. I loved the way they moved over each other. . . . I'm as easily amused by the movement of a line or gesture as I was by the real things along the way." In *Infestation: A Floor Cloth*, she used the social order of the insect world to depict the conflicts and complications arising in human society. "People come together with others to work on a project," she says, "but bring their own agendas with them. This can make the accomplishment of even simple tasks impossibly complicated. At worst, decisions . . . are not based on the best outcome at all." Still, the artist is interested in other interpretations of her art and says she does not want to work only "in the vacuum of my own thoughts."

While insect and worm imagery comes naturally to her, its effect on the viewer ranges from interest to repulsion. *Infestation: A Floor Cloth* is a kind of bas-relief, described by art historian Glenn Brown as "producing the effect of an organic mass swelling up from the floor." If viewers react negatively, it does not seem to concern this artist. She wants to convey a message and she does it effectively. There was another source of inspiration for the quilt's format, however. Impatient with the tendency of art quiltmakers to describe their quilts as wall hangings, she deliberately positioned this one horizontally.

For *Insecurity,* Upshaw used ordinary plastic packaging materials as a metaphor for the mind and the lack of privacy of thought.[5] "The piece is about the use of technology as detection and the possibility of threatening privacy," she said in March 2006, a few months before the installation opened. "There will be a fitting room with open curtains and each will contain a life-sized stitched figure on organza. There are mirrors so the images are both sheer and reflected. There will also be a rack with hospital gowns that are

embroidered with germs, tumors, etc. I think of it as a triptych of detection: walk through metal detector, fitting room surveillance, and medical detection (like MRIs). The gowns, drapes, and embroidery all reference the personal aspect of privacy and also the connection to the traditions of fiber."[6] Even studies such as *Emotional Baggage: Material Discomfort* (Plate 95) for the installation are unsettling.

In the 1970s when artists were beginning to stretch beyond the boundaries of the traditional craft, they sometimes found their works excluded from traditional exhibits. While the definition of a quilt has become more inclusive, Upshaw still finds herself frustrated by criteria she must meet for entry in quilt exhibitions. She has dealt with the problem humorously in some of her utility quilts, including potholders and gigantic quilted ironing boards, but the issue is a serious one for her. While she plans to keep on making quilts, they are more likely to be quilted walls than wall hangings.

Plate 95.

Emotional Baggage: Material Discomfort, 2003, 27 × 21. Layered vinyl; paint; thread-drawn line.

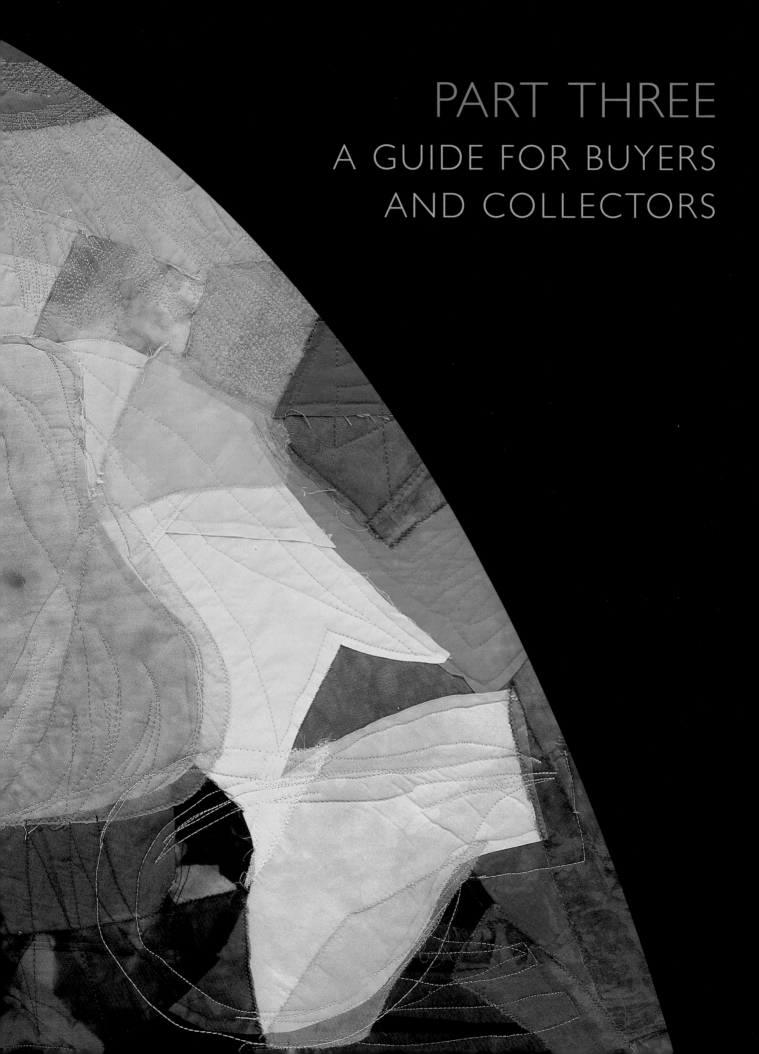

PART THREE
A GUIDE FOR BUYERS
AND COLLECTORS

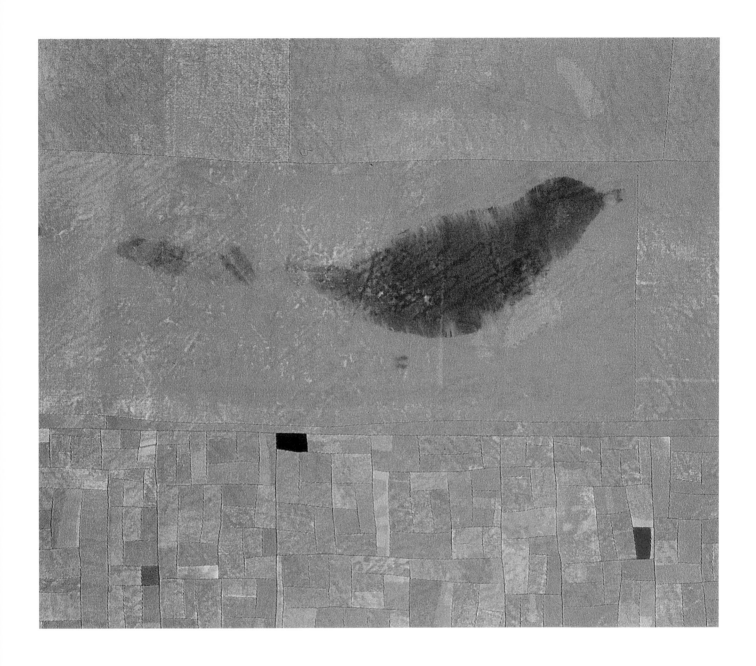

Carmen Grier, *Forage*, 2003, 9½ × 16, unframed. Rayon;
sewn and pieced, multiple printing and dyeing processes.
Grier does not typically quilt her art, although she uses
techniques of surface design and intricately pieces the
surface. Private collection

21
Educational Resources
and the Market

It all begin with my going to Haystack in 1978. There I became
aware of what makes a fine weaving or a fine pot. It whetted my
appetite and we began collecting in a small way . . . what appeals
to me is the work in which the artist has taken an old art form
and revitalized it in a more modern way. The challenge and the innovation that these artists have found in using any art form is
just wonderful. . . . It is not just making another pot or another
quilt. It is beyond that.
—Eleanor Rosenfeld, collector of contemporary craft

Good fiber art will almost always engage the viewer. But the serious buyer
needs sound criteria to evaluate it when considering a purchase. Artist
and teacher Susan Brandeis suggests that we keep certain questions in
mind when looking at textile art:

Is the idea behind the piece a good one?

Is the use of the material innovative?

Does the work show a good sense of composition and an effective use of color?

Is the craft good or appropriate to the idea?[1]

Material, craftsmanship, and composition are important. Experts may give emphasis, however, to different aspects of the art. Art consultant Robert Shaw advises buyers to look for originality and power of expression, balance in the formal
elements including color, line, pattern, texture, and scale, and "cohesion and in-

tegrity of the overall work." He emphasizes looking for the way in which the artist has "mined the rich history, symbolism, and meaning of the traditional quilt."[2]

The pleasure that the quilt gives the viewer is just as important as a more intellectual evaluation. "I don't intellectualize," craft collector Robert Pfannebecker told an interviewer. "I see something and I really like it. You can talk to collector after collector and they'll say, 'It's something that kept me up last night.' I see things that I just have to have. I just think they're wonderful, and I react on an emotional and visual level."[3] But Pfannebecker has been looking, learning, and collecting for almost forty years. He intuitively understands what makes an object "good art," whether it is a quilt or ceramic sculpture.

Curators and collectors alike stress the importance of spending time *looking*, especially if enjoyment in a particular quilt is to last. But studio quilts are not always easy to find. They are not in every museum or art gallery. For this reason, some guidance, especially for the newcomer, is necessary. In the following pages, you will find an overview of the studio quilt world—where it interacts with the art world and where it does not. Following the trail can be adventurous and exciting, but it can also be confusing and disheartening if you are more used to the quiet reflection possible in a museum or gallery. It is better to be prepared.

Museums

Collections and Acquisition Policies

We will begin at the museum, the pre-eminent art institution and an important arbiter of what can be called art and whose art should be held in esteem. Fortunately, there are many different kinds of museums, and the views of their directors and curators are not all the same. Studio quilts are found mostly in those devoted to craft, design, and textiles. Their representation in museums of fine art is low, although it is slowly increasing. They are also represented in the collections of numerous city, state, and historical museums. And while not all museums collect studio quilts, many exhibit them. Quilt shows of all kinds—antique, ethnic, avant-garde—always attract crowds.

Generally, museum collections vary widely. The first requirements for a fiber collection are a storage facility and a conservation staff. Assuming this basic need is met, acquisitions of new works are determined by budgets and a museum's collection policy, which is the framework within which the director, curator, and board make their choices. That policy sets up the parameters and guidelines as to what the museum is going to collect.[4] Collecting may be shaped somewhat by what is already in the collection. Since textile and quilt collections are usually begun with private donations, unless the museum has a staff which is interested in contemporary fiber art, its textile collections will often reflect the vision of the original collector/donor(s).

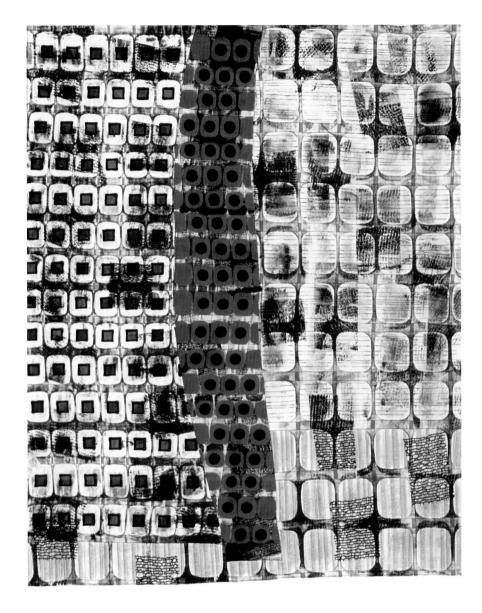

Jeanne Williamson,
Orange Construction Fence Series # 29,
2004, 46 × 38. Whole cloth, cotton;
mono-printed, hand stamped, machine
printed. Photo: David Caras

Collecting policies vary. When the Art Institute of Chicago made a commitment to build its textile collection, the textile curator was charged with seeking out "unusual contemporary interpretations of historic techniques." She was to use the following criteria: "[T]he contemporary application of an ancient technique must be combined with a form of expression that is 'neutral and not a fad' for the item to fit into the AIC's textile collection."[5] Most quilt museums were established to preserve the legacy of traditional quilts and their makers. The Rocky Mountain Quilt Museum, founded in 1990, recently expanded this mission to include building a "comprehensive collection of quilts that would represent the history of studio quiltmaking in the United States."[6] This attempt to attain both depth and breadth is the way many museums approach collecting.

The Museum of the American Quilter's Society (MAQS), founded in 1991, seeks to "honor today's quiltmaker" by focusing on "the best of quiltmaking from the second quilt revival of the 20th century."[7] Most of its acquisitions are award winners in the Society's annual competition. The San Jose Museum of Quilts and Textiles seeks "to promote the art, craft, and history of quilts and textiles. . . . Its exhibits and programs promote the appreciation of quilts and textiles as art and provide understanding of their role in the lives of their makers, in cultural traditions, and as historical documents."[8] The museum recently changed its name and its collecting policy to include textiles as well as quilts and expects to begin slowly adding contemporary works to its traditional collection. Its exhibitions over the last ten years have consistently included studio quilts.

Another approach to museum collecting is rooted in the belief that quilts should not be singled out as more—or less—special than other objects in the visual arts. This leads to a collecting policy which considers acquisitions in terms of how innovative they are and how they fit into and add to the scope of the total collection, not just quilts. It is the policy of the Mint Museum of Craft + Design, according to Mark Leach, founding director of the museum. The Mint's objective is to collect "singular moments" in every medium, objects that are innovative and stand out in the broader field of visual arts. These different approaches to collecting represent the varying contexts into which museums place studio quilts, or art quilts, as they are often called. Museums draw attention to those aspects of the art form that they find noteworthy, or they direct the viewer's attention to the ways in which these objects, among others, reflect certain aspects of life in our culture.

Acquisition policies often include works of regional artists. If a fine arts museum already has the facilities to care for textiles, it is possible its collections will include studio quilts. For example, the Indianapolis Museum of Art includes in its textile collection a small but important group of studio quilts which are the work of nationally known, regional artists.

Making Use of Museum Resources

Each museum has its own policies regarding accessibility of works not on display. None will have them all on display at the same time for reasons having to do with both space and conservation. Check the museum's website for a listing of the artists represented or get a list from the registrar. The National Museum of American History has an enormous collection and has set up a formal schedule for visitors. Smaller museums may be more relaxed, and if the staff has time, you might be able to examine works in storage. Other museums require you to write for an appointment or might give access only to scholars. The contemporary fiber art in the collection of the Renwick Gallery and the Museum of Arts & Design in New York City are in off-site storage facilities, making access more difficult. The Renwick's policy is to exhibit work in its collections on a rotating basis.

Many museums offer educational programs for learning about the art in their collections. Tours and lectures given by the museum director, curator,

and experts in the field are often scheduled in connection with particular exhibits. With advance notice, it is often possible to arrange a personal or small group tour.

Additional options for learning, such as "study days," are offered by some museums. Participating in a museum support group can provide opportunities for behind-the-scenes tours of the museum's collection, tours of collections in other museums, visits to artists' studios or collectors' homes, and educational tours to exhibits or textile centers. Seeing fiber art in these various contexts and having an opportunity to meet and talk with artists help

Emily Richardson, *Triumphs of Oriana,* 2005, 73 × 48. Silk, painted and layered; stitched.

participants to recognize quality and to define their own interests. The newsletters of these support groups usually carry information about upcoming educational activities and exhibits.

The International Quilt Study Center The International Quilt Study Center is a scholarly institution but provides opportunities for the public to participate in some of its programs, both at the Center and through its website. The IQSC has a collection of more than 2,000 American and international quilts, including nearly 200 contemporary ones. "Its acquisition priority at this time is focused on building a solid base of early quilts made by prominent contemporary artists and on more recent ground-breaking or cutting-edge quilts," writes Carolyn Ducey, curator of collections.[9] A new building scheduled for completion in 2008 will house three exhibition halls. An ambitious exhibition schedule will regularly feature studio quilts. The Center records lectures given by faculty and visiting scholars during monthly programs and makes some of these available through its website. Although these have been concerned with traditional quiltmaking, it is expected that the growth of its contemporary collection will lead to presentations of greater interest to a studio quilt audience.

Since 2003 the entire collection of the IQSC has been online. Nearly 200 studio quilts are included, beginning with work made in the early 1960s. The collection affords the viewer a glimpse of changing quilt aesthetics as artists began to expand the boundaries of the tradition and experiment more freely.

The Quilt Index In addition to the online collection of the IQSC, there is a second source of quilt images online called the Quilt Index. The Index is a growing research and reference tool designed to provide access to information and images about quilts held in private and public hands. The great majority of these quilts are traditional. Images from the Rocky Mountain Quilt Museum, the International Quilt Study Center, the Museum of the American Quilter, and the New England Quilt Museum will be integrated into the Index in 2007 and 2008, adding historically important studio art quilts to the collection. Future plans call for expanding its search capabilities. The project has been funded in part by the National Endowment for the Humanities and is a collaborative effort of the Alliance for American Quilts and Michigan State University.

Internet Galleries The internet is an important tool giving artists wide exposure for their work. It also serves buyers, museum curators, and other researchers by providing an overview of the market and quick access to an artist's portfolio. Artists who do not have their own website or a presence on an online gallery site are becoming rare. The internet's capacity to provide graphic imagery is unmatched. What it cannot do is convey what is unique about the art form—the language of cloth—which is what people find most

Jeanne Lyons Butler, *White 10: 87*, 2005, 59 × 41. Diptych. Cotton, linen, cheese cloth; paint and graphite; machine appliquéd and quilted. Photo: Karen Bell

engaging about textile art. Colors on the computer monitor may not match precisely with the colors of the actual art object and the details of craftsmanship may not be visible. For these reasons, it is wise to be cautious about online purchasing unless you are already familiar with the artist's work.

In addition to presenting their portfolios, artists post résumés and provide links to the galleries that represent them. Artist group websites such as Art Quilt Network/New York (AQN/NY), Professional Art Quilt Alliance (PAQA) in Chicago, FiberScene, a San Francisco–area group, Studio Art

Quilt Associates (SAQA), and Surface Design Association (SDA) also have online galleries which feature the work of members. Search terms such as "art quilters" or "fiber artists" will link the researcher with numerous artist group websites as well as individual ones.

The internet serves buyers and collectors in other ways, too. For example, the Guggenheim Museum's website provides descriptions of contemporary art movements and offers illustrations from works in its collections. The Textile Museum's website provides information on the care and display of textiles as well as a list of textile collections in the United States. A search of "ethnic textiles" leads to information and illustrations of textiles and techniques from all over the world. From the websites of the Alliance for American Quilts and the Archives of the Smithsonian American Art Museum, users can read interviews with contemporary quiltmakers. The Alliance's website also has a glossary of technical terms used in quiltmaking. The internet is also a source for both print and online reviews of exhibits. A recently developed website invites readers to review art quilt exhibits which they have seen. Its purpose is to publish reviews in a more timely fashion than is possible in the magazines and journals which usually cover them.

Private Galleries

An Overview

Private galleries representing and exhibiting the work of studio quilt artists include fine art, mixed media art, craft, and decorative art galleries. Only a small proportion of these are fine art galleries. The reasons are varied. Bruce Hoffman, director of Snyderman-Works Galleries in Philadelphia, which represents artist Nancy Crow and which holds a biennial exhibition of fiber art, believes that survival is an important factor. "It is very hard to maintain a gallery," he says. "The decorative arts are in decline and many galleries are closing their doors. There are numerous shops around, but these are not galleries. Now we have shows like SOFA (Sculptural Objects Functional Art) which we have to do. Many galleries attend the shows and then use the internet for selling and marketing. They do not go to the expense of maintaining their retail space anymore." He adds: "Art quilts sell, but I do not think that galleries have the patience to establish the market. What Gross McCleaf Gallery [Philadelphia] has been doing is wonderful. . . . They have built an audience. It takes an investment in time for a gallery and time is money."[10] Hoffman believes the studio quilt continues to be hampered in its search for recognition by the public perception of quilts as "women's work" and, therefore, as not comparable in price or quality with fine art. Another problem, he says, is the difficulty all but a few craft artists have had breaking into the "old boys" club of the mid-town New York galleries.

Realistically, however, the number of professional studio artist quiltmakers is very low relative to the numbers of artists in the country. And within

this small group—and this is true in all of the visual arts—while there are many wonderful artists, they are not all exceptional.

Apart from museums, galleries continue to be the best setting for viewing the aesthetics of the art form. The exhibition of quilts in both museums and art galleries has been criticized by some for stripping them of their domestic and utilitarian history, but this criticism is not relevant to all art in this genre. Like small art centers, galleries also allow for closer examination of the work than is possible in the museum.

The Gross McCleaf Gallery in Philadelphia is one of a small number of fine art galleries—the American Art Company Gallery in Tacoma, Washington, is another—which has opened its doors to studio quiltmakers. Director Sharon Ewing has held an exhibit of their work each year since 1993. She says it is just a small part of what they do, but the exhibits have been successful. The gallery's approach is invitational; it exhibits several pieces by each artist and rarely shows the work of more than a few artists at a time. Philadelphia artist and quiltmaker Emily Richardson is represented by Gross McCleaf. Several years ago the gallery was introducing a few abstract artists into its stable of primarily realist painters. "We felt Emily's work related more to painting in

Sue Benner, *BODY PARTS* (*Zebra Sleeve, Paisley Sleeve*), detail, 2006. Silk and cotton, dyed and painted; found fabrics, fused, mono-printed, machine quilted. See preface for full image. Photo: Eric Neilsen

some ways than it did to traditional quilting. Her work is beautifully done and loosely fulfills the criteria for quilts. But we see it as bringing abstraction to the gallery through a different medium. Although Emily paints on silk, she is still painting" (see Richardson's *Triumphs of Oriana*).[11]

What to Expect

Art exhibited in private galleries must meet criteria that are established by the director or owner. Aesthetics and prices must be matched with client interests and expectations. The style of the studio quilts shown in galleries in different parts of the country may, therefore, vary according to regional tastes. Geometric or organic form, abstraction, landscape, figurative art, color, hand processes, and the significance given to the material aspects of the quilt are among the variables. Prices include a commission for the gallery, which covers rental space for the art, sales assistance, financial management and record keeping, advertising, and the costs and services involved in arranging for exhibition of the artist's work and opening night receptions when the public can meet the artist.

For customers who are genuinely interested in an artist's work, the director can be a valuable source of information. Galleries also provide installation services, if needed, and advice on caring for the art. Their role in providing exposure of the art form to the public, and to the still hierarchical art world, is critical. Sales through galleries validate artistic merit in the art world. The director who pushes up the price of an artist's work, when he or she firmly believes in its value, takes risks but signals other galleries and the art world to pay attention to this art. In the long run, good artists will benefit. Despite the low numbers of galleries that represent studio quiltmakers, those that do play a key role in assuring the long-term appreciation of the genre as a whole.

When artists have gallery representation, their contracts usually require them to refer direct inquiries from customers to their gallery. It is not uncommon, however, for an artist or gallery director to give a small discount to a buyer who is a collector of the artist's work. Buyers who seek a cheaper price by buying directly from the artists represented by private galleries may be contributing to the delayed acceptance of studio quilts as art.

Cooperative Galleries

In the absence of private galleries to represent them, and in an effort to increase the amount of the purchase price that they pocket, some artists participate in cooperative galleries. All administrative and financial responsibilities and costs are divided among members. Co-op galleries exist for both fine arts and crafts; studio art quiltmakers participate in both. In fine art, the galleries draw from a broader audience and tend to offer a greater range and diversity in art than is currently fashionable in the art world.

Prices in cooperative galleries may be lower than in private ones, but this is not always true. Artists are more accessible to the customers than when

Erika Carter, *Time Series: Frozen in Time,*
2002, 53 × 37. Discharged cotton fabric;
stitching. Collection of the artist

they are represented by some private galleries. The Noho Gallery (fine art) in New York City gives its members solo exhibitions, just as private galleries do. The Ariel Gallery (contemporary craft) in Asheville, North Carolina, has not yet had solo exhibits, instead staging them for three or four artists at a time. Fiber artist and member Carmen Grier typically has six to eight pieces on exhibit at a time. Paper portfolios and computer folders of each artist's work are accessible. Noho Gallery also maintains a portfolio for each artist member.

National and International Competitions   There are two major competitive exhibits that serious collectors should try to attend: *Quilt National* (Athens, Ohio) and *Quilt Visions* (sponsored by Quilt San Diego). These are the oldest and most highly regarded among the artists. *ArtQuilt Elements* (Wayne, Pennsylvania), formerly known as *Art Quilts at the Sedgwick*, is newer but has become increasingly more competitive. Like museums, these competitions have missions that guide the selection process. The purpose of *Quilt National*, for example, is "to carry the definition of quilting far beyond its traditional parameters and to promote quiltmaking as what it always has been—an art form."[12] Both *Quilt Visions* and *ArtQuilt Elements* seek to promote the contemporary quilt as an art form. All three exhibits publish catalogs in book or digital format.

In addition to these competitions, there are many excellent and long-running smaller ones which attract entrants from across the country. These include, for example, the biennial *Artist as Quiltmaker* exhibit in Oberlin, Ohio, and the annual *Quilts = Art = Quilts* exhibit at the Schweinfurth Memorial Art Center in Auburn, New York. These exhibitions and others like them are usually found listed on the websites of the Studio Art Quilt Associates and *AmericanStyle* magazine. They are also published in the calendar pages of *Fiberarts* magazine and kept up to date on the website of the American Craft Council.

In competitive exhibits, the winning entries are chosen by a juror or a panel of jurors from among hundreds, sometimes thousands, of slides sent by artists. There are differing opinions among artists and art professionals about who should be on these panels; organizations take different approaches. Artist-jurors in the field are more likely to recognize derivative (copied) work, but museum curators, art historians, and other art professionals are more likely to have a deeper knowledge of art and design and to keep in mind the broader context of the arts when making their selections. The outcome may also be influenced by the small size of the community of professional artist-quiltmakers and the likelihood that jurors are familiar with one another's work. *Quilt National*'s jury is different for each exhibit, as are those of *Quilt Visions* and *ArtQuilt Elements*. *Quilt National*'s jury consists of two artists with a longstanding relationship to the organization and one museum professional.[13] An effort is made to select a significant number of quilts from artists who have not previously entered the competition. The *Quilt Visions* panel includes one artist plus two different art professionals. Some small exhibits use just one juror, usually someone with a broader view of the field than most artists would have.

Not all studio artists submit their work to quilt-only competitions. Some seek recognition from a broader audience than quiltmakers, who make up the majority of the people who attend these shows. These artists are more likely to enter competitions for mixed media fine art, fiber art, or craft. Two such competitions are *Fiberart International,* a biennial exhibition of contemporary fiber art sponsored by the Fiberarts Guild of Pittsburgh, and *Materials: Hard & Soft,* an annual exhibition of craft held in Denton, Texas. Both shows have achieved national recognition. Exhibits like these are found listed in the pages or websites of publications like *Fiberarts* and *Art Calendar.*

Regional and Traveling Exhibitions   Shows are also organized by artists who have joined together in critique or support groups. Among the oldest of these are the Art Quilt Network in Ohio and the Contemporary Quilt Association of the Northwest. These networks find venues at small museums and at community, arts, craft, and textile centers. After a regional exhibition, the show might travel to other parts of the country. University museums, too, host fiber art exhibits, sometimes, but not always, featuring the work of the host school's faculty and artists who teach in other schools. These exhibits

Facing. Susan Shie, *The Punch Bowl/Star,* 2006, 86 × 63. The Star card in the artist's Kitchen Tarot art quilt deck. Whole cloth painting on white cotton. Hand drawn with paint markers, airbrushed; diary writing with airpen and fabric paint; hand sewn, machine crazy grid quilted.

Dominie Nash, *Stills from a Life*, 2002, 40¼ × 40¼. Fabric collage with cotton and silk organza; dyed and printed using a variety of surface design techniques. Raw-edged, machine appliquéd, and quilted.

are posted on the university's website, the arts or style sections of local news-papers, and occasionally in magazines devoted to art, textiles, and craft.

Small shows in the kinds of settings described above give viewers an opportunity to view studio quilts from a close perspective, an advantage over larger museum settings. If they are traveling exhibits, viewers have a chance to see art from other parts of the country. You should be aware, however, that group exhibits may include the work of artists working in very different styles and having different levels of skill. This may result in a show of uneven quality or one which does not seem well composed.

For invitational exhibits, studio quilts (or the artists) are selected by an art professional, usually a museum curator or gallery director, from a pool of artists whose work is familiar to the professional. This method of choosing works for a group show allows the curator to have control over the quality and overall composition of the exhibit.

Fiber Art Destinations Professional conferences in the textile arts and major quilt exhibitions frequently offer the public opportunities for viewing a wide spectrum of studio quilts and other forms of textile art within a single geographical area and within a compressed time span. For example, during its biennial conference in Kansas City, Missouri, the work of the Surface Design Association's most accomplished artists is exhibited at numerous local art galleries, churches, and community and art centers. Faculty and students in the fiber art program of the Kansas City Art Institute have work on display in the Institute's galleries. Not all the work is for sale, but the exhibits survey a wide range of professional-level work. Recently another exhibit has been added which is open to all members wishing to show a sample of their work. Every June, when the Quilt Surface Design Symposium meets in Columbus, Ohio, several galleries and art centers in the city and surrounding areas display contemporary quilts, including those of the Symposium faculty. Every other spring, the Gross McCleaf Gallery of Philadelphia has its invitational art quilt show, and the Snyderman-Works Galleries, also in Philadelphia, holds an invitational fiber art exhibit. The *ArtQuilt Elements* exhibit, formerly *Art Quilts at the Sedgwick,* in nearby Wayne, Pennsylvania, runs at the same time. Numerous private, non-profit, and university art and textile centers and galleries exhibit studio quilts and other forms of textile art. Undoubtedly, there are other cities where, at times, conferences and convocations afford similar opportunities. All are subject to change, of course, as exhibitions, galleries, and art centers cope with changing rents and space requirements.

Open Studio Days   "Open studio days" are specific days during the year when artists open their studios to visitors. They are often sponsored by city and regional art and cultural affairs departments and commissions of local government. Studio artists Judith Trager in Denver and Joan Schulze in San Francisco have found the program to be a good means of educating the public about fiber art. For the visitor, it is an opportunity to visit the studio of participating artists and to speak with them about their work without pressure to buy. Open studio days are advertised in local newspapers. In some communities, sponsoring organizations provide maps to the artists' studios.

Large Quilt Shows and Festivals   Far removed from the quiet atmosphere of galleries and artists' studios are quilt festivals and shows, typically held over a period of three to five days. With exceptions made for charitable causes and the vendors who sell quilts from booths set up within the exhibition halls, the shows are not venues for the sale of exhibited quilts. The majority of the quilts are traditional. There are separate categories for amateurs and professionals, but most winning entries are made by stellar hobbyists, not professional quiltmakers. This may be the reason for their continuing popularity. Quiltmakers, and their friends and families, make up the majority of those attending. Educational workshops taught by professional quiltmakers are an important part of these shows, as are the vendors, who sell not only quilts but also the latest fabrics and tools for quiltmakers. The shows tend to have a fair-like atmosphere.

The longest running of the festivals is the International Quilt Festival

Patricia Autenrieth, *Red Dot Study*, 2006, 12 × 10. Inkjet (pigment) printed, machine embroidery, quilted, crocheted border.

(IQF), which was founded in 1975 and is held each fall at the convention center in Houston, Texas. Within its large embrace are several small exhibits of studio quilts. In 2005 roughly 35 percent of all the quilts exhibited at the festival were "art quilts."[14] These included quilts made by both professionals and amateurs. One regular feature at IQF is a segment of *Quilt National*. IQF routinely showcases the work of individual quiltmakers, including studio artists. Jean Ray Laury, Yvonne Porcella, Katie Pasquini-Masopust, and Nancy Crow are among those who have been featured. In addition to exhibits, lectures on topics related to studio quilts have become part of each year's program. Quilts, Inc., the owner of the IQF, sponsors a second quilt festival each March in Chicago.

The American Quilter's Society (AQS) Annual Quilt Show and Contest, founded in 1985, is equally well known and popular with traditional American quiltmakers. The show, held each spring, brings thousands of enthusiasts to the small town of Paducah, Kentucky. The AQS represents traditional quiltmaking but has added a "nontraditional" category. "Aren't they all art quilts in different styles?" asks Bonnie Browning, the executive show director. "We strive to provide a mix of quilt styles in the special exhibits, in addition to the contest quilts."[15] Quilts selected for the exhibition and award winners must demonstrate exceptional craftsmanship and be linked to the craft's traditions; its jurors use traditional criteria in judging. AQS sponsors a similar but smaller competition and show in Nashville, Tennessee, each August. There are many studio artists who choose not to participate in these competitions, but others do take part. Represented among AQS award winners and in its museum collections are studio artists Ruth McDowell, Judi Warren Blaydon, Carol Bryer Fallert, Erika Carter, Alison Goss, and Lonni Rossi, among others.

Serious collectors of studio quilts insist that there is value for both the casual buyer and the beginning collector in attending, at least once, events like the IQF and the AQS Show and Competition, even though most of the quilts are traditional and the setting is not always ideal for appreciating the quilts as art. Karey Bresenhan, co-owner of Quilts, Inc. and a founder of IQF, says, "Large shows help you to define your interests." She suggests that newcomers not try to see the show in a single day, that they isolate the kinds of quilts that appeal to them, and that they try to determine why some may have won awards and not others. Doing this will help "to educate your eye."

Local Guild Exhibitions   Quilt guilds are the center of the quiltmaking community in many cities. During their meetings, members share ideas and recent quilts with one another, organize activities to meet community needs, and arrange educational lectures and workshops. Their exhibits tend to be traditional, but you might discover a talented emerging artist there. For the new collector, these shows are a good place to learn about "derivative" work, a practice which has negative connotations in art but is a longstanding practice among quiltmakers. Sharing designs is part of the craft's tradition. It is not uncommon to see several quilts by different makers that were begun in a workshop and which bear a strong resemblance to the style of the workshop teacher. Guild exhibits are not venues for sale, but you should be able to initiate communication with a quiltmaker whose work interests you by leaving contact information with one of the volunteers.

Student Work   There are many people who enjoy discovering young talent. The work of MFA students at schools such as Cranbrook Academy of Art in Bloomfield, Michigan, and many universities is exhibited in their galleries during the academic year, especially in the spring.

Charitable Auctions   One final source for studio quilts are the fundraising auctions held by schools, craft centers, and arts organizations. Schools such as Arrowmont School of Arts and Crafts, Penland School of Crafts, and Haystack Mountain School of Crafts hold these events several times a year.

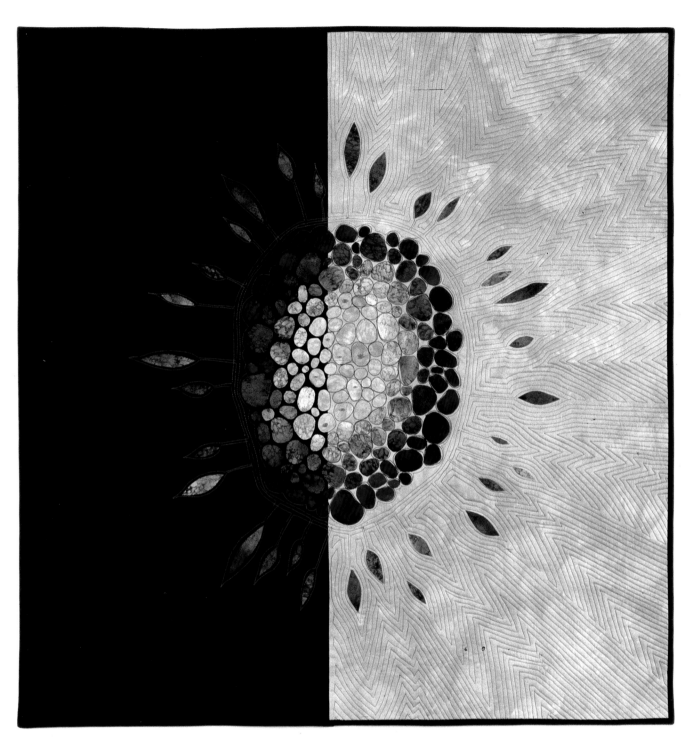

Charlotte Bird, *Fruiting Body, #1*, 2005,
31½ × 30½. Cotton; hand dyed and
commercial; hand cut and fuse appliquéd,
machine quilted, hand embroidered.
Photo: Jack Yonn

22

Suggestions for Buyers

If you see a piece and you really like it, what difference does it
make if no museum has that person's work? You respond to it.
Buy what you want to live with.
—Rebecca A. T. Stevens, curator of contemporary textiles,
the Textile Museum, Washington, D.C.

Price is not always an indicator of worth.
—Penny McMorris, art consultant

- Attend exhibits—in museums, art centers, colleges. Get on the mailing
  lists of sponsoring organizations and read local papers for exhibit openings. Go to your local guild's quilt show.
- If you are not familiar with studio quilts or the market, but you want to
  buy a quilt quickly, and if it is important that you buy an original piece,
  then select work from a juried exhibit, buy through a reputable gallery,
  or use an art consultant. (See chapter 25, "Working with an Art Consultant.") Do not feel obliged to accept the consultant's recommendations.
- Use the internet to get an overview of the field and the market. If an
  artist's website has only a few images, ask him or her to send more.
  Inquire at exhibitions about how you can reach an artist whose work
  interests you.
- When you attend an exhibit, be aware that the setting in which the art is
  displayed affects your perception of it. Good works are easily overlooked
  in crowded settings. Work which is not exceptional can look very good
  when grouped with pieces of lesser quality.
- Remember that your judgment will be influenced by other works you
  have seen the same day and by those hanging in the immediate vicinity
  of the work in front of you.

- Quilts that have an immediate visual impact should have other qualities that engage your interest over a more sustained period of time.
- By itself, technique is not art, and dazzling technique can mask a lack of deeper significance.
- Embellished quilts (beads or other objects attached to the surface) should be carefully examined. They may present storage problems. Be sure that the embellishments are not covering design failures. (See chapter 27, "Displaying, Caring for, and Storing Studio Quilts.")
- When looking at a quilt, consider the whole composition. If frayed edges or crude workmanship are important to the composition, they cannot be considered sloppy technique.
- Technique should be related to content. Small, even stitches and perfectly matched points are not important in a studio quilt unless they are required to carry out the artist's intent, as, for example, in a sharply defined geometric piece.
- Work should always be finished and well presented by the artist, even if the composition is "crude."
- An artist who uses a technique developed by someone else is not necessarily copying, but the technique should not be used in work similar enough in style to the original artist's as to be identifiable as his or her work. The compositions of each artist should be recognizable as his or her own.
- If you see work that interests you, try to find out more about the artist. Look for a website that illustrates his or her work. Most artists will make their portfolios available for review if you are sincerely interested. Look for evidence of a cohesive body of work. Serious artists develop their own voice, styles, and techniques over time. They do not repeatedly change them.
- Ask the artist to notify you of upcoming exhibits.
- When an artist sells an original work of art made on or after 1978, the copyright for that work remains with the artist for his or her lifetime plus seventy years. (Regulations vary slightly for art made before 1978.) The buyer is not permitted to have copies made or to have the art published without permission from the artist.
- If you buy a quilt over the internet, get a written guarantee that it can be returned if the colors or level of craftsmanship are not what you expected.
- Do not be surprised or put off by irregularities you may detect in comparing the prices of various artists. In general, artists learn how to price their art through the process of selling it in a gallery. Gallery directors know what prices the market will bear, or they would not be able to remain in business. Because only a small proportion of studio art quiltmakers are represented by galleries, artists without a history of sales may have little guidance when pricing their work. The prices they set may not accurately reflect their talent, skill, and accomplishments. Recent graduates may overestimate the value of their work. Some artists charge for

their work based on what they *think* it is worth relative to what others charge. Excellent artists from less populated parts of the country may underestimate the value of their work when it is sent to venues on the East or West Coast where the market sustains higher prices. Occasionally, quiltmakers price a quilt very high because they have no intention of selling it. Buyers should not take these problems as evidence that the artists are not serious about their work.

- The quilt prices of artists represented by galleries may be higher than you expect, but galleries rarely charge more than their regular customers are willing to pay for art.
- Artists do not usually have more than one gallery representing them unless the galleries are located in different parts of the country. Prices will be the same in all galleries.
- If an artist who is represented by a gallery also sells art from a website, website prices will be consistent with the gallery prices.
- If you find a quilt which you love but cannot afford, ask the artist if you can make monthly payments. Most artists will accommodate you. The same is true for work sold through galleries. The art remains with the artist or gallery until payments are completed.
- Expect to pay higher prices for the work of artists whose quilts are in important museums and private collections or who have had work accepted into major competitions and won awards. Art which represents a turning point for an artist might be priced higher for historical reasons.
- Be careful about spending a lot of money for work by someone about whom you know nothing. That is not to say you should not buy it. If you really love the work, if it is exactly what you want, if you are not put off by the price, and if it is not important whether or not you can sell it in ten years for what it costs now, then buy it.
- Prices are influenced by trends. Color, style, and aesthetics (landscape, abstract, etc.) are all variables that change over the years. Likewise, trends in the popularity of one art form over another can also affect price. In the 1980s and early 1990s, there was a "buzz" in the quilt market; both traditional and contemporary quilts sold well. In the 1990s, glass art became a "hot commodity," and its prices skyrocketed while the price for studio quilts stagnated.
- Size is a factor in the price of all art. Larger works cost more. Some quiltmakers use a square foot method to determine their prices, with more accomplished artists charging a higher figure. Using this measure as a guide, potential buyers can compare the prices of students and emerging artists with mature and well-known artists.
- The price of a studio art quilt should not be determined by the length of time an artist spends making it.
- Think about buying student work. Art students are always encouraged when someone thinks well enough of their work to buy it. It gives them confidence. Keep in mind, though, that students do not have a record

of sales or accomplishments to justify a high price. If you pay too high a price, you may give them an unrealistic expectation of the value of their art in the marketplace. If you are a collector and they are aware of it, your interest may influence their future direction before their careers have even begun. Student work is usually on exhibit at university galleries in the spring. Many schools also have sales of student work in early December.

- Do not buy fabric art (or watercolors, drawings, or even oil paintings) if you are looking for something to hang on a sunlit wall. (See chapter 27, "Displaying, Caring for, and Storing Studio Quilts.")
- Windows can be screened with UV filters to protect fabric art from the most harmful rays of light.
- If you are buying a very large studio quilt and plan to display it for an extended period of time, you may need to have a professional framer. Over time, gravity will distort the shape of freely hanging large quilts. A supportive frame that bears the weight of the quilt can keep this from happening. (See chapter 27, "Displaying, Caring for, and Storing Studio Quilts.")
- If it is important to you that a large quilt hang freely and unattached to a frame, buy two quilts for the same space and allow one to rest every six months.
- Studio quilts can be framed if done so properly. (See chapter 27, "Displaying, Caring for, and Storing Studio Quilts.")

Katie Pasquini-Masopust, *Grapes*,
60 × 96, 1996. Hendricks Collection.
Photo: Scott Turner

23

Collecting

Some Well-Known Collectors and
What We Can Learn from Them

The most enjoyable aspect of collecting is the selection process and determining which quilts demonstrate the highest level of artistry and unique design. I also enjoy meeting the quilt artists and learning about their particular passion and the driving interest which led to the creation of their art work. It may be because I quilt myself that I appreciate design and I treasure the detailed workmanship, stitching and dedication to quality that are the hallmarks of noted quilt artists.

—Maureen Hendricks, collector

If you look at something and you are looking for the sake of learning, you start to see things that are too subtle to see at a glance. You don't ever really see something in its entirety the first time. And if it is great art, it is likely you will never fully understand it. But over time, you can be drawn to different facets of the object, such as the technique. You may see how the artist is stitching a quilt in a variety of different ways, but it is still the same object. This is what is normally taught in connoisseurship courses, the notion of comparing and contrasting and trying to learn more about what excellence is. Excellence manifests itself in many different ways, the quality of someone's ability to get across an idea, excellence in the concept, the execution of technique. These are all things that are subtle yet substantive and require time and effort to see and understand. Often, effort can be understood simply as the ability to be still and to look.

—Mark Leach, founding director and chief curator of craft,
Mint Museum of Craft + Design

Collectors approach their search for art differently from casual buyers. They tend to have a passionate interest in and love for the objects they seek, a passion that extends to the activities involved in collecting. It is an important part of their lives, and they find it not only fun but also exhilarating. This is true for most art collectors; what distinguishes collectors of fiber art is their willingness to look beyond the art institutions' hierarchy of "high and low" art to an aesthetic form that is personally meaningful. As critic and curator Polly Ullrich noted recently: "To be a collector of fiber art takes individuality. It takes toughness and the ability to be comfortable with a certain distance from the mainstream art world."[1]

The motivations for collecting and the aesthetics which appeal to collectors are varied. Some collectors are interested only in studio quilts; others are drawn to other forms of art as well. The passion is a constant, however. In a panel discussion at the International Quilt Study Center in 2005, art and antique quilt collector Jonathan Holstein expressed it this way: "Talking about the Amish quilts, no matter how many times I have seen these quilts, every time I unfold one, I experience exactly the same thrill and excitement that I did when I saw them for the first time thirty years ago. That to me is about extraordinary art objects and also about the way they pull collectors into collecting."[2]

Asked what they look for in an art object or what is the focus of their collecting, collectors frequently respond by saying "I buy what I like" or "The work speaks to me." This does not mean they have no focus, but that their collections are personal. Fiber art collector Sharon Hoogendoorn says: "We all come from a different perspective and that is what makes your collection your own. You may not create the pieces, but you create the collection. This reflects who you are." Craft collector Robert Pfannebecker bought what he liked for nearly forty years: "Everything I have has associative and idiosyncratic value to me. I knew the people; I know where I bought it. It had an importance when I bought it. It may have less value, but it has value. . . . In terms of a mistake, I don't really use that term."[3] Camille Cooke often buys works that she and her husband admire before an artist makes a name in the craft field. "It's not that we do not like to buy established artists; it's that there is pleasure in supporting a newcomer and a genuine rush of pride when they 'make the grade' into an important show or are collected by a major museum."[4]

Art advisors sometimes tell clients who are interested in building a collection to choose a theme to guide their purchases. Such advice is partly based on the assumption that in the future, a cohesive collection will be more valuable.[5] A theme might mean concentrating on a particular artist or time period. Nancy and Warren Brakensiek, for example, have confined their collection mostly to the work of studio quilt artists living in the Northwest. Brakensiek, a retired corporate attorney, and his wife, a retired certified public accountant, have one of the larger collections in the country. They also collect other forms of contemporary art.

Most collectors do not buy fiber art for investment purposes, but having a focus to collecting can be beneficial in other ways. John M. Walsh III has been collecting studio art quilts since the early 1990s. He is a chemical engineer and the CEO and principal shareholder of Waltron, LLC, which manufactures water quality analyzers for the electric power industry worldwide. His life's work has been to make water safe to use. Shortly before beginning to collect, Walsh chanced upon a television show in Britain about the artist Michael James. It sparked his interest. Returning to the United States, he attended a conference in Kentucky which included, among other exhibits, one of contemporary quilts. One of the speakers he heard at the conference was Penny McMorris, the historian, television show producer, and curator, who spoke of the lack of serious collectors in the field. Not long afterward, with McMorris as his advisor, Walsh set out to document the artistry and range of art in the genre. Walsh's focus is to look for the best works of the best artists. He believes that having a goal and a focus makes the collecting experience more rewarding. "This way," he says, "collecting is like creating a work of art. If done well, the whole is more than the individual pieces."[6]

People rarely buy their first work of art with the intention of accumulating a collection, however. "I purchased a few small quilts," said Del Thomas, "but did not think of my activity as collecting. Then I saw one of Ruth McDowell's quilts. I wanted it so much, that I bought it with the money I had saved for a new sewing machine. That is when I became a collector. I began to set aside a certain amount of money each year for quilts."[7] "In the beginning," say Nancy and Warren Brakensiek, "you see a piece of art which you love and you buy it. You do not think about how this piece will be part of a collection. As you buy more, at some point you realize that you have become a collector and with that realization comes the responsibility to educate yourself regarding the medium, maintain and preserve the artwork, promote the medium, and protect the rights of the artists."[8]

When do a few studio quilts become a collection? Penny McMorris, who has been a corporate art curator and advisor to Walsh as well as to Ardis and Robert James (see below), observes: "An individual can begin buying art quilts because she likes them and then buy more. These quilts do not constitute a true collection. A true collection is formed with real intent and with a desire to learn, as well as to acquire pieces that give you satisfaction."[9] This definition does not assign a size to a true collection nor does it assess a value to anyone but the collector.

Walsh's desire to learn is an earnest one. He has taken a workshop in quiltmaking in order to better understand the process and the artists. Like the Brakensieks, he realizes that collecting entails responsibilities. He does not see himself as the owner of his collection, but as its curator and caretaker for future generations. He frequently lends the quilts out for exhibition. Even this experience has proven educational. By watching curators decide how to arrange the quilts for exhibition, he says, he has realized how important the presentation of an exhibition is. "I think being a serious collector means having a serious interaction with the medium, perhaps with the artists, spending some time and getting to know what is going on. It is very helpful to have assistance from someone who understands the medium, knows what is going on, and can improve your vision and understanding."[10] Walsh has a second goal to his collecting, which involves support for promising artists. He commissions quilts from them, thereby providing the financial support and enabling them to pursue experimental work. The Brakensieks, too, have supported artists. They funded a lecture series for the Contemporary Quilt Association of the Northwest and sponsor an award at the *Quilt National* and *Quilt Visions* competitions. They have also provided counsel to the Studio Art Quilt Associates by serving on its board of directors.

Ardis and Robert James have taken a somewhat different approach to collecting quilts. In the late 1960s they began accumulating what became one of the largest, if not the largest, private collection of antique quilts in the country. In later years they added contemporary works to their interests. Ardis James owned a fabric store in the 1960s and became a passionate collector of antique quilts. She took quilt design classes with the artist Michael James (no

Frank Connet, Untitled, 2000,
63 × 33. Shibori (stitched resist)
wool used to create the shapes
and patterning; natural dye
(indigo, walnut, and madder);
cut, pieced, and hand quilted.
Photo: George Pfoertner

relation) and was an early supporter of his work. Her husband Robert James was a professor of economics at Massachusetts Institute of Technology prior to becoming a vice president for Mobil Oil in Houston, Texas, and then co-founding Enterprise Development Associates, which built shopping centers and is now known as Enterprise Asset Management. He not only encouraged his wife in her collecting, but he joined her and found it to be a great deal of fun. Collecting involved pricing, negotiating, and deal making, just as his entrepreneurial activities did. The two realized that they could put an outstanding collection together for far less money than Robert's colleagues in New York were investing in other forms of art. In 1997 the Jameses, who were originally from Nebraska, donated 950 quilts from their collection to the University of Nebraska–Lincoln and pledged additional support. Their donations led to the establishment of the International Quilt Study Center which encourages interdisciplinary study of all aspects of quiltmaking. A few years later, they funded the first academic chair in quilt studies, a position filled by artist Michael James. Additional support from the couple has helped the IQSC to build a new facility to house and exhibit its collections. In addition to antique quilts, they have donated nearly 90 untraditional, contemporary quilts to the Center.

The enjoyment of art and the pleasures of collecting outweigh interest in making a profit for most collectors in this field. Prices, with some exceptions, have not risen much in the last ten years, although the art world is slowly beginning to pay more attention. This makes it an ideal time for people who love art to take a look at studio quilts. Experienced gallery dealers expect the value of studio quilts made by the best artists to hold.[11] The art form is not yet fifty years old, and a secondary market is only beginning to develop, but there is plenty of wonderful art out there.

24

Suggestions for Beginning Collectors

I began collecting to fill my wall, but I personally enjoy it. I have embroidery and two collages and love them for the same reason as my quilt—the depth. Our house is unusual, angular and very modern. The piece really does complement it. The silk background is very much like a watercolor.
—Colleen Piersen, collector

Look at as much stuff as you can. Go to as many exhibitions as you can. Try to find somebody who isn't just trying to sell you whatever they have on the market and have a discussion with them about why they show what they show. Try to talk to artists whom you respect and who are articulate. . . . I listened a lot more than I talked until I learned something about it. I would spend hours just listening to an artist discuss the whole field. I just think that if you are interested enough, you can find a mentor, perhaps an artist or a gallery owner. You want to be a little careful. Some people have their own bias, their own agenda. Try to find your own particular niche in what you are really interested in.
—Robert Pfannebecker, collector

Serious artists work intensely on an idea for a long period, and then naturally, as they read and think, new ideas come to them which require them to work in a different direction. But their work evolves from previous work; they take risks. There are peaks and valleys when they are thinking and learning. Every piece they make is not going to be exceptional.
—Penny McMorris, art consultant

Nancy Herman, *Blue Waltz*, Liberty
Ridge, Liberty Property Trust, Malvern,
Pennsylvania. Photo: Weaver Lilley
Photography

• Read widely about all the visual arts. Find out what museums collect in contemporary quilts and what is in their collections. Try to make an appointment with the curator to see works that are not on view. Make use of other opportunities for learning what the museum offers in the area of contemporary quilts.

• By accepting an artist's quilt into its collection, the museum is saying that it believes in the value of the artwork artistically, historically, and technically. Spend time with these pieces. Go back and see them more than once. Ask the curator why they are important.

• See as many exhibitions as you can, major and minor ones, especially when you are just beginning to collect. Talk with people about the art—artists, gallery owners, other collectors. Artists are often happy to talk about their art. Gallery owners can be very important in your education. Ask them why they represent particular artists and not others. Be wary if they try to rush you into a purchase.

- Get exhibit catalogs for shows you are not able to attend. Request that your name be put on the mailing and e-mail lists of galleries.

- If you are not relying on a consultant and are just beginning to collect, begin with a price cap even if you can afford to spend more. It will force you to be selective. As you gradually learn what interests you most and your confidence in your selections grows, you will be ready to make a larger purchase.

- Before spending a lot of money on a quilt, make sure the art is truly original and not derived from work done ten or even a hundred years ago. If you are not sure, ask a quilt historian or consultant.

- Think carefully about whether you will still like the piece in ten years.

- Some advances in technology have led to new materials being used in art which cannot be guaranteed to last as long as the traditional cotton and linen. (Silk has always been more fragile, and wool vulnerable to insects.) If you are concerned about this, request a list of components used in the quilt from the artist and ask if any special care is required. Most care measures are simple procedures.

- If you do not like a quilt that your art consultant recommends, you are under no obligation to buy it. (See chapter 25, "Working with an Art Consultant.")

- If you are buying work from someone other than the artist, make sure to ask for documentation of its provenance (names of previous owners and history of sales). Check databases for lost or stolen quilts and art. If the owner says it was sold through a gallery, check with the gallery. Find out if the quilt was ever damaged and the name and qualifications of the person who restored it.

- As studio quilts begin to develop a secondary market (re-sale), they will most likely be sold in the decorative arts category of auction houses and online auction sites. If you are going to bid, do your homework before-hand. Look at comparable items in museums, books, and galleries. Make sure to read descriptions carefully. Inquire about the piece's condition, including damage and restoration. Get accurate information about the quilt's provenance.

- As your collection grows, you will need a system to manage information about each object in it. This information should include the following: an image of the artwork, a written description, the name of the art-ist, its provenance, the appraiser, the insurer, insured value, condition, and a means of keeping track of it, particularly if you lend pieces out for exhibition. There are several computer software programs that have been developed for collectors that serve this purpose.

- There are costs connected with collecting that are not included in the purchase price. These include insurance, storage, and transportation. If you send parts of your collection out for exhibition from time to time, there will be additional costs, such as extra insurance and packaging. (See chapter 29, "Insuring Your Art.")

- Think about how and where you are going to store your artwork. A collector must be able to store quilts when they are not being displayed. Ideally, they should lie flat in rooms where the temperature and humidity are stable. (See chapter 27, "Displaying, Caring for, and Storing Studio Quilts.")

- Unless you are planning to sell your collection or leave it to your children, you should begin planning for its disposition while you are still able to do the research involved. If you plan to donate it to a museum, you must find a match between what you have and what a museum wants. A museum may already have art by the same artist and not want any more. Staff may not believe that your piece is a particularly good example of an artist's work.

- Generally, museums do not like to accept art with conditions attached, although if you are also making a major contribution to the museum, they might accept it. Remember, every donation made to a museum requires expenditure for staff time, research, conservation, and space.

- You, as donor, should be sure that your intentions for the art and the museum's intentions are similar. What is the current focus of the museum's collecting? What is the attitude of the textile and contemporary art curators toward the exhibition of studio quilts? What about de-accessioning (the selling of donated work)?

- Do not assume that if your collection is accepted by a museum, the museum's standards of care will meet your own. It is important to ask specific questions about the care it would receive. Inquire about the storage facility. Is it climate controlled? Does it protect artwork from sprinklers? Is there a fire suppression system? What kind of emergency planning does the museum have? Are there periodic inspections for insects? And although you want to make sure your quilts are not locked away in storage for years, unseen by anyone, you do not want them to be exhibited constantly without a periodic rest.

- If you are planning to donate your collection to a charitable institution and to obtain a tax deduction, you will need an appraisal that conforms to IRS regulations. These regulations became more rigorous in 2006. (See chapter 28, "What You Should Know about Appraisals.") A museum might give you some suggestions regarding where you can go for an appraisal, but it is not ethical for the museum to appraise your collection.

- Read chapter 22, "Suggestions for Buyers." The suggestions in that chapter are also applicable to collecting.

25

Working with an Art Consultant

A lthough most people who are interested in buying fiber art do not need the services of an art consultant or advisor, such professionals can be a knowledgeable and unbiased source of advice and can save the buyer a considerable amount of time.

Art consultants can be engaged by individuals as well as institutions or other organizations. Their responsibilities depend on the intentions of their clients. If the client is seeking to build an art collection, the consultant, for example, may help his client to "focus his collecting activities, set realistic goals, and find and acquire appropriate objects."[1] The focus is usually on acquiring existing art. If the client is a museum, business, professional organization, hospital, or hotel, the consultant's responsibility may be either to build a serious art collection or to provide art to enhance the workplace. Much art obtained for this latter purpose is newly commissioned work. While the academic requirements are the same for both kinds of art consulting, some of the skills required, the experience, and the manner in which fees are paid differ.

Training and Responsibilities   Whether retained by a serious collector or a business wanting decorative art, art advisors should have an education in art history. This gives them the analytical framework necessary to assess quality. Specialists in studio art quilts should have a broad and deep knowledge of the field based on experience coming from involvement as a curator, writer, dealer, and/or juror. Their knowledge should include familiarity with traditional quilt design. Potential clients should always ask about consultants' education and experience.

When clients are serious collectors seeking to develop a true collection, that is, "one formed with real intent and with a desire to learn as well as to acquire pieces that give satisfaction," consultants have a responsibility to be as knowledgeable as possible, says Penny McMorris, former art advisor to collectors Ardis and Robert James and John M. Walsh III. This means they must be able to distinguish an artist's work from his or her students. They must also be familiar with the artist's whole body of work and know what is the best available. They must know which of an artist's work interests their clients and suggest the names of artists whose works should be sought. McMorris places great importance on consultants' responsibility to educate their clients. "The agent should never be in a hurry with the client and the client should never be in a hurry to buy," she says. And the client and agent must have a good working relationship.[2]

Art consultants who work primarily with business clients must be familiar with a broad range of visual art. They are not likely to have specific training in textile art, and most of the companies that employ consultants are not buying art with the intent to build museum-quality collections. Nonetheless, many of these consultants are savvy about quilts and textiles. "We find the most interesting spaces tend to have different kinds of material, different sizes, and different kinds of art," says Judy Lepow of Galman Lepow Associates. "That is why we include textile arts."[3]

The "eye" and experience of consultants are important to their work with businesses. They must be able to envision the kind, scale, and color of art that will work in spaces ranging from lunchrooms to boardrooms, from stairwells to atriums. Because the art required is often "site-specific," consultants seek artists who will take commissions much more often than they look for existing artwork. Unless companies have an ongoing art-collecting program, consultants are hired for a limited period of time during which they assess the space, work with the clients to determine what interests them most, present clients with various art options that will work, arrange for commissions, and oversee the installation. Their responsibilities begin with being well versed in the contemporary (and/or antique) art and design trends.

Maxine Manges of MKM Fine Art, Inc. has used contemporary quilts in her projects for many years. She reads art publications, attends the major art quilt exhibitions when possible, and keeps copies of their catalogs to locate artists. Art consultants who are grounded in art history, she believes, are able to find artists whose work is not tied to a particular period, to find work that is timeless; good design practices are common to all great art, as much as new trends test those limits. Manges also believes it is important that her clients love the art she puts forward as much as she does and that the work echo the mission of her client, whether it is corporate, health care, professional, or hospitality based. "I build a collection for a company and give them the wherewithal to keep track of it. Once they have the data saved, including résumés of the artist and the essential information about the work, we can keep up with the appraised value and augment the collection as the client grows."[4]

Fees   Fees paid to art consultants by companies are included in the company's art budget. Consultants limit presentations made to corporate clients to works whose prices fall within the budget they are given.

Fees paid by collectors or other individuals can be structured in several different ways. It is important for clients and art consultants to speak openly about fees, says McMorris. Assistance purchasing just a few quilts can be based on an hourly rate. Otherwise, she believes, the only truly ethical way to structure fees is to pay consultants a retainer fee that is not based on a particular sale. "The fee itself must make it worthwhile for the consultant to spend her time carrying out her responsibilities which include looking for works for her client, making herself available to answer her client's questions, working with curators and assisting when art is exhibited."

McMorris believes that when fees are based on the price of a quilt, it leaves open to question the possibility that consultants might be urging their clients to buy higher-priced quilts in order to make more money. Payment plans based on consultants negotiating a discount with gallery directors and then keeping the difference are also subject to easy abuse. This method can result in consultants encouraging several galleries to compete with each other. In this situation, says McMorris, advisors are not concentrating on finding the best art for their clients.

This long-time specialist in studio art quilts offers one last piece of advice: It is important that clients and art consultants have a good working relationship, one that is based on a clear understanding of intentions, expectations, and budgets.

Anne McKenzie Nickolson, *Who Will Lead Us?*
2006, 64½ × 57. Cotton, pieced, appliqué. In this
contemporary quilt, the basic scheme for cutting
and piecing was developed on a computer.

26

Commissioning a Quilt

The elements of a successful commission are the same whether the studio quilt is for a home or a business—good communication between the artist and the client and clarity from the beginning about all aspects of the process. John M. Walsh III, who has commissioned many studio quilts, advises that before any steps are taken, it is important to answer two questions: "Who is the commission for?" and "What do I hope they will get out of it?"[1] Walsh is a generous patron; his support in the form of commissions has given promising and talented artists the freedom to experiment. But his questions are relevant and important to anyone commissioning a work of art.

With these questions settled, the next step is to become familiar with the whole body of an artist's work and the range of his or her prices. This can be done by attending exhibits, conducting an internet search, and requesting slides or electronic images from the artist. Artists who accept commissions are usually happy to accommodate a potential buyer.

If the buyer has not seen the artist's work in person, a first meeting might take place in the artist's studio. Otherwise, the location where the art would be installed is a good place to meet. During this meeting, the artist will be interested in learning what draws the potential buyer to his or her work, what is liked about the previous work, and what is expected from the commission. The artist will acquaint the client with his or her style of working so that the client can decide if it is acceptable. When an artist's style is improvisational, for example, it is not possible to predict what the finished piece will look like.

The nature of some of the processes employed by the artist, fabric-dyeing for example, may come into play. "With all good intentions," says artist Jean Williams Cacicedo, "the creative process of art-making can often produce an element of surprise in the final work even if the artist's intentions were clearly defined."[2] On the other hand, the approach of landscape artists Gayle Fraas and Duncan Slade holds no surprises. After preliminary consultations which might require a site visit if specific landscape imagery is to be used, they produce a drawn-to-scale painting of their design on paper for approval by their clients. Once approved, it is rarely changed before final execution.

Before designs or plans are drawn up, both parties need to assess, through questions and careful listening, whether a good working relationship is possible. Few artists will agree to create art that is not aesthetically consistent with their current or evolving body of work. When this is what the client is requesting, artists usually will advise the client to look for a different artist. Nor do many artists wish to copy work they have already done or to do so in a different color. "Each art work is subject to the flow of ideas," says Joan Schulze. "If you want the best from an artist, be prepared for something you could not 'see in advance.' Art is about change. . . . A re-do of existing work is not art but production."[3]

The key element of a good relationship is trust. "It is really important," says Walsh, "to respect the fact that the artist is an artist to start with and not just someone involved in a commercial enterprise." When artists sense that a client needs rigid control, they may turn down the project. Clients who have not previously commissioned work may have a natural anxiety about the outcome, and some artists do take time to lead them through the process, keeping them informed and educating them as to the reasons for their artistic decisions. The commission process is founded on trust. "It is most important that the client allow me to be the artist," says Elizabeth Busch. "They commission me for my work and must trust that I need freedom to create and will not disappoint them."[4]

Size, location, color, and price should be discussed from the beginning. Some artists will not accept a commission for works under a certain size. They will often want to know where the work will hang; a client's plan to install it in direct sunlight will most likely be rejected. With respect to color, artists differ. Some will accept suggestions and attempt to use at least a bit of a requested color, but they will not agree to precisely match the upholstered furniture. For business projects, however, artists typically provide sample color palettes or fabric swatches to the art consultant, designer, or architect. A mutually agreeable decision is made before work begins.

A deposit of one-third to one-half of the full price is expected when the commission agreement or contract is signed. Preliminary design fees are often folded into the total price. Clients should expect that travel expenses and numerous consultations will increase the price. Although the base price varies from artist to artist and takes the cost of materials into account, the price of commissioned work is often determined by square footage.

A contract is signed when an agreement about the commission is reached. This legal document should provide clarity to the process and expectations for both client and artist. It spells out the materials to be used, the size, the price of the completed work, and conditions whereby additional charges such as framing, shipping, and installation may apply. It contains a schedule for payments and a completion date, and it defines the terms that apply if the purchaser wishes to terminate the agreement. It should specify that the artist is responsible for insurance coverage until delivery takes place, and it may serve to notify the purchaser that the copyright remains with the artist after sale.[5] Some fiber artists insist on a clause requiring the purchaser to have restorative work, necessitated by damage to the quilt, approved by them. The agreement may also specify the terms of the client's access to the art while it is being made and legal options for "adjustments" if the client is dissatisfied.

If the client wishes to add something to the project after the contract has been negotiated, and such options are not included in the contract, the additional requests should be put in writing along with additional costs involved. Artists want their clients to be happy with the outcome of the commission. They will often accept some modifications if what is asked for remains consistent with the original idea and quality. They do not want art to be sold under their name if it does not meet their standards.

When clients have done their homework and have found an artist whose work meets their own standards, and when both client and artist are willing and able to meet each other's needs, the commission will have a happy outcome for both.

Ludmila Uspenskaya, *Hot & Sunny,* 2003, 93 × 57.
Silk and cotton; hand painted, wax resist; collage,
machine and hand quilted. Photo: Karen Bell

27

Displaying, Caring for, and Storing Studio Quilts

I really see my work as something to be enjoyed now and for many years to come," writes Jan Myers-Newbury. "But I don't worry about 100 years from now. My goal is to have each quilt be a pleasure, not a burden, for the folks who have it in their lives."[1]

There is a common misperception that textile art is more troublesome to maintain than other forms of visual art. This view fails to take account of the many problems that have arisen with contemporary art in other media. The acrylic paint, enamels, and other synthetic substances that artists have substituted for oil paint since the 1950s, and the ready-mades and found objects they have incorporated into or turned into art have, in some instances, become curatorial nightmares. The relatively softer surface of acrylic paint attracts dirt, is vulnerable to scratches and dents, and is susceptible to mold. Presently, there is no completely acceptable means of cleaning it.[2] A deep red Rothko painting that has become pale blue; cracked gloss enamel on a Pollock canvas; Rauschenberg's famous combine *Monogram,* which consists of a stuffed goat encircled by a rubber tire; and Don Flavin's fluorescent lights are just a few examples of the challenges faced by conservators. In 2002 the Getty Museum, working with the Tate Museum in London and the National Gallery in Washington, D.C., began a major project to address the paint problems.[3] These problems have not kept museums from acquiring modern art, nor collectors from buying it.

The long-term prospects for studio quilts are at least as good as they are for most contemporary art. The fiber-reactive dyes many artists use have been proven to have "excellent fade resistance in indirect sunlight," according to artists who have been using them for thirty years.[4] And the new synthetic fabrics are undergoing study by museum textile conservators working to preserve their fashion collections.

For most textile art, however, conservation is mostly a matter of good sense, good housekeeping, climate control, and familiarity with archival materials. For anyone who does not have time or interest in taking studio quilts off the wall for vacuuming, there is no reason these quilts cannot be framed.

Where you hang a textile is important, however. If it is unframed and hung in a kitchen or child's playroom, an airport terminal or a sunny atrium, it will eventually need to be replaced. This does not mean that you should not buy a quilt for these environments. It means that it will not remain in pristine condition forever, and it might not be wise to spend thousands of dollars on it.

Displaying Your Quilts

- Many studio quiltmakers prefer to have their work hang freely. If that is your choice, you should vacuum it twice a year and observe a few precautions.
- Textiles collections (and all art) should be kept in reasonably controlled climate conditions. High humidity, warmth, and lack of air circulation encourage the growth of mold. Sudden, extreme changes in temperature and humidity can damage the fibers of the fabric. Textiles should not be displayed above heating vents, radiators, or air conditioners.
- Interior walls are the best for hanging textiles. Outside walls can condense moisture from a warm room, producing conditions conducive to the growth of mold.
- Museums generally keep the lighting in their galleries low for paintings and textiles. The reason is that sunlight and fluorescent lights emit imperceptible ultraviolet rays which cause damage and fading over time. Studio quilts should not be hung in the direct path of the sun or on a wall that receives substantial reflected light. Exposure can be greatly reduced by either framing your textiles with glass or Plexiglass containing a UV filter or by covering your windows with a flexible UV filter which can be purchased in clear, flexible sheets and applied directly to them.
- Incandescent lighting generates heat. Its source should not be placed too close to textile art. A spotlight aimed directly at the surface of any art can be harmful; floodlights are preferable. Lighting should be oriented so that the surface is evenly lit.
- Family members and guests should be reminded not to touch the art, as textiles readily absorb the oil from fingers, and not to smoke in the room where the art hangs.
- The shape of very large quilts that are suspended on a rod indefinitely

can be distorted over time by the force of gravity. It is advisable to take them down after six months and give them a rest for several months before re-hanging them. If you are going on a lengthy trip, it is a good idea to take down the quilts, lay them flat on a bed, and cover them with a sheet.

• Very large quilts that are stitched to a fabric panel for support and then framed can be displayed for an extended period of time.

• There are several ways to display studio quilts. When you purchase a quilt from a gallery or directly from the artist, you will likely receive instructions and the hardware for mounting it. These instructions should be followed. If you wish for your art to be framed, and it is a commissioned piece, the framing should be discussed with the artist beforehand. The artist may include the frame as part of the project.

Hanging Quilts   If your studio quilt does not come with instructions or materials for mounting it, there are several ways in which this can be done. Most textile conservators advise using Velcro. The following method for hanging "textiles in sturdy condition" is recommended by the chief conservator of the Textile Museum in Washington, D.C. It is printed here with permission from the museum.[5]

Velcro Mount

There have been a variety of systems used to hang textiles and rugs for display. These range from sleeve casings and twill tapes fitted with rings, to mounts that require overall stitching of the textile to a backing fabric and framing. A Velcro mount has replaced the use of sleeve casings and tapes and ring systems as the technique of choice by most conservators for the following reasons: 1) it is relatively easy to execute, 2) the points of stress on the hanging edge are minimal, and 3) it allows for adjustments and repositioning to compensate for dimensional movement and ripples in the textile caused by changes in humidity, or because of the natural uneven quality of many handmade textiles. A caveat: this hanging method is not appropriate for all textiles. Evaluate the textile carefully to see if it can truly support its own weight. If in doubt, consult a conservator to select the appropriate hanging method. This [Velcro] method is most often recommended for sturdy blankets, quilts, and rugs. It is not appropriate for thin or fragile textiles, such as silk, or for textiles with heavy surface embellishments like beads.

Materials

Undyed cotton tape (such as the canvas webbing used by upholsterers); 2" width for lightweight textiles and 3" width for heavier pieces.

Velcro brand hook and loop fastener: The 1" width loop side of the tapes is adequate for lightweight textiles and 2" width for heavier pieces. The 2"-wide hook side of the tape is attached to the wooden slat for hanging.

Cotton sewing thread: The weight of the thread and color will need to be matched to the textile.

Wooden slat: Select a poplar or other low-resin wood. The slat should have a

½" × 3" profile and be cut approximately ½" shorter than the width of the hanging edge of the textile. (For smaller, lightweight textiles, a ¼" × 1½" profile may be sufficient.) To protect the textile from wood acids, apply two coats of a water-borne polyurethane varnish to the slat.

Non-rusting staples or tacks are used to attach the hook tape to the wooden slat.

Fasteners such as mirror plates, "D" rings, or eye screws can be used to attach the slat to the wall.

Steps to Hanging

1. The easiest way to attach the loop tape (soft side) to the cotton canvas webbing is with a sewing machine. Center the loop tape on the webbing and sew down the length of the tape as shown in the diagram below. Note: the tape should never be sewn directly to your textile. Because of its stiffness, it is very difficult to work a sewing needle through it. The stress of trying to pull a needle through the tape may cause damage to your textile.

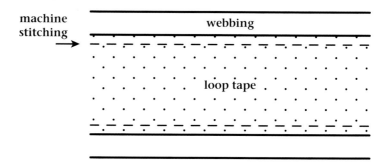

2. Place your textile face down on a clean, flat surface. Hand-woven textiles are not perfectly square. Allow the textile to assume its natural shape. Lay the webbing with the loop tape in a straight line across the top of the back of the textile. Do not try to follow the line of the upper edge if the textile is uneven. So as not to be visible from the front, the webbing should be placed at least 3'8" below the upper edge of the textile.

3. Mark the straight line of the upper edge of the webbing with a few pins, but do not pin the webbing to the textile. The line of pins will allow you to ease the webbing as you sew and still maintain a straight line.

4. When sewing, you will work from the center to one edge of the textile, and then from the center to the other edge. This technique is used to prevent the textile from stretching in one direction along the top edge. Thread a sharp needle with cotton thread that matches the background color of the textile. (Try to work the needle between the threads of the textile rather than piercing textile warps and wefts.) Working from the back, stitch through the webbing and textile above the loop tape. Make a zigzag stitch over two or three warp threads and bring the needle back through the textile and webbing as shown in the diagram below. The zigzag stitches illustrated in the third drawing are a modification, recommended by the museum's curator, of the original drawing, which still appears on its website. Continue stitching to the edge. Returning to the center, complete the row of stitching. Place another row of stitching through the webbing below the tape, as shown on the diagram.

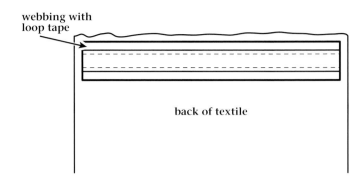

webbing with
loop tape

back of textile

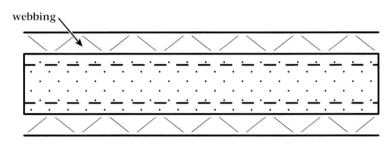

webbing

zig-zag stitching

5. The wooden slat, coated with varnish and thoroughly dried, is now ready to prepare with the hook tape. Using staples or tacks, attach the hook tape in a straight line along the slat the same distance from the top of the slat as the loop tape is from the top of the textile. The staples should be placed about 1" apart and staggered for greater strength.

There are a variety of hangers available to attach the slat to the wall. Mirror plates, "D" rings, and eye screws are all possibilities. Install the hardware.

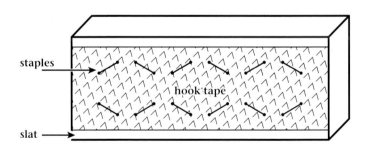

staples

hook tape

slat

6. Match the two halves of the loop and hook tape together, working from one side of the textile to the other. Be careful not to stretch the upper edge of the textile as you work across the slat. If it is necessary to make adjustments, slide your hand in between the two tapes to release. Do not pull the tapes apart, as this can place strain on the textile.

7. Install slat on the wall.

(*Reprinted with permission from the Textile Museum, Washington, D.C.*)

Sleeve Casing Method

A second method for displaying a studio quilt involves a sleeve casing. A sleeve is a tube of fabric that is sewn to the backside of a quilt that allows the quilt to be hung with wood or metal hangers, either flat or round. No part of the hanger touches the body of the quilt. Owners should still take the precaution of sealing wood slats or rods with a polyurethane sealant and allowing it to cure before using it to hang the quilt. Over a period of years, the sleeve absorbs acid from unprotected wood.

The method described here will make a casing that is 4" wide—a standard size. Individual artists, however, determine which width works best for their art.

Steps

1. To make the sleeve, prepare an 8"-wide strip of fabric in a length that is 1" less than the width of the top of the quilt. Hem the ends.

2. Fold the strip in half lengthwise, right sides together, and sew the entire length.

3. Turn right side out. Press.

4. Hand-stitch the top and bottom edges of the sleeve to the top of the quilt. The finished sleeve should be 1–2" shorter than the quilt width so that hanging hardware (nails or screws) is hidden behind the quilt.

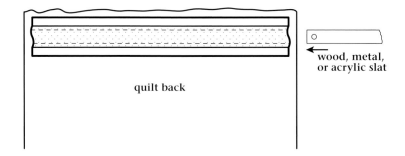

quilt back

wood, metal, or acrylic slat

5. For small or lightweight quilts, have wood lattice strips cut to size slightly less than the quilt width. Heavier quilts will need more substantial wood or metal rods. The wood should have two coats of cured polyurethane sealant on it to prevent acid in the wood from damaging the fabric.

6. Drill holes in the ends of the lattice strips or attach screw eyes. Quilts may also be hung with decorative drapery hardware if appropriate.[6]

7. Sometimes a second sleeve is added to the bottom of a quilt and another rod or slat inserted. This rod is not attached to the wall, however. It helps to keep the quilt from rippling.

There are several commercial display systems that the studio quilt owner, especially a collector, might employ with components designed for free-hanging textiles. Walker Display Inc. of Duluth, Minnesota, offers users a choice between a metal rod which slides through a sleeve or a bar with Velcro attachments.

Framing   Framing a studio quilt not only protects it from most dust and dirt. It provides very large quilts with the support they need for extended hanging. By using UF-3 and UF-4 Plexiglas or glass with a UV filter, the danger of fading is greatly reduced. However, a quilt should be framed only by someone who has experience with textiles.

There are several requirements. It should never be wrapped directly around a wood frame, not only because its acidic content will damage the fabric, but also because wrapping causes stress on the fibers and may weaken them. If the art is to be wrapped, the corners and edges of the frame must be padded. The quilt could also be stitched to a background fabric which can be wrapped around a stretcher or acid free board. Spacers should be used to ensure that the quilt does not come in contact with the glass or Plexiglas. The frame should be backed with archival material. Framing must allow for air circulation.

Care Instructions

- Studio art quilts should be treated as paintings. They should not be washed or dry-cleaned unless the artist suggests otherwise. The same is true for spot cleaning. Dyes can run or be rubbed out, even when the artist has used the best quality available. Water leaves marks on some fabrics that are difficult if not impossible to remove. Rubbing may stretch the fabric out of shape. Steam cleaning sometimes changes its drape.
- If the piece is seriously dirty, the owner should first seek help from the artist. If the artist is unable to help, or if the owner has reason to think there is insect damage, it is advisable to find a textile conservator who will know how to clean the quilt, assess the damage, and take appropriate measures to stop it. Conservators Harold F. Mailand and Dorothy Stites Alig advise that a written report be requested before work begins. It should include an assessment of the problem, a proposal for treatment, and a cost estimate. The purpose of this documentation is to provide a baseline record of the textile's condition and to provide documentation for insurance purposes.[7]
- Vacuum unframed textile art twice a year to remove dust and dirt, which can damage the fiber and attract insects. The procedure involves laying the artwork flat on top of a clean cloth and covering it, or a section of it, with a piece of fiberglass screening. Reduce the suction on your vacuum cleaner; using a non-rotating brush duster, go over the surface of the quilt until it is completely cleaned on one side. Shake the underlying cloth thoroughly and lay the quilt down with the reverse side on top. Repeat the procedure.
- If the quilt has embroidery stitches, beads, or other embellishments, instead of using a fiberglass screen, cover the nozzle of the vacuum cleaner with a piece of nylon and vacuum through the nylon. Use a

lift-and-press method rather than dragging the nozzle over the quilt. The finer nylon mesh should prevent the yarn and beads from being sucked up.

- Do not use pins or staples to attach labels to textile art.

- If you find creases in your studio quilt after storage or exhibition, do not use a commercial steamer or a steam iron to remove them. Application of steam stretches some polyester and other synthetic fabrics, changing its drape and causing permanent damage. Steam irons can cause water damage on silk and rayon which cannot be removed. Contact the artist for instructions or ask a conservator for advice. It is advisable to get a list of the fiber contents from the artist when you buy your art. A conservator could perform tests and tell you. Never spray starch on a quilt, as starch attracts insects.

- Good housekeeping and climate control are the best means of preventing insect damage to studio quilts. Examine them every six months when they are vacuumed for any sign of insect activity. Insects can find their way even into framed art. The website of the Textile Museum in Washington, D.C., has information that will help you identify the problem. Consult a textile conservator for advice.

- If your art becomes damaged or stained, specialized care should be sought. There are two professionals who work with textiles—restorers and conservators. "The primary objective of a restorer is to return a work of art to its assumed original appearance, sometimes at the expense of original material, sometimes by adding new material," according to Mailand and Stites. "A conservator endeavors to stabilize a work of art and minimize further damage so that it can be fully enjoyed and interpreted. . . . One of the guiding principles of conservation is reversibility: The material or treatment method used should be fully reversible, allowing the work of art to be treated again at a later date, should better materials or methods become available."[8] This principle should guide the owner who contemplates self-help remedies.

Storage

- When storing textile art, avoid locations where the humidity is high or the temperature fluctuates markedly. The area should be regularly cleaned.

- If possible, textile art should lie flat when stored. An unused bed in a spare room is perfect. Cover the quilt lightly with a sheet. If you layer several quilts on top of one another, separate them with a sheet to protect embellishments from getting tangled in threads from another quilt.

- Stored textile art should not come in contact with any wood, cardboard, or paper unless they are acid-free. Shelves and drawers should be lined with several layers of acid free tissue paper or with washed unbleached muslin. The muslin should be washed yearly and the tissue replaced every five years. Wood can be coated with polyurethane for additional protection.

- Avoid plastic sheeting or bags. They hold moisture.
- If it is not possible to store your studio quilts in a flat position, they can be wrapped around a large (minimum diameter 3 to 4") cardboard tube that has been covered with several layers of washed, unbleached muslin. Roll the quilt around the covered tube loosely, avoiding creases and making sure the quilt top faces outward. If the quilt is embellished with plastic or metal objects, these should be wrapped in acid-free tissue paper before rolling. Wrap the entire role with more muslin and loosely wrap a tie around both ends. If possible, the roll should be suspended so that no part of it rests on a flat surface. The simplest way to do this is to rest the ends on blocks that are elevated above floor level. Various suspension systems can also be devised.
- Most studio art quilts should not be folded. Ask the artist or a conservator before folding.

28

What You Should Know about Appraisals

An appraisal is a written document that states the value of an object in the marketplace. Valuation depends partially on the reason for the appraisal; thus an appraisal of an art object for insurance purposes is likely to differ from an appraisal of the same object if the owner wishes to donate it or a fractional interest in it to a museum. Other reasons for obtaining an appraisal include the assessment of estate or gift taxes, equitable distribution (e.g., divorce), bankruptcy, and damage/loss. There is also an appraisal value for art that earns an income for its owner.

Appraised value is arrived at after an analysis of numerous factors. These include identification of the object, evaluation of its quality and its condition, and a thorough analysis of the market in which it was bought and the market in which the owner may want to sell it. Studio art quilts are bought and sold in markets for fine art, textile and fiber art, and fine craft or decorative art. There is also a craft and boutique market and an aspiring art quilt market.[1] The marketplace in which the valuation is made, however, depends on the purpose of the appraisal. Insurance appraisals, for example, reflect replacement costs, not what the owner might get if the quilt is sold.

All tax-related appraisals are based on what the Internal Revenue Service calls fair market value, defined as "the price at which property would change hands between a willing buyer and a willing seller, neither being under any compulsion to buy or sell and both having reasonable knowledge of relevant facts." Tax-related appraisals include, among others, donations for which the donor intends to claim a charitable deduction and those used for the determination of gift and estate taxes. Appraisals are required if the deduction exceeds a certain amount.[2] The Internal Revenue Service requires that marketplace analysis occur within a limited period of time prior to the date of the donation.

With the recent passage of the Pension Protection Act of 2006 (Public Law 109-280), Congress made major changes in the law affecting all tax-related appraisals. At present, there is uncertainty about how these changes will affect the appraisal profession. Until now the profession has been self-regulated and without licensing requirements. One concern in the profession is the possible increase in educational requirements for appraisers, many of whom have not completed college or professional-level coursework relevant to the property they value. However, they may already be certified, have many years of experience, and carry out their work in accordance with the Uniform Standards of Professional Appraisal Practice (USPAP).

The USPAP were developed by the Appraisal Foundation, an organization funded and empowered by Congress for that purpose. Appraisal associations such as the American Society of Appraisers (ASA) and the Appraisers Association of America (AAA) have required members to apply these standards to their work. The Professional Association of Appraisers—Quilted Textiles (PAAQT) does not, although members are advised to do so.[3]

Now that Public Law 109-280 has introduced governmental regulation for some appraisals, it is likely that the same rules will eventually affect the entire profession. "Provisions of this act," writes Leatrice S. Eagle, a senior appraiser in the ASA, "make changes in a number of the qualifications related to the preparation of tax-related appraisals including the valuation standards that are used to determine the fair market value of tangible and intangible property. The act redefines both the term Qualified Appraiser and Qualified Appraisal. Both definitions raise requirements for the appraiser and specify the valuation approach that determines the value of the property. The third area of change requires stricter accuracy of valuation and increased accountability for both the donor and the appraiser. In addition the new law specifies the terms governing fractional gifts of tangible personal property when being valued for estate, gift, and income purposes." Eagle continues: "The implementation of this act will be done through the issuance of proposed regulations. These regulations will specify how the new valuation requirements will be enforced and used by appraisers in their work."[4] While insurance valuations are not affected by the new law, it is possible that insurance companies will choose to apply the same standards as the IRS for insurance appraisals.

Until the redefinitions of *qualified appraiser* and *qualified appraisal* are fully clarified and published, Shelly Zegart, a quilt appraiser and member of the Appraisers Association of America, offers this advice: "When you are choosing an appraiser, you should ask about the appraisal association of which they [are] a member and determine what skills are required for membership in that association. In addition, if you need the valuation for tax-related purposes, make sure the appraiser you choose can meet all of the legal requirements that went into effect in February, 2007, so that your appraisal is valid."[5]

If satisfied with the standards of the appraiser after a review of his or her professional credentials and association, there is still the question of how skilled he or she is at the job. "A good appraiser," says Eagle, "must understand the marketplace and understand the requirements of appraisal. . . . A fine arts background is important, but there is more. You need to be out in that marketplace seeing art, whether it is quilts, pots, glass, or painting. You have to be out there every day. You have to be really knowledgeable about the field. . . . You need to go to galleries, openings of museum shows and be familiar with art in many fields. You need to know about all types of things going on in the marketplace, because trends are the marketplace, and the marketplace won't just include a trend for quilts."[6]

Zegart agrees emphatically with this emphasis on the responsibilities of the appraiser. She states: "Appraising is not a question of personal preference for a particular kind of quilt. Regardless of the aesthetic, the history and the workmanship must be evaluated against the daily wisdom of the marketplace that sets new values daily on everything in the world, including art objects. After all the connoisseurship is considered, if an appraiser is not linked to the material personally or through contact in the field on a daily basis, he has no business appraising."[7] Julia Zgliniec, quilt appraiser and former president of PAAQT, adds: "There is student-level and master-level work. I have to know the difference. I must know what is derivative."[8]

The redefinition of both *qualified appraiser* and *qualified appraisal* that is called for in new law should assure more accurate valuation. At present, not all textile appraisers are knowledgeable about quilts, and not all quilt appraisers are knowledgeable about studio art quilts. Those who value donations of craft to museums are more likely to be familiar with the markets for both traditional and studio art quilts than appraisers who usually value donations of paintings. Many quilt appraisers are more knowledgeable about traditional quilts than about art. Since studio quilts are rooted in both fine art and quiltmaking, it is important that the appraiser have the necessary knowledge of fine art and contemporary quilts.

Unless owners have received references from professional or trustworthy sources, they should be cautious about using appraisers who are art dealers. There is a possibility that unscrupulous dealers would undervalue an art object in order to purchase the item and then sell it at a profit. On the other hand, art dealers are in the market buying and selling on a daily basis and might be more astute about value. Donors should not seek appraisals from people connected to the museum to which their donation will be given. It is unethical for such people to do an appraisal in this circumstance even if they meet the qualifications.

An appraisal is a legal document between the owner of the property and the appraiser and should be typewritten. The following list of the elements necessary for a correctly prepared appraisal has been adapted from the list prepared by the Appraisers Association of America in 2007.[9]

1. Name and address of client
2. Name, contact information, and qualifications of the appraiser:
    Statement of the appraiser's education and experience, both as
        defined by law, which qualify him or her to value the type of
        property being valued
    Statement of financial disinterest on the part of the appraiser
    Statement of the fee structure (the fee should not be contingent on
        the value of the object being appraised)
    Statement that the appraisal is prepared in accordance with USPAP
    Statement of personal physical inspection of the art object by the
        appraiser and the method by which it was carried out
3. The purpose of the appraisal
4. The valuation method used and defined (a description of the method
    of valuation used for tax-related appraisals is no longer sufficient)
5. The market place in which valuation is applied
6. Type of valuation:
    Replacement value
    Fair market value
    Market value
    Marketable cash value
7. Relevant dates (date of inspection, effective date of appraisal,
    date of report)
8. Description of the appraised object:
    Item
    Name of the artist/craftsperson
    Country of origin
    Title
    Date of creation
    Medium
    Detailed description (including style, dimensions, condition)
    Firm statement of value (no estimates)
9. Additional statements:
    Statement of belief in authenticity
    Statement of assumptions and limitations
10. IRS requirements for appraisals:
    Statement that the appraiser has not been disqualified by the IRS
    Appraiser's Tax ID number
    Statement of the appraiser's qualifications specific to the object
        appraised
    Statement of how the object was acquired
    Statement that the appraiser understands that a substantial or
        gross valuation misstatement may subject the appraiser to a
        civil penalty (a new requirement of Public Law 109-280)

11. Additional description:
  Provenance
  Frame information
  Exhibition history
  Publication history
  Photographs
12. Support for valuation conclusions

Even if the purpose of an appraisal is not related to taxes, says Eagle, who has appraised many fine art and craft objects and collections for donation to museums, "I feel it is very important to follow the guidelines given by the IRS. If you are looking to sell your art, the next buyer wants to know all this."

Most people seek quilt appraisals for insurance purposes. This is primarily because the overwhelming majority of quilts made today are traditional craft objects made by hobbyists for family and friends. Zgliniec says that it is not uncommon for their owners to think, incorrectly, that having a quilt appraised is having it judged. She emphasizes that valuation is based only on the object's worth in the current market and adds that condition of the object counts, but only the condition in which it is brought to the appraiser. The possibility of future fading or deterioration has no bearing, although the appraisal will note if fading or deterioration is already occurring.

Remaining objective about an appraisal may be difficult for both the owner and quiltmaker. The appraised value is neither more nor less than the quilt's value in a particular marketplace at a particular time. It is important to remember that it is not proof or disproof of artistic merit, and it has nothing to do with its importance to its owner.

29

Insuring Your Art

S tudio quilts have been known to disappear from exhibitions, workshops, and their owners' homes. They have been lost and damaged in transit to museums. Thoughtless viewers, people with mental disorders or deficiencies, and thieves, as well as fire, water, and smoke, have damaged quilts and caused their owners anguish. Although insurance coverage can never replace a loved or valued art object, in the event of loss or damage it can at least provide protection for the owner's monetary investment.

It is common practice for owners of small art collections, those valued at less than hundreds of thousands of dollars, to obtain coverage for them through home insurance policies. These policies, however, place limits on how much they will pay for expensive property in the event of loss or damage. These limits should be clear to owners before choosing this kind of coverage. Owners should also understand how the company will assess the value of the lost or damaged art. Under home insurance plans, owners usually have the option of listing each work in their collection as scheduled property. If they choose not to, artwork may be subject to depreciation, just as other household goods. There is an added premium, but in the event of loss or damage there would be no deductible and owners would receive the amount listed in the contract. Owners should be aware that if a loss of any kind occurs for items covered by a "package policy" such as homeowner insurance, it is likely to cause an increase in the premium, even if the loss has no impact on the owner's art collection.

Homeowner insurance policies are not adequate for owners who exhibit their art. Most policies cover goods only when they are in the owner's possession. In these instances, it may be necessary to obtain additional insurance. Mail carriers offer insurance, but there is often an upper limit to the coverage. The per-pound liability coverage of many moving companies is completely unsuitable as a basis for insuring value in art. Before relying on any transit company's insurance, owners should also find out how the company would determine the value of the lost or damaged art, be aware of all limitations and exclusions that apply, and ask how it would handle a loss or damage suit. Most insurance claims for fine art are for damage sustained in transit. When an art object that is irreplaceable is damaged, most owners want to have it restored if possible. That may require a very particular kind of specialist. Owners may wish to engage a moving company that specializes in fine art.

Museums and organizations which sponsor exhibits usually have insurance coverage for all art in the exhibit. There may, however, be a limit to the amount their policies will pay out for any single work that is stolen or damaged.[1] Owners must ask about this and also find out when that coverage begins and ends. When the exhibit is over, will the museum cover damage if the damage was caused by its own poor packing? Many moving companies will not cover damage that occurs during transit unless the goods have been packed by their own agents.

Insurance policies that are designed especially for fine art or quilts provide broader coverage than home insurance plans. They may have a threshold limit on the premium, but they are less likely to have a limit on what is paid for art that is lost or damaged. Their coverage may be worldwide and usually extends to art in transit, on exhibition, or in the possession of a gallery where it is for sale. It is damage rather than total loss that is the basis of most insurance claims by owners of fine art. Companies offering this insurance have expertise in finding good restorative services. Claims, however, must be filed by the insured if these restoration services are to be covered, and clients must work through the agency to obtain payment. These companies also keep abreast of changes in the art market and use this knowledge to advise their clients if new appraisals are warranted. Fine art policies have fewer exclusions than homeowner policies, but they do have the standard exclusions, such as wear and tear (fading and soil) and pest damage.[2]

One insurance policy currently available was developed especially for quilts. It provides broader coverage than homeowner insurance and will cover quilts which are in transit and on exhibit in museums or other locations in the United States and Canada. The policy recognizes that many collectors are also professional artists and quiltmakers. They travel often and teach in workshops where their own quilts are used as class samples. At home, their studios are equipped with valuable machinery, fabric, and thread. This policy's coverage extends to these quilt-related items in addition to quilts.[3]

No matter what kind of insurance policy is chosen, it is the owner's responsibility to keep on file as much documentation as possible about his or her art. Any certified appraisals, the bill of sale, two photos (a full image and a detail), a verbal description which includes color and size, and any other documents relating to its value should be kept stored in a safe location. If the studio quilt has been given to or inherited by the owner, and she does not have a bill of sale, a certified appraisal is necessary. Some companies advise owners to obtain an appraisal for works valued over a certain amount. These documents are essential in the event of loss or damage.

One final word of caution: never rely on verbal assurance from an insurance agent that a particular situation would be "covered." Owners should insist on a written and signed statement to that effect if it is not spelled out in their insurance policy.

30

Resources

The following lists are ordered alphabetically by state, or by name of event or publication.

Museums (Selected)

Oakland Museum
Oakland, California
Collection of Artwear; occasional exhibits of art quilts.

The Visions Art Quilt Gallery
San Diego, California
Exhibits the work of established and emerging artists in rotating exhibitions.

The Museum of Craft and Folk Art
San Francisco, California
No permanent collections; occasional exhibits of textile art.

The San Jose Museum of Quilts and Textiles
San Jose, California
Expects to increase its small collection of studio quilts; contemporary works
frequently exhibited.

Denver Art Museum
Denver, Colorado
Extensive textile art collection which includes contemporary works in fiber.

Rocky Mountain Quilt Museum
Golden, Colorado
Large collection of traditional and studio quilts.

The Renwick Gallery of the Smithsonian Museum of American Art
Washington, D.C.
Collection of studio quilts. Works in the collection rotate in the galleries.

The Textile Museum
Washington, D.C.
Does not collect contemporary textile art but does exhibit it. Excellent educational
   resource.

The Art Institute of Chicago
Chicago, Illinois
Collects "unusual contemporary interpretations of historic techniques."
Antique quilts and textiles.

Indianapolis Museum of Art
Indianapolis, Indiana
Extensive textile collection. Small but growing collection of studio quilts.

Kentucky Museum of Art and Craft
Louisville, Kentucky
Collection of contemporary quilts by regional and national artists.
Frequently has quilts on exhibition.

The Museum of the American Quilter's Society
Paducah, Kentucky
Large collection of contemporary quilts; most are award-winning quilts from
   AQS's annual competitions. Focus is traditional quiltmaking, although there
   are "boundary breakers" in the collection.

The Museum of Fine Arts, Boston
Boston, Massachusetts
Collection of fiber art from collector Daphne Farago includes several studio quilts.

Fuller Craft Museum
Brockton, Massachusetts
Small collection of studio quilts; craft exhibitions include these works; has had
   solo exhibitions by artists in this genre.

The New England Quilt Museum
Lowell, Massachusetts
Growing collection of quilts made by New England pioneers of the studio quilt
   movement.

Cranbrook Art Museum
Bloomfield, Michigan
Fiber art collection highlights the contributions that Cranbrook artists have
   made to the field. Includes historic textiles. Graduate degree exhibition held
   each spring.

Michigan State University Museum
East Lansing, Michigan
Collection of contemporary ethnic quilts including African American and
   Native American quilts. Small number of studio art quilts.

The Mississippi Museum of Art
Jackson, Mississippi
Collections include narrative quilts by contemporary southern quiltmakers.

International Quilt Study Center
University of Nebraska–Lincoln
Lincoln, Nebraska
Comprehensive collection of antique and contemporary quilts. Frequent exhibitions
    of antique and studio quilts.

The Newark Museum
Newark, New Jersey
Collection contains antique and contemporary studio quilts, including works
    commissioned from contemporary artists.

The Museum of Arts and Design
New York, New York
(Formerly known as the Contemporary Craft Museum and the
    American Craft Museum)
Large collection documents the beginning of the studio art quilt movement
    to the present.

Mint Museum of Craft + Design
Charlotte, North Carolina
Small but significant collection of contemporary quilts; expected to grow.

Ohio Craft Museum
Columbus, Ohio
Small number of studio quilts in its collection. Contemporary craft exhibitions
    include studio quilts; biennial exhibition of contemporary quilts.

Coos Art Museum
Coos Bay, Oregon
No studio quilts in the permanent collection; however, the museum has textile
    and contemporary quilt exhibitions.

The Museum of Contemporary Craft
Portland, Oregon
Collection represents the development of West Coast craft; traveling exhibitions.

Museum of Fine Arts, Houston
Houston, Texas
Collection includes Gee's Bend quilts but does not focus on contemporary fiber art.

The Virginia Quilt Museum
Harrisonburg, Virginia
Exhibits include both historic and contemporary studio quilts.

La Conner Quilt Museum
La Conner, Washington
Small collection of donated studio quilts. Ambitious exhibition schedule includes
    contemporary quilts.

The Milwaukee Museum of Art
Milwaukee, Wisconsin
Collections include twelve contemporary quilts, four of which are by artists
    from Gee's Bend.

Racine Art Museum
Racine, Wisconsin
Small current collection, but long-term plans call for building a collection that will
  document the history of contemporary fiber art. Museum regards studio quilts
  as an important part of this history.

Art Centers, Textile and Textile Art Centers (A Sampling)
Several additional art centers are listed under "Juried Art Quilt Exhibitions."

Atlantic Center for the Arts
New Smyrna Beach, Florida
Artist in residency program; schedule of exhibits includes national and internation-
  al contemporary studio quilts, artist lectures open to the public.

Indianapolis Art Center
Indianapolis, Indiana
Classes, periodic fiber and quilt art exhibitions.

The Textile Center of Minnesota
Minneapolis, Minnesota
Exhibitions of traditional and innovative textile art, large library, workshops, sales.

Houston Center for Contemporary Craft
Houston, Texas
Exhibitions, gallery, classes, sales.

Artist Networks (A Sampling)
*Below is a sampling of artist groups and their websites. Some, such as Fiberscene, are
online galleries. Links to individual artists' websites and scheduled exhibitions are posted
at these groups' websites.*

African American Art Quilt Network
http://www.AfricanAmericanArtQuilt.com

Art Quilt Network New York (includes artists from outside the N.Y. region)
http://www.artquilt.net/network.html

Art Quilt Network Ohio
http://www.artquiltnetwork.com

California Fiber Artists
http://www.cafiberartists.com

Contemporary Quilt Art Association (Northwest)
http://www.contemporaryquiltart.com

Fiber Revolution
http://www.fiberrevolution.com

FiberScene (California, includes all fiber media)
http://www.fiberscene.com

Kansas Art Quilters
http://www.kansasartquilters.org

Professional Art Quilt Alliance (Chicago area)
http://www.artquilters.com

Studio Art Quilt Associates
http://www.saqa.com

Textile Study Group of New York (includes all fiber media)
http://www.tsgny.org

Galleries (A Sampling)

Below is a sampling of commercial and non-commercial galleries which sometimes exhibit fiber art; studio quilts may or may not be on exhibit at any particular time.

La Jolla Fiber Arts Gallery
La Jolla, California

The Visions Art Quilt Gallery
San Diego, California

Mobilia Gallery
Cambridge, Massachusetts

Detroit Gallery of Contemporary Crafts
Detroit, Michigan

Robert Hillestad Textiles Gallery
University of Nebraska–Lincoln
Lincoln, Nebraska

Jane Sauer Gallery
Santa Fe, New Mexico

Noho Gallery
New York, New York

Ariel Gallery
Asheville, North Carolina

Tyndall Galleries
Chapel Hill, North Carolina

Gross McCleaf Gallery
Philadelphia, Pennsylvania

Snyderman-Works Gallery
Philadelphia, Pennsylvania

James Gallery
Pittsburgh, Pennsylvania

The American Art Company Gallery
Tacoma, Washington

Juried Art Quilt Exhibitions

Quilt Visions/Quilts San Diego
Oceanside Museum of Art
Oceanside, California
(biennial, winter)

Quilt National
Dairy Barn Cultural Center
Athens, Ohio
(biennial, late spring and summer; travels after closing in Athens)

ArtQuilt Elements
(formerly *Art Quilts at the Sedgwick*)
Wayne, Pennsylvania
(biennial, spring)

Juried Mixed Traditional and Studio Art Quilt Exhibitions/Competitions (A Sampling)

American Quilter's Society Show and Competition
Paducah, Kentucky (annual, mostly traditional, spring)
Nashville, Tennessee (annual, late summer)

Quilters' Heritage Celebration
Lancaster, Pennsylvania
(annual, March; two-thirds of each *Quilt National* exhibition is shown during this event)

International Quilt Festival
Houston, Texas (annual, fall)
Chicago, Illinois (annual, spring)

Juried Fiber Art Exhibitions

Fiberart International
Pittsburgh, Pennsylvania
(triennial, spring and summer; last exhibit 2007; travels after closing in Pittsburgh)

Juried Craft and Studio Quilt Exhibits (A Sampling)

Form, Not Function
Carnegie Center for Art and History
New Albany, Indiana
(annual, winter)

Quilts=Art=Quilts
Schweinfurth Memorial Art Center
Auburn, New York
(annual)

Artist as Quiltmaker
Firelands Association for the Visual Arts (FAVA)
Oberlin, Ohio
(biennial, late spring and summer)

Materials: Hard and Soft
The Center for the Visual Arts
Denton, Texas
(annual, winter)

Studio Art Quilt Associates
Regional and national juried exhibits for professional members
(annual; venues change; check website for listings: http://www.saqa.com)

Fine Craft Shows and Fairs

American Craft Council Fairs
San Francisco, California; Sarasota, Florida; Atlanta, Georgia; Baltimore,
    Maryland; St. Paul, Minnesota; Charlotte, North Carolina
(check website for dates: http://www.craftcouncil.org)

Bellevue Art Museum Craft Fair
Bellevue, Washington
(annual, summer)

Craft Fair of the Southern Highlands
Asheville, North Carolina
(semi-annual, summer and fall; contemporary and traditional)

Philadelphia Museum of Art Craft Show
Philadelphia, Pennsylvania
(annual, late fall)

Smithsonian Craft Show
Washington, D.C.
(annual, spring)

SOFA—Sculptural Objects Functional Art
Chicago, Illinois (fall)
Palm Beach, Florida (winter)
New York, New York (spring)

Overseas Exhibits

European Art Quilts
Traveling biennial exhibit sponsored by the European Art Quilt Foundation
http://www.europeanartquilt.com

Festival of Quilts
Birmingham, England
(annual, August; very large; approximately 15% of the quilts are contemporary)

Quilt Japan
Tokyo, Japan
(biennial, February; contemporary quilts are one of three categories)

Publications of Interest

Most quilt magazines are written for non-professional quiltmakers. They provide patterns, instructions, and reviews of new tools. For this reason, they are not cited here. Publications such as Art News, Art and Antiques, *and* Art in America *occasionally cover textile and fiber art.*

American Craft
Published by the American Craft Council and sold in many bookstores. Stated purpose is to provide "intellectual and visual interest for the reader on today's craft." Covers craft in all media. The American Craft Council's website, under the category "Events," has a state-by-state monthly listing of exhibits of fine craft. The listing includes museum, gallery, and university exhibitions.
www.craftcouncil.org

AmericanStyle
Sold in bookstores and at newsstands. An arts lifestyle publication which seeks to "nurture" collectors. Features crafts in all mediums; includes collector profiles and regional arts tours. Provides state listings of museum and gallery craft exhibitions, retail craft fairs, and annual craft events.

Fiberarts
Sold in bookstores and at newsstands. Includes news about people and events in all fields of fiber art; features stories about artists; reviews new books and exhibits; occasionally spotlights collectors. State-by-state listing of fiber exhibitions and events held in museums, galleries, textile centers, and universities. Updates to this listing are provided on its website.
http://www.fiberarts.com

Portfolio
Published annually by Studio Art Quilt Associates; contains illustrations of members' work.
http://www.saqa.com

Quilters Newsletter
Has occasional articles on the history of the art quilt movement.

The Sourcebook of Architectural and Interior Design and *The Artful Home: The Guild Sourcebook of Residential Art*
Published by The Guild, Madison, Wisconsin, each year; useful for both professional designers and homeowners; illustrates the work of textile artists who use the publications as a means of gaining exposure for their work and obtaining commissions.
http://www.guild.com

Surface Design Journal
Quarterly journal published by the Surface Design Association. Features innovative artists and emerging issues in surface design and includes interviews and reviews of exhibitions and books. "Every issue covers a theme, e.g., stitching, creative process, pushing the edge, that allows for in-depth coverage of different aspects of surface design." It does not provide an instruction guide. SDA provides an on-line, state-by-state calendar of events which includes a link to the sponsors, so additional information can be obtained. Listings include museum, university, gallery, and artist group shows and cover all areas of surface design and fiber arts.
http://www.surfacedesign.org

Additional Educational Resources

The Alliance for American Quilts
Online access to interviews with traditional and studio art quiltmakers.
http://www.quiltalliance.org

The Archives of American Art
Oral interviews and online transcripts of interviews with a small group of studio quilt artists.
http://www.aaa.si.edu

Friends of Fiber Art International
P.O. Box 468
Western Springs, IL 60558
708-246-9466
An association of collectors and fiber artists. Organizes programs for members in conjunction with important contemporary fiber art events. These include symposia; expositions that serve collectors, such as SOFA Chicago; important serial exhibitions, such as *Quilt National* and the International Triennial of Tapestry in Poland; and artist conferences. Most Friends programs are designed to attract and educate potential collectors by including visits to fiber art collectors' homes.

The International Quilt Study Center
Online collection of antique and contemporary quilts.
http://www.quiltstudy.org

The Quilt Index
Access to images of thousands of quilts in private and public collections (mostly traditional, will eventually include studio art quilts).
http://www.quiltindex.org/

The Textile Museum
Washington, D.C.
Private museum with an extensive, non-circulating library; e-mail requests for bibliography on specific topics are answered by staff. Extensive international directory of textile collections can be accessed online. Books covering a variety of textile art forms are sold in the museum shop and over the internet.
http://www.textilemuseum.org

The Textile Society of America
Provides an international forum for the exchange and dissemination of information about textiles worldwide from a variety of perspectives including artistic, cultural, and technical. Member benefits include a CD-ROM of biennial symposia pro ceedings, newsletters with information about upcoming events, and opportunity to participate in textile study tours.
http://www.textilesociety.org

Event Calendars

See publications listed above including *American Craft, AmericanStyle, Fiberarts, Quilter's Newsletter,* and *Surface Design Journal.*

Studio Art Quilt Associates, Inc.
Another event calendar can be accessed on the website of the SAQA. (The home page features a rotating slide show of more than 400 pieces of artwork with links to the artists' galleries.) The calendar includes gallery exhibits as well as major

festivals. The collector's corner contains information on history, artwork care, insurance, appraisals, and collection donation.
http://www.saqa.com

Care Resources

Textile conservators might be found by contacting a museum with a textile collection in your area. Museum conservators should be able to recommend a restoration specialist if your textile art has sustained damage. Additional resources that you may wish to consult first are listed below.

The American Institute for Conservation of Historic and Artistic Works (AIC)
Washington, D.C.
Professional association of conservators; website provides information about conservation professionals and lists members by specialty and region. Studio quilts might be included in "Objects" or "Quilts and Blankets."
http://aic.stanford.edu/

Preserving Textiles: A Guide for the Non-Specialist by Harold F. Mailand and Dorothy Stites Alig (Indianapolis: Indianapolis Museum of Art, 1999).

The Textile Museum
Washington, D.C.
Website provides full information about care, display, and storage of textile art.
http://www.textilemuseum.org

Display Systems

Suppliers of archival materials, UV Plexiglas for framing and storage purposes, and display hardware can be found on the internet. One such supplier is listed below.

Walker Display Incorporated
P.O. Box 16955
Duluth, MN 55816
800-234-7614
218-624-8990
http://www.walkerdisplay.com

Insurance

AXA Art Insurance
http://www.axa-art.com

Chubb Masterpiece Personal Insurance
http://www.chubb.com

Christine Johnston
1750 E. Glendale Ave.
Phoenix, AZ 85020
602-749-4282

Art Consultants

Judy Lepow and Elaine Galman
Galman Lepow Associates
Cherry Hill, New Jersey
http://www.glappr.com
(corporations, professional)

Penny McMorris: an independent curator who served as a corporate art curator at Owens Corning Corporation for twenty years. She co-authored *The Art Quilt*, the first book focusing on twentieth-century quilt design development. She was the American consultant for the British Craft Council's *Contemporary American Quilts* exhibition (1993) and has curated two exhibitions at the Museum of Arts and Design in New York City. Currently vice president of the Electric Quilt Company, makers of software for quilters.
Bowling Green, Ohio
Penny@electricquilt.com
(museum consulting only)

Maxine Menges
MkM Fine Art, Inc.
Glen Mills, Pennsylvania
http://www.mkmfineart.com
(corporations, healthcare, hospitality, professional)

Jane Sauer: a fiber artist and owner and director of Jane Sauer Gallery, Santa Fe. She has a BFA from Washington University and has her art in the collections of more than twenty museums, including the Museum of Art and Design in New York, the Mint Museum of Craft + Design in Charlotte, North Carolina, and the Cleveland Institute of Art. As a gallerist, she has placed artwork in many residences, corporations, and museums. She is a former chairperson of the American Craft Council and an independent curator.
Santa Fe, New Mexico
jsauer@sauergallery.com

Robert Shaw: an independent curator and art historian who has written extensively on American folk arts and contemporary studio crafts (*Quilts: A Living Tradition*, 1995; *The Art Quilt*, 1997). He is former curator of the Shelbourne Museum and consulting curator to the *International Quilt Festival*. He has curated exhibitions at the National Gallery of Art and the Renwick Gallery of the Smithsonian Museum of American Art, as well as international expositions.
Shelburne, Vermont
http://www.roberteshaw.com
(business, museum, and private collectors)

Alice Zrebiec: an independent curator; consulting curator of textile art for the Denver Art Museum. She has a Ph.D. in art history from the Institute of Fine Arts–New York University. For sixteen years she worked as a curator of textiles in the Department of European Sculpture and Decorative Arts at the Metropolitan Museum of Art. Her interests include contemporary works of art in fiber and ethnographic textiles. She has lectured and published widely on diverse aspects of textiles and tapestry.
Santa Fe, New Mexico
Alice_Zrebiec@compuserve.com

GLOSSARY

Abstract Expressionism: An art movement which encompassed several kinds of non-objective painting including Gestural or Action Painting. The imagery of art and the gestures of the painter as he or she painted were believed to emanate from the unconscious mind. Jackson Pollock was the most widely known painter who worked in this style. His paintings had no central focus, had no figure-ground relationship, and were characterized by an "edge-to-edge format." Late 1940s and 1950s.

airbrush: An atomizer used to spray paint and other liquids.

all-over pieces: Art which lacks a focal point and extends from edge to edge.

appliqué: A needlework technique which involves cutting pieces of fabric and stitching them onto a background cloth. Reverse appliqué involves the layering of cloths of different colors. Sections are cut from the upper layer or layers, revealing shapes or designs in the colors of the lower layers.

arashi ("storm") shibori: A **resist** technique in which cloth is wrapped around a pole, wound with thread, and then compressed to one end before dyeing. The distinctive design it produces looks like wind-driven rain.

backing: Cloth which forms the underside of a quilt.

batik: Indonesian term for a dyeing process using a wax resist. *See* **resist**.

batting: The middle layer of a quilt of three layers (top-batting-backing). Usually cotton, wool, or polyester.

block: A basic unit of quilt construction. Blocks are joined to form the top.

clamp resist: A **resist** process in which cloth is folded and clamped or bound tightly between a pair of wooden boards before dyeing.

collage: An art form which involves the layering of elements to make a composition. It tends to imply a "fragmented cluster of diverse images and materials" producing a synergy, or an effect that none of the individual elements could produce on its own.

Color Field painting: Color Field painters were associated with **Abstract Expressionism**. They used color to express an emotional state and tried to draw the viewer into this state. Mark Rothko's large abstract washes of color typified this approach. 1950s through 1970s.

Conceptual Art: An art movement whose proponents have sought to redefine art. They challenge the "preciousness" of the art object and believe that the essence of art is the idea or concept. In its extreme version, the words, propositions, actions, ideas, and gestures recorded by the artist *are* the art.[1] This movement embodies a variety of art forms including installation, performance, video, and environmental art. Mid 1960s to present.

crazy quilt: A quilt made from a **patchwork** technique in which irregularly shaped pieces of fabric are joined to a cloth foundation to form the quilt top. It is frequently embellished with embroidery.

digital printing: A process involving the printing of computer-scanned or -generated imagery or patterns onto fabric or paper. Computer design software makes possible the manipulation of color and scale, the layering of design elements, and other alterations in the images before printing. Some small ink-jet printers use a pigment-type coloring agent in their ink which has been found to be colorfast if heat is applied. Some large-scale digital printers can be altered to print with fabric dyes on properly pre-treated fabrics.

direct dyeing: A process in which dye in either a liquid or paste form is applied directly to the fabric without a **resist**.

discharge dyeing: A process in which a chemical agent is used to remove or diminish color from a previously dyed fabric.

dyebath: A solution of water, dye, and a chemical agent into which fabric is immersed for dyeing. The chemical agent sets the color in the fabric.

dyeing: Process through which molecules imparting color are chemically bonded to fiber, which produces deeply saturated color.

embellish: A process of adding elements such as embroidery, beads, buttons, or other objects to the quilt top.

embroidery: A needle art in which an extensive variety of stitches and materials are used to **embellish** fabric.

fabric paint: Pigment paste formulated to a thin consistency which can be brushed onto fabric. It is made colorfast by applying heat, which activates the adhesive in the formula; it does not bind with the molecules of the fiber like dye.

felting: A process for making felt by subjecting wool fibers to agitation or compression and to shrinkage, which causes them to interlock and mat together. For a similar process using woolen textiles, see **fulling**.

Feminist Art Theory: A perspective that encourages artists to look at experience from the perspective of gender and gender power. Its analysis of art is often concerned with how women are stereotyped.[2] Late 1960s to present.

fiber: A hair-like component of plant or animal tissue used to make yarn or textiles.

fiber-reactive dye: Dye which bonds chemically with fiber molecules, creating a permanent bond.

fragmentation: An art strategy for "capturing a transitory moment." Planes and images are split and disjointed.

French knot: An **embroidery** stitch formed when yarn is wrapped around a needle before the needle is re-inserted into the fabric.

frottage: A process for making an image by pressing cloth or paper against a three-dimensional surface and rubbing or brushing a coloring agent against it.

fuse: *See* **lamination**.

fulling: A process in which loosely woven or knitted woolen textiles are subjected to agitation and shrinkage, causing the fibers to interlock and mat. It results in dense, heavy cloth. For a similar process using wool fibers, see **felting**.

hand: Characteristics of cloth that can be perceived by touch such as softness, drape, and resilience.

ikat: A **resist** technique in which the yarn or thread is wrapped before it is dyed and woven.

improvisational quiltmaking: Originally an African American process in which the design and color combinations are not pre-determined but take shape as the quiltmaker assembles pieces and units of fabric to make the quilt top. The resulting combinations typically have a spontaneity and liveliness to them resulting from the quiltmaker's skill, experience, and intuition.

installation art: Art that is arranged in a place or site. The installation may be permanent or not and specific to the site or not.

kantha: Indian and Bangladesh quilts made with layered, worn silk saris and held together by straight stitch **embroidery**. The stitching became a way for women to express their lives through narrative imagery.

lamination: A process by which two or more materials are united; it usually involves the application of heat.

Minimalism: An art movement which rejected the inward focus of **Abstract Expressionism** and excluded human content, emotion, and sensuality in art. Minimalist painters reduced works to the barest essentials of line, shape, and even color. Their art is defined by rigid, geometric forms and flat planes of color executed with mathematical precision. The movement's founder, Frank Stella, believed that art should be taken in at a glance, removing the possibility of confusion about its meaning. Late 1950s through 1960s.

mola: A textile art form of the Kuna people of Panama and Colombia. It consists of multiple layers of variously colored cloth in a reverse appliqué technique. The design is formed by cutting away parts of each layer.

Mylar: A strong polyester film made by the Dupont Company in the 1950s.

narrative quilt: A quilt, usually with an appliquéd or painted top, whose elements tell a story.

Optical Art: Art that evokes a perception of movement by using color (or black and white), line, and shape with extreme precision. 1940s onward.

optical quilt: A quilt in which the colors and shapes of the top give the illusion of movement and/or dimension.

organdy: A sheer, lightweight woven cotton fabric.

organza: A crisp sheer, lightweight woven fabric that is made from silk, rayon, nylon, and polyester.

patchwork: A process of combining fabrics to make a quilt top.

pattern: Generally refers to repeated elements in the design of a quilt. The same pattern may have several names.

piecing: A needlework technique carried out by hand or machine for joining two pieces of cloth.

plaiting: A fabric technique in which several elements are interlaced diagonally.

plangi: A Malay term for silk **shibori** textiles which have been bound, stitched, and dyed in several colors.

Pop Art: An art movement that explored the image of popular culture. Artists based "their techniques, style, and imagery on certain aspects of mass production, the media, and consumer society." 1950s.[3]

Post-Minimalism: An art movement that involved artists who worked in a minimalist style but who eventually reacted against the movement's "purity" and impersonality. Introduced unconventional media, and personal and social concerns into art. Late 1960s.

Postmodernist Art Theory: Proponents "believe we are all prisoners, to some degree, of identities constructed for us by artistic and popular media. . . . There is no visual style associated with postmodernism; instead, any and all styles and visual vocabularies are valid, and pluralism rules." Appropriation of subjects, compositions, and details of art and design from art history and popular culture are combined into an "eclectic visual pastiche." Challenges as elite the idea that originality and innovation should be celebrated.[4] Late 1970s onward.

printing: A process of applying dye, ink, or colored pigment to the surface of paper or fabric. The color particles are suspended in a thickening agent to ease application. Printing on fabric can be accomplished using sophisticated equipment or simpler means such as block printing, stamping, and **screen printing**. The particular coloring agent used will determine the type of chemistry or post-printing processing required to make the print permanent on fabric.

quilt: Traditional quilts are textile bedcovers which typically have a top, **backing**, and a filling (**batting**) between them. The layers are held together by stitches or knots. *See* **studio art quilts**.

quilt top: The uppermost layer of a quilt.

quilting: The process of sewing layers of fabric together. A running stitch is commonly used. Quilting may be decorative or plain.

ready-mades: Term given to unaltered objects used in the making of art. May be assembled or used alone.

resist: A technique or material which creates designs on cloth by preventing or impeding dye or paint from penetrating it. The covered area remains undyed. *See* **arashi shibori, batik, clamp resist, ikat, shibori, stitch resist, wax resist.**

rotary cutter: A tool for cutting fabric consisting of a rotating circular blade which is attached to a handle and pushed by hand across the surface of the fabric, cutting through one or more layers.

rubbings: *See* **frottage**.

running stitch: A hand needlework technique in which a threaded needle is taken in and out of the fabric several times before it is pulled through. It is used for **piecing** and **quilting**.

satin stitching: A technique of hand or machine **embroidery** in which individual stitches are laid down exactly parallel to each other, creating a sharply defined shape and edge. It is used for making monograms and may be used for attaching shaped fabric to a background.

screen printing: A process of forcing **fabric paint** through a mesh screen attached to a screen by using a squeegee. Stencils allow the paint through certain areas to create a design.

Seminole patchwork: A term applied to a **patchwork** pattern used by the Seminole Indians to decorate clothing. Strips of fabric of varying widths are sewn together to form a panel. The panel is then cut either vertically or diagonally. The resulting segments are re-arranged and stitched into patterned bands.

shibori: A Japanese term which encompasses a variety of techniques for manipulating and securing fabric before dyeing. The process creates resistance to dye penetration and results in a variety of unique patterns.

stamping: Technique for applying ink, a **dye discharge** agent, paint, or **resist** to fabric using a carved, cut, or incised wood block or rubber material which is compressed firmly onto the fabric.

stenciling: Technique for reproducing a design by passing paint over a thin firm material in which a design has been cut.

stitch resist: A resist process encompassing a variety of stitches to gather the fabric tightly before dyeing.

studio art quilt (or studio quilt): An art form which retains a link through its material elements and/or structure to the traditional **quilt**.

Surrealism: An art movement which stressed the importance of the unconscious mind, free association, and dreams as the source of imagery. 1920s through 1950s.

template: A precisely measured, re-usable shape made from paper, cardboard, or plastic. It is used to size and trace individual pieces of fabric when they are cut for patchwork and to mark designs for quilting the top.

textile: Anything made from fibrous materials, including felt, woven material, baskets, knitted fabrics. It may include objects made from "synthetic linear elements" like nylon window screens.

tjanting: A fountain pen–like tool used to apply a **wax resist** to fabric before dyeing.

Vandyck brown print: A printing process utilizing the action of light on ferric salts. The name derives from its similarity in color to the brown pigment used by the Flemish painter Van Dyck.[5]

warp: The vertical thread in woven cloth.

wax resist: A process in which hot wax is applied as a **resist** before dyeing. Also known as **batik**.

weft: The horizontal thread or yarn that interlaces with the **warp** threads.

NOTES

Preface

1. Robert Pfannebecker, interview by Helen Drutt English, 21 May 1991, Smithsonian Institution Research Information System (SIRIS): Archival, Manuscript, and Photographic Collections, transcript, 221.

1. Introduction

1. In warmer regions of the country, or for summer use, quilts were sometimes made without a middle layer.

2. Janet Catherine Berol and Patricia Cox Crews, *Wild by Design: Two Hundred Years of Innovation and Artistry in American Quilts* (Lincoln: International Quilt Study Center, University of Nebraska–Lincoln, in association with the University of Washington Press, 2003).

3. Robert Shaw, *Quilts: A Living Tradition* (Westport, Conn.: Hugh Lauter Levin Associates, 1995).

4. Harriet Powers's quilts are in the collection of the National Museum of American History and the Museum of Fine Arts, Boston. African American quilts include the traditional pieced-block design, appliqué, folk art, improvisational, contemporary narrative or storytelling, the unique pieced quilts made by quiltmakers in Gee's Bend, Alabama, and studio art quilts.

5. Bernard L. Herman, telephone interview by the author, 14 July 2005.

6. Margolit Fox, "Ruth C. Bond Dies at 101; Her Quilts Had a Message," *New York Times,* 13 November 2005.

7. This observation was made by artist Dorothy Caldwell while she was studying mending, patching, and utilitarian samplers at the Textile Museum of Canada. Dorothy Caldwell, e-mail correspondence with the author, 6 August 2006.

8. Penny McMorris and Michael Kile, *The Art Quilt* (Chicago: Quilt Digest Press, rev. ed., 1996).

9. In the late 1920s, when the Arts and Crafts movement was waning, several cottage industries were organized in the southeast United States which produced and sold handmade quilts. During the Depression, some of these groups received support from the Southern Highland Craft Guild.

10. The Bauhaus School, founded by the architect Walter Gropius in Weimar, Germany, in 1919, was an effort to unite all forms of visual art, including craft, into architecture. It was forced to disband in 1933 by the Nazis.

11. Bets Ramsey, "Art and Quilts: 1950–1970," *Uncoverings* 14 (1993): 16.

12. Edward Lucie-Smith, "Craft Today: Historical Roots and Contemporary Perspectives," in *Craft Today: Poetry of the Physical*, ed. Paul J. Smith and Edward Luc-

ie-Smith (New York: American Craft Museum and Weidenfeld & Nicolson, 1986), 31–32.

13. "American Craft Council, 1943–1993: A Chronology," *American Craft*, August/September 1993, 137–138. In 1979 the Museum of Contemporary Crafts was renamed the American Craft Museum. In 2002 the name was changed again to the Museum of Arts & Design.

14. "American Craft Gold Medalists," *American Craft*, August/September 1993, 109.

15. Ramsey, "Art and Quilts," 4.

16. Jean Littlejohn and Jan Beaney, *Conversations with Constance: A Celebration of the Life of Constance Howard, MBE* (Maidenhead, Berkshire, UK: Double Trouble Enterprises, 2000), 10.

17. Sandra Sider, "My Mother Was Not a Quilter," *Jean Ray Laury: A Life by Design*, catalog essay (San Jose, Calif.: San Jose Museum of Quilts and Textiles, 2006), 4.

18. Ibid. One of Laury's most popular books is *The Creative Woman's Getting-It-All-Together at Home Handbook* (New York: Van Nostrand Reinhold, 1977; reprint, Fresno, Calif.: Hot Fudge Press, 1985).

19. Katherine Westphal, telephone interview by the author, February 2006.

20. Katherine Westphal, "A Contemporary History: Surface Design Today," *Surface Designer's Art: Contemporary Fabric Printers, Painters, and Dyers* (Asheville, N.C.: Lark Books, 1993), 14.

21. This movement was "rooted both in art and studio fiber art and sought to define itself as separate from fashion. . . . Most of it is intended for formal or everyday wear, but it also had links to performance and conceptual art, and in these cases may or may not be wearable." Melissa Leventon, *Artwear: Fashion and Anti-fashion* (New York: Thames and Hudson, with the Fine Arts Museum of San Francisco, 2005), 8.

22. While the interest of the public in handcraft was helpful economically to craft makers without teaching positions, there was concern among some academics that the value of their own work was being undermined by the flood of macramé and other easy-to-make craft objects.

23. Eleanor Levie, *American Quiltmaking: 1970–2000* (Paducah, Ky.: American Quiltmaker's Society, 2004), 20.

24. *The National Survey of Quilting in America Survey 2006* (Golden, Colo.: CK Media), 3.

25. Radka Donnell, personal correspondence with the author, 31 March 2007.

26. Robert Shaw, *The Art Quilt* (Westport, Conn.: Hugh Lauter Levin Associates, 1997), 48.

27. Jean Ray Laury, "My Journey through Quilting," *Quilter's Newsletter Magazine*, March 2003, 31.

28. Shaw, *The Art Quilt*, 51.

29. Jonathan Holstein, *Abstract Design in American Quilts: A Biography of an Exhibition* (Louisville, Ky.: Kentucky Quilt Project, 1991), 58.

30. Robert Shaw, "Five Decades of Unconventional Quilting," *Quilter's Newsletter Magazine*, April 2004, 59.

31. "Art: Quilts Find a Place at the Whitney," review by Hilton Kramer, *New York Times*, 3 July 1971, 22.

32. Gayle A. Pritchard, *Uncommon Threads: Ohio's Art Quilt Revolution* (Athens: Ohio University Press, 2006), 5.

33. Shaw, *The Art Quilt*, 48.

34. Nancy Halpern, telephone conversation with the author, 8 February 2007.

35. Michael James, *The Second Quiltmaker's Handbook* (New York: Prentice-Hall, 1981; Los Altos, Calif.: Leone, 1993), 47.

36. Patricia Malarcher, telephone interview by the author, 13 January 2007. Malarcher has been editor of *Surface Design Journal* since 1993.

37. The definition and description of processes of surface design appear on the title page of each edition of *Surface Design: The Journal of the Surface Design Association*.

38. A definition of these terms is provided in the glossary.

39. Gayle Fraas and Duncan Slade, e-mail correspondence with the author, 5 December 2006.

40. Linda Fowler, interview by the author, 28 November 2005.

41. See "Resources" for a list of some of these networks. Requirements for membership vary. In some instances applicants go through a screening or jurying process and are required to submit a portfolio for review. Other networks are loosely organized and allow anyone who wishes to join to become a member.

42. McMorris and Kile, *Art Quilt*, 60. Michael Kile was a well-known quilt dealer in 1986 and co-editor of a new journal called *Quilt Digest*. Penny McMorris, now a quilt historian, art consultant, and vice-president of the Electric Quilt Company, was a corporate art curator and the creator and producer of several public television series about quilts.

43. Janet Koplos, "When Is Fiber Art 'Art'?" *Fiberarts*, March/April 1986, 34–35.

44. Ibid.

45. Kim LaPolla, "The Birth of a Vision," Studio Art Quilt Associates website (accessed 12 January 2007), http://saqa.com/aboutus//history.aspx.

46. Nancy Crow, interview by the author, 27 November 2005.

47. Sol LeWitt, "Paragraphs on Conceptual Art," *Artforum*, Summer 1967, 80.

48. David J. Hornung, telephone interview by the author, 24 July 2006.

49. Lois Martin, "The Making of Quilts; The Maker of Quilts," *American Craft*, June/July 1995, 35.

50. Patricia Malarcher, "In Search of Quiltness," *Surface Design Journal* 16:3 (Spring 1992): 8.

51. Ted Gooden, "Thunder and Lightning," *Ontario Craft*, Winter 1988, 17.

52. Paul J. Smith, telephone interview by the author, 17 May 2005 and 18 January 2007.

2. Liz Axford

1. Bernard L. Herman, "Architectural Definitions," *Gee's Bend: The Architecture of the Quilt* (Atlanta: Tinwood Books, 2006), 207–214.

2. Liz Axford, interview by the author, 26 October 2005.

3. Liz Axford, e-mail correspondence with the author, 25 July 2006. These remarks and subsequent quotations are derived from correspondence on this date.

3. Susan Brandeis

1. Susan Brandeis, e-mail correspondence with the author, 17 August 2006.

2. Susan Brandeis, "Post-Digital Textiles: Rediscovering the Hand," *Surface Design Journal* 28:4 (Summer 2004): 44–51.

3. Bhakti Ziek, "Digital Technology for Textiles," *Technology as Catalyst*, ed. Rebecca A. T. Stevens (Washington, D.C.: Textile Museum), 2002.

4. Rachel Brumer

1. Sandra Kroupa, "Ordinary to Extraordinary: Books of Rachel Brumer," *Fiberarts*, November/December 2000, 8.

2. Rachel Brumer, telephone interview by the author, October 2006.

3. The opera was performed at the Brooklyn Academy of Music.

4. Brumer, interview, October 2006.

5. "Portfolio: Rachel Brumer," *American Craft*, December 1997/January 1998, 57.

6. Elizabeth Hendricks, "Cover Them—A Quilt Installation: The Work of Rachel Brumer," *Art/Quilt Magazine*, no. 11 (2000): 35.

7. Matthew Kangas "Rachel Brumer and Isabel Kahn: Patterning the Past," *Surface Design Journal* 28:2 (Winter 2003): 40.

8. Hendricks, "Cover Them," 35.

5. Pauline Burbidge

1. Pauline Burbidge, *Quilt Studio* (Chicago: Quilt Digest Press, 2000), 128.
2. Ibid., ix.
3. Ibid., 128.
4. Judith Duffey Harding, "Quiltmaking in an Age of Mechanical Inspiration: Pauline Burbidge," in *Portfolio Collection: Pauline Burbidge* (Bristol, England: Telos Art, 2004), 16.
5. Pauline Burbidge, e-mail correspondence with the author, August 2006.

6. Elizabeth Busch

1. Patricia Malarcher, "In Search of Quiltness," *Surface Design Journal* 16:3 (Spring 1992): 8.
2. Elizabeth Busch, e-mail correspondence with the author, 17 July 2006. All quotations of the artist in this essay are derived from this correspondence.
3. Malarcher, "In Search of Quiltness," 10.

7. Jean Williams Cacicedo

1. Jean Williams Cacicedo, e-mail correspondence with the author, 13 August 2006. Additional quotations from the artist, unless otherwise attributed, come from this e-mail correspondence.
2. Matthew Kangas, *Jean Williams Cacicedo: Explorations in Cloth* (San Francisco: Museum of Craft and Folk Art), 7.
3. Melissa Leventon, *Artwear: Fashion and Anti-fashion* (New York: Thames and Hudson and Fine Arts Museums of San Francisco, 2005), 93.
4. Because of the vulnerability of wool to the common clothes moth, Cacicedo lines her quilts in linen and soaks the wool cloth in a solution to make it moth proof.

8. Dorothy Caldwell

1. Sarah Quinton, *Dorothy Caldwell: In Good Repair* (Toronto, Ontario, Canada: Textile Museum of Canada, 2003); catalog essay.
2. *The Surface Designer's Art: Contemporary Fabric Printers, Painters, and Dyers* (Asheville, N.C.: Lark Books, 1993), 112.
3. Kantha quilts are made from worn saris. See the glossary.
4. Quinton, *Dorothy Caldwell.*
5. John E. Vollmer, "Field Notes: An Exhibition of Quilts by Dorothy Caldwell," in *Dorothy Caldwell: Field Notes* (Peterborough, Ontario, Canada: Art Gallery of Peterborough, 1996), 8.

9. Kyoung Ae Cho

1. Kyoung Ae Cho, "Reminiscences," in *Portfolio Collection: Kyoung Ae Cho,* (Winchester, England: Telos Art, 2003), 24.
2. Ibid., 22.
3. Ibid., 25.
4. Catherine S. Amidon, "Reordering Nature: The Work of Kyoung Ae Cho," *Surface Design Journal* 21:4 (Summer 1997): 18–20.
5. Gerhardt Knodel, foreword to Kyoung Ae Cho, *Portfolio Collection,* 6.

10. Nancy Crow

1. Nancy Crow, interview by the author, 27 November 2005.
2. Nancy Crow, Oral History Interview by Jean Robertson for the *Smithsonian American Archives of American Art: Nanette L. Laitman Documentation Project for Craft and Decorative Arts in America,* 18 December 2002; transcript obtained through the

website of the Smithsonian Archives of American Art (accessed 19 May 2005), http://artarchives.si.edu/oralhist/crow02.htm, 6.

3. Nancy Crow, e-mail correspondence with the author, 23 February 2007.

4. Nancy Crow, unpublished interview by Jean Robertson, 17 August 1988. This interview was donated by Jean Robertson to the Smithsonian Archives of American Art.

5. Nancy Crow, *Quilts and Influences* (Paducah, Ky.: American Quilter's Society, 1990), 158.

6. Nancy Crow, *Nancy Crow* (Elmhurst, Ill.: Breckling Press, 2006), 69.

7. Ibid., 89.

8. Crow, interview, 17 August 1988.

11. Nancy Erickson

1. "Textured Narratives: Nancy Erickson and Dana Boussard," *Art/Quilt Magazine,* no. 7 (1996/97): 41.

2. Barbara Lee Smith, *Celebrating the Stitch: Contemporary Embroidery of North America* (Newtown, Conn.: Taunton Press, 1991), 91.

3. Margaret Kingsland, "Bearing Witness: Nancy Erickson's Fiber Art, Drawings, and Paintings," *Nancy Erickson: Recent Work,* catalog essay (Missoula, Mont.: Art Museum of Missoula, 2003), 4.

4. Ibid., 5, 6.

5. Bonnie Lee Holland, "Nancy Erickson: Linked to the Narrative Tradition," *American Craft,* June/July 2002, 43.

12. Carole Harris

1. Carole Harris, e-mail correspondence with the author, 22 September 2006. Unless otherwise identified, quotations from the artist come from this correspondence.

2. The name of the American Craft Museum has been changed to the Museum of Arts and Design.

3. Bill Harris, "Eye Music," in *African American Quiltmaking in Michigan,* ed. Marsha L. MacDowell (East Lansing: Michigan State University Press, 1998), 93.

13. Ana Lisa Hedstrom

1. Ana Lisa Hedstrom, e-mail correspondence with the author, 20 January 2007. All quotations from the artist come from this correspondence.

2. Michael James, catalog essay, *Process = Pattern* (Lincoln: University of Nebraska, Robert Hillestad Textiles Gallery, 2004), 11.

3. These artist-quiltmakers are African American residents of the small, isolated town of Gee's Bend, Alabama. Their quilts are a distinctive, graphic, and improvisational art form.

4. James, *Process = Pattern,* 12.

14. Marilyn Henrion

1. According to the art historian Robert Hughes, Ellsworth Kelly made this remark when he returned to the United States from a trip to Paris in 1948. Robert Hughes, *American Visions: The Epic History of Art in America* (New York: Alfred A. Knopf, 1999), 567.

2. Marilyn Henrion, telephone interview by the author, 16 December 2004.

3. Marilyn Henrion, e-mail correspondence with the author, 11 August 2006.

4. Lois Martin, "Timeless Moments: Marilyn Henrion," *Surface Design Journal* 26:2 (Winter 2001): 48.

5. ArtLinks Partnership is devoted to fostering excellence in the arts between the United States and the countries of the former Soviet Union.

6. Ed McCormack, "Geometry Unmoored," in *Marilyn Henrion: Disturbances,* catalog for solo exhibition, Noho Gallery, New York, September 2006.

15. Michael James

1. Michael James, Oral History Interview by David Lyon for the *Smithsonian Archives of American Art: Nanette L. Laitman Documentation Project for Craft and Decorative Arts in America,* 4–5 January 2003; transcript obtained through Smithsonian Archives of American Art (accessed 19 May 2005), http://artarchives.si.edu/oralhist/james03.htm, 28.

2. Michael James, *Michael James: Art and Inspirations* (Lafayette, Calif.: C&T, 1998), 16.

3. James, Oral History Interview, 28.

4. Glen Brown, "Michael James: Interference and Innovation," *Surface Design Journal* 31:1 (Fall 2006): 21.

5. Patricia Harris and David Lyon, "Ideas of Order: The Art of Michael James," in James, *Michael James,* 16.

6. Ibid., 57.

7. Ibid., 104.

8. Michael James, "The Digital Quilt," *Fiberarts* 30:3 (November/December 2003): 29.

9. Ibid.

10. Michael James, interview by the author, 23 February 2005.

11. Brown, "Michael James," 21.

16. Jan Myers-Newbury

1. Jan Myers-Newbury, e-mail correspondence with the author, 12 August 2006. All quotations attributed to the artist come from this correspondence.

2. Yoshiko Iwamota Wada, *Memory on Cloth: Shibori Now* (Tokyo: Kodansha America, 2002), 133.

3. *MAQS Quilts: The Founders Collection* (Paducah, Ky.: Museum of the American Quilter's Society, 2001), 85.

4. Yoshiko Iwamoto Wada, Mary Kellogg Rice, and Jane Barton, *Shibori: The Inventive Art of Japanese Shaped Resist Dyeing* (Tokyo: Kodansha International, 1983, 1999), 7.

5. Vicky A. Clark, "A Search for Light: Jan Myers-Newbury's Adaptation of Shibori," *Surface Design Journal* 22:1 (Fall 1997): 21.

17. Risë Nagin

1. Risë Nagin, "Artist's Statement and Additional Remarks," 2006. Correspondence with author (in 2006).

2. Patricia Malarcher, "The Imagined Image: Looking with the Inner Eye," *Surface Design Journal* 21:3 (Spring 1997): 22.

3. Risë Nagin, telephone interview by the author, 21 September 2006.

4. Patricia Malarcher, "Risë Nagin," catalog essay (Pittsburgh: New Image Press and the Pittsburgh Center for the Arts, 2000).

5. Nagin, interview.

6. "Risë Nagin: Biography," Smithsonian American Art Museum (accessed September 2006), http://www.americanart.si.edu/index3.cfm.

7. Malarcher, "Imagined Image," 22.

18. Joy Saville

1. Joy Saville, "Artist's Statement" (2005). Correspondence with author (in 2006).

2. Ed McCormack, "Exposing the Significance of Contemporary Art Quilts in Noho Gallery Exhibition," *Gallery & Studio,* February/March 2006, 9.

3. Patricia Malarcher, "Review: Joy Saville at the Newark Museum," *Surface Design Journal* 17:3 (Spring 1993): 28.

4. Patricia Malarcher, "Indian Patchwork on View in Newark," *New York Times* (New Jersey supplement), 10 July 1983.

5. Joy Saville, e-mail correspondence with the author, 10 October 2006.

6. Betty Freudenheim, "5000 Tiny Bits of Fabric in Quilts That Scintillate," *New York Times* (New Jersey supplement), 20 September 1992.

19. Joan Schulze

1. Poem by Joan Schulze published in *Quilts: Joan Schulze,* catalog of an exhibit of the author's quilts at the *Festival of Quilts,* Birmingham, England, August 2005 (Sunnyvale, Calif.: Schulze Press), 8.

2. Joan Schulze, interview by Le Rowell, *Quilters' S.O.S.—Save Our Stories* (Asheville, N.C.: Alliance for American Quilts), 4 August 2003 (accessed 17 November 2005), http://www.centerforthequilt.com, 9; now available at http://www.quiltalliance.org/index/html (accessed 4 July 2007).

3. Judith Tomlinson Trager and Heidi Krakauer Row, eds., *Rooted in Tradition: Art Quilts from the Rocky Mountain Quilt Museum* (Virginia Beach, Va.: Donning, 2005), 45.

4. Joan Schulze, e-mail correspondence with the author, 14 August 2006.

5. Joan Schulze, interview by the author, 11 November 2005.

20. Julie John Upshaw

1. Julie John Upshaw, "Artist's Statement," 2006. Correspondence with author (in 2006).

2. Ibid.

3. Julie John Upshaw, e-mail correspondence with the author, 28 August 2005.

4. Robin Treen, *Art about Art: Weavings from Virginia Davis, Insecurity: An Installation by Julie John Upshaw* and *Katherine Westerbout: After/Image* (San Jose, Calif.: San Jose Museum of Quilts and Textiles, 2006), 5.

5. Ibid.

6. Julie John Upshaw, e-mail correspondence with the author, 12 March 2006.

21. Educational Resources and the Market

1. Susan Brandeis, interview by the author, 28 October 2004.

2. Robert Shaw, *The Art Quilt* (Westport, Conn.: Hugh Lauter Levin Associates, 1997), 12.

3. Kathleen McCann, "The Art of Collecting," *Fiberarts* 18 (January/February 1992): 36.

4. Michael Monroe, former curator-in-charge, Renwick Gallery of the Smithsonian Museum of American Art, and director, Bellevue Art Museum, Bellevue, Washington; telephone interview by the author, 8 October 2005.

5. Sharon Hoogendoorn, "Art Institute of Chicago Curator on Collecting Criteria," *Friends of Fiber Art International News,* no. 38 (January 2006): 4.

6. Judith Tomlinson Trager and Heidi Krakauer Row, eds., *Rooted in Tradition: Art Quilts from the Rocky Mountain Quilt Museum* (Virginia Beach, Va.: Donning, 2005), vii.

7. Judy Schwender, e-mail correspondence with the author, 22 November 2006. Schwender is the curator of the Museum of the American Quilter's Society.

8. This statement of the museum's mission appears on its website (accessed 24 November 2006), http://www.sjquiltmuseum.org/about_us.html.

9. Carolyn Ducey, e-mail correspondence with the author, 28 November 2006. The IQSC offers the only graduate degree in quilt history in the world as well as classes for individuals who want to learn more for their own sake, including a small selection of classes that are offered online to anyone.

10. Bruce Hoffman, interview by the author, 31 March 2005.

11. Sharon Ewing, interview by the author, 1 April 2005.

12. This statement of purpose was obtained from the *Quilt National* website (accessed 24 November 2006), http://www.quiltnational.com.

13. Hilary Fletcher, interview by the author, 2 August 2004.

14. Karey Bresenhan, interview by the author, 28 October 2005.

15. Bonnie Browning, e-mail correspondence with the author, 14 November 2006.

23. Collecting

1. Polly Ullrich, unpublished panel presentation, Sculptural Objects Functional Art (SOFA), Chicago, 11 November 2006.

2. Jonathan Holstein, panel presentation, "Collectors, Collecting, and Collections," a symposium sponsored by the International Quilt Study Center, University of Nebraska–Lincoln (24, 25, 26 February 2005).

3. Kathleen McCann, "The Art of Collecting." *Fiberarts* 18 (January/February 1992): 36.

4. Camille J. Cooke, *AmericanStyle* 5 (Summer 1996).

5. Cathleen McCarthy, "Anatomy of an Art Purchase," *Wall Street Journal,* special advertising section (2–3 December 2006), s4.

6. John M. Walsh III, telephone interview by the author, 16 February 2005.

7. Del Thomas, interview by the author, 9 January 2005.

8. Nancy and Warren Brakensiek, telephone interview by the author, 14 January 2005.

9. Penny McMorris, interview by the author, 7 December 2004.

10. Walsh, interview.

11. Bruce Hoffman, interview by the author, 31 March 2005.

25. Working with an Art Consultant

1. Robert Shaw, "Consulting Services for Artists, Collectors & Organizations," website of Robert Shaw (accessed 2 December 2006), http://www.roberteshaw.com /Quilts.html.

2. Penny McMorris, telephone interview by the author, 7 December 2004. Subsequent quotations in this section which are attributed to McMorris come from this interview.

3. Judy Lepow, telephone interview by the author, 11 May 2005. Lepow's firm provided art advising services for Fortune 500 companies in the 1980s and early 1990s.

4. Maxine Manges, telephone interview by the author, 14 May 2005.

26. Commissioning a Quilt

1. John M. Walsh III, telephone interview by the author, 16 February 2005.

2. Jean Williams Cacicedo, e-mail communication with the author, December 2006.

3. Joan Schulze, e-mail communication with the author, December 2006.

4. Elizabeth Bush, e-mail correspondence with the author, 6 December 2006.

5. Under the 1976 Copyright Act and the 1998 Copyright Term Extension Act, copyright protection for visual art created after 1 January 1978 begins at the moment of a work's creation and extends through the artist's lifetime plus seventy years. See the U.S. Copyright Office website (accessed 11 December 2006), http://www.copyright .gov/.

27. Displaying, Caring for, and Storing Studio Quilts

1. Jan Myers-Newbury, e-mail correspondence with the author, 26 October 2006.

2. "Caring for Your Acrylic Paintings," *Smithsonian Museum Conservation Institute* website (accessed 18 February 2007), http://www.si.edu/MCI/english/learn_more /taking_care/acrylic_paintings.html.

3. Randy Kennedy, "Paints Mysteries Challenge Protectors of Modern Art," *New York Times,* 14 February 2007.

4. Gayle Fraas and Duncan Slade, "A Question of Intent: Quilts and Durability," *Surface Design Journal* 23:4 (Summer 1999): 36.

28. What You Should Know about Appraisals

1. Julia Zgliniec, interview by author, 11 January 2005. Zgliniec is a quilt appraiser and member of the Professional Association of Appraisers—Quilted Textiles.

2. In 2006, deductions of more than $5,000 required a written appraisal. This figure is subject to change. Information (accessed 17 February 2007) from publication 561 on the Internal Revenue Service website: http://www.irs.gov/publications/p561/ar02 .html#d0e589.

3. PAAQT was formed by appraisers certified by the American Quilter's Society as "qualified to give fair market and insurance values to quilts and quilted textiles." The association holds classes to keep members current and yearly conferences to address issues of common concern.

4. Leatrice Eagle, JD, ASA, AAA, e-mail correspondence with the author, 13 February 2007.

5. Shelly Zegart, telephone interview by the author, 21 February 2007.

6. Leatrice S. Eagle, interview by the author, 24 August 2005. Unless otherwise noted, quotations attributed to Leatrice S. Eagle come from this interview.

7. Shelly Zegart, interview by the author, March 2005.

8. Zgliniec, interview.

9. "Elements of a Correctly Prepared Proposal," Appraisers Association of America website (accessed 17 February 2007), http://www.appraisersassoc.org.

29. Insuring Your Art

1. Bill Lyle, telephone interview by the author, December 2006. Mr. Lyle is a retired insurance agent and author of "Insuring Quilts," *Professional Quilter,* Summer 2005, 1–3.

2. Ida Ziewacz, telephone interview by the author, December 2006. Ms. Ziewacz is a senior underwriter for AXA Art Insurance Corp. in Chicago.

3. The company offering this policy, Milne & BNC, was sold in July 2007. The policy is still available through Christine Johnston at 1750 E. Glendale Ave., Phoenix, AZ 85020. Phone: (602) 749-4282.

Glossary

1. Robert Hughes, *American Visions: The Epic History of Art in America* (New York: Alfred A. Knopf, 1999), 574.

2. Jean Robertson and Craig McDaniel, *Themes of Contemporary Art: Visual Art after 1980* (New York: Oxford University Press, 2005), 26.

3. Guggenheim Museum (N.Y.) website, "Pop Art" (accessed 20 August 2007), http://www.guggenheimcollection.org.

4. Robertson and McDaniel, *Themes of Contemporary Art.* See pp. 22–27 for an expanded account of Postmodernism and Postmodernist Art Theory.

5. Wynn White, "Vandyck Notes" (accessed 18 July 2007), http://www .wynnwhitephoto.com/altphoto.html.

SUGGESTED READINGS

Art Quilts: A Celebration. New York: Lark Books, 2005. (A compilation of quilts exhibited at *Quilt National* between 1995 and 2003)

Benberry, Cuesta. *Always There: The African American Presence in American Quilts.* Louisville: Kentucky Quilt Project, 1997.

Berlo, Janet Catherine, and Patricia Cox Crews. *Wild by Design: Two Hundred Years of Innovation and Artistry in American Quilts.* Lincoln: International Quilt Study Center, University of Nebraska–Lincoln, with the University of Washington Press, 2003.

Brandeis, Susan. "Post-Digital Textiles: Rediscovering the Hand." *Surface Design Journal* 28:4 (Summer 2004): 44–51.

Constantine, Mildred, and Laurel Reuter. *Whole Cloth.* New York: Monacelli Press, 1997. (Contemporary artists working in cloth; conceptual, installation, performance, and environmental art; includes wearable art and the work of several quiltmakers)

Contemporary Art Quilts: The John M. Walsh III Collection. Lexington: University of Kentucky Art Museum, 2001.

Dormer, Peter, ed. *The Culture of Craft.* Manchester, England: Manchester University Press, 1997. (Essays cover topics as diverse as the history of craft, writing about craft, craft and a consuming society, and textiles and society. Dormer wrote an earlier book, *The Art of the Maker* [London: Thames and Hudson, 1994], but this book is hard to find, even through online used book sites.)

Holstein, Jonathan. *Abstract Design in American Quilts: A Biography of an Exhibition.* Louisville: Kentucky Quilt Project, 1991. (An account of the 1971 Whitney Museum exhibit and tour of antique quilts)

Hughes, Robert. *American Visions: The Epic History of Art in America.* New York: Alfred A. Knopf, 1999. (Only Amish quilts are included in this very readable text; nonetheless, it is good background for understanding the fine art context in which studio quilts developed.)

James, Michael. "The Digital Quilt." *Fiberarts* 30:3 (November/December 2003): 26–31.

Koplos, Janet. "When Is Fiber Art 'Art'?" *Fiberarts,* March/April 1986.

Korwin, Laurence. *Textiles as Art: Selecting, Framing, Mounting, Lighting and Maintaining.* Chicago: by the author, 1990.

MAQS Quilts: The Founders Collection. Paducah, Ky.: Museum of the American Quilter's Society, 2001.

Mazloomi, Carolyn. *Spirits of the Cloth: Contemporary African American Quilts.* New York: Clarkson Potter, 1998.

McMorris, Penny, and Michael Kile. *The Art Quilt.* Rev. ed., Chicago: Quilt Digest Press, 1996.

Passantino, Erika D., ed. *The Eye of Duncan Phillips: A Collection in the Making.* Washington, D.C.: Phillips Collection and New Haven, Conn.: Yale University Press, 1999. (A large and sumptuous book which includes Phillips's own views about the art he collected)

Pritchard, Gayle A. *Uncommon Threads: Ohio's Art Quilt Revolution*. Athens: Ohio University Press, 2006.

Pulleyn, Rob. "It's How Much?!" *Fiberarts* 28:1 (Summer 2001): 40–45. (Published interview between the publisher of *Fiberarts* and Bruce Hoffman, director of Snyderman-Works Galleries, about prices and textile art)

Quilt National. New York: Lark Books and Dairy Barn Cultural Arts Center. (Published biennially in connection with the exhibit; includes all quilts shown in that year's exhibition)

Quilt Visions. San Diego, Calif.: Visions. (Published biennially in connection with the exhibit; includes all quilts shown in that year's exhibition)

Ramsey, Bets. "Art and Quilts: 1950–1970." *Uncoverings* 14 (1993): 9–39.

Saarinen, Aline B. *The Proud Possessors: The Lives, Times and Tastes of Some Adventurous American Art Collectors*. New York: Random House, 1958.

Shaw, Robert. *The Art Quilt*. Westport, Conn.: Hugh Lauter Levin Associates, 1997.

———. "The Art Quilt in 2003." *Fiberarts* 30:3 (November/December 2003): 37–43.

Smith, Barbara Lee. *Celebrating the Stitch: Contemporary Embroidery of North America*. Newtown, Conn.: Taunton Press, 1991.

The Surface Designer's Art: Contemporary Fabric Printers, Painters, and Dyers. Asheville, N.C.: Lark Books, 1993.

Trager, Judith Tomlinson, and Heidi Krakauer Row, eds. *Rooted in Tradition: Art Quilts from the Rocky Mountain Quilt Museum*. Virginia Beach, Va.: Donning, 2005.

Wada, Yoshiko Iwamoto. *Memory on Cloth: Shibori Now*. New York: Kodansha International, 2002.

ARTIST BIOGRAPHIES

Liz Axford
Houston, Texas

Education: B.A., Architecture and Fine Arts, Rice University, 1976; B. of Architecture, 1978

Awards/Honors: Quilt Japan Award, *Quilt Visions;* 1st Prize, *Artist as Quiltmaker;* Honorable Mention, *Materials Hard and Soft;* Cultural Art Council of Houston/Harris County, Individual Artist Grant

Exhibitions (selected): *Quilt National,* Athens, Ohio; *Quilt Visions,* San Diego; *Art Quilts at the Sedgwick,* Philadelphia; *Materials Hard and Soft,* Denton, Texas; *Tactile Architecture,* International Quilt Festival, Houston; *The Artist as Quiltmaker,* Oberlin, Ohio

Related Professional Experience: Instructor, Southwest School of Art and Craft, San Antonio, Texas; Arrowmont School of Arts and Crafts, Gatlinburg, Tennessee; Quilt Surface Design Symposium, Columbus, Ohio; Juror, *Quilt National;* Judge, International Quilt Festival; Lecturer; Curator

Susan Brandeis
Raleigh, North Carolina

Education: B.A., Indiana University, Bloomington, 1971; M.S., Art Education, Indiana University, 1979; M.F.A., Textile Design/Fiber Art, University of Kansas, 1982

Awards/ Honors: North Carolina Arts Council, Visual Artist Fellowships, 2002–2003, 1996–1997, and 1991–1992; North Carolina State University College of Design nominee for Alumni Distinguished Graduate Professor, 2006–2007

Exhibitions (selected): *Recursions: Material Expressions of Zeros and Ones,* Museum of Design, Atlanta, Georgia, 2005; *Technology as Catalyst: Textile Artists on the Cutting Edge,* the Textile Museum, Washington, D.C., 2002; *Cheongju International Craft Competition,* Cheongju Arts Center, Cheongju, Korea, honorable mention, 2001; *Contemporary American Quilts,* Crafts Council of Great Britain, touring, 1993–1994; *14th International Biennial of Tapestry,* Musée Cantonal des Beaux-Arts, Lausanne, Switzerland

Collections and Commissions (selected): Renwick Gallery of the Smithsonian American Art Museum, Washington, D.C.; Bank of America/Charlotte Gateway Village, Charlotte, N.C.; Duke University Medical Center, Durham, N.C.; Embassy Suites Hotel, City of Toyama, Japan

Related Professional Experience (selected): Professor, North Carolina State University, College of Design; Instructor at several schools of arts and crafts; Author: "A Creative Life," *Surface Design Journal* 31:2 (Winter 2007); "Post-Digital Textiles: Re-Discovering the Hand," *Surface Design Journal* 28:4 (Summer 2004); "Crossing Boundaries/ Maintaining Traditions," exhibition catalog essay, Center for Craft, Creativity and

Design, University of North Carolina–Hendersonville (August 2005); Juror: *Fine Contemporary Crafts,* Raleigh, N.C., 2006; *Conversations about Roots,* 24th annual Women's Artist Registry of Minnesota, Minneapolis, 2006; Lecturer

Rachel Brumer

Seattle, Washington

Education: B.F.A., Mills College, Oakland, Calif., 1978

Awards/Honors: *Quilt National* Juror's Award, 2003; *Fiberarts International* Best of Show, Narrative Category, 1999; Artist Trust Gap Grant, 1997, 2000

Exhibitions (selected): *Building Tradition: Gifts in Honor of the Northwest Collection,* Whatcom County Museum of History and Art, Bellingham, Wash., 2007; *Textile Works,* Carl Solway Gallery, Cincinnati, Ohio, 2005; *Slumber the Nights,* Cultural Development Authority, Seattle, Wash., 2004; *Sewn: Documents Northwest,* Seattle Art Museum, Washington, 2000; *Quilt National,* Athens, Ohio, 2003

Collections: Seattle Art Museum, Seattle, Wash.; Tacoma Art Museum, Tacoma, Wash.; Museum of Arts and Design, New York; Brakenseik Collection of Contemporary Quilts, Los Angeles; John M. Walsh III Collection, Martinsville, N.J.

Related Professional Experience: Professional modern dancer, 1978–1987; Interpreter, American Sign Language, 1988–1990

Pauline Burbidge

Berwickshire, Scotland

Education: Dip A.D., Fashion/Textiles, St. Martin's School of Art, London, 1973

Awards/Honors: Scottish Arts Council, 1996; East Midlands Art, 1981–1989; Award of Excellence, *Quilt National,* 1983; John Ruskin Craft Award, Crafts Council

Exhibitions (selected): Solo: *Quiltworks—Visions of the Natural World,* Shipley Art Gallery, Gateshead, England (and subsequent tour), 2004–2005; Works Gallery, Philadelphia, 1991; Ruskin Craft Gallery, Sheffield, England; Group: *Ground Cover: Contemporary Quilts,* Niceville, Fla., 2001; *New Perspectives on the British Art Quilt,* Manchester, England, 1998–1999; *Contemporary Quilts from the James Collection,* Purchase, N.Y.; *New Wave Quilt Collection II,* touring Japan, 1992

Collections: John M. Walsh III Collection, Martinsville, N.J.; International Quilt Study Center, Lincoln, Neb.; Victoria and Albert Museum, London; National Museums of Scotland, Edinburgh; Whitworth Art Gallery, Manchester, England; Aberdeen Art Gallery, Aberdeen, Scotland; Nottingham Castle Museum (Textiles Collection), Nottingham, England

Related Professional Experience: Taught workshops worldwide, 1981–2002, including Slide Lecture at the Victoria and Albert Museum; Quilt Surface Design Symposium, Columbus, Ohio; Split Rocks Arts Program, University of Minnesota; *Quilt National,* Athens, Ohio; Co-curator for *Contemporary American Quilts,* Crafts Council Exhibition, London, 1993

Elizabeth Busch

Glenburn, Maine

Education: B.F.A., Rhode Island School of Design

Awards/Honors: Presidents Award, *Quilt Visions,* 2006; Surface Design Award, *Quilts=Art=Quilts,* Schweinfurth Memorial Art Center, Auburn, N.Y., 2005; Quilts Japan Award, *Quilt National,* 2003; Best of Show, *Quilt National,* 1989, Athens, Ohio; Mentor of the Year, Women's Business Development Corporation, Maine, 1995

Exhibitions (selected): *Quilt Visions* (4 exhibitions); *Quilt National* (7 exhibitions); *Art Quilts: Playing with a Full Deck,* Smithsonian Museum of American Art, traveling exhibition, 1995; *Contemporary Quilts USA,* Boston, 1990; *The Contemporary Quilt,* Japan, 1984

Collections (selected): Museum of Art and Design, New York; Nortel Corporation, Calgary, Alberta, Canada; Ropes and Grey, Boston; First USA Bank, Orlando, Fla.; Airport Hotel, Haneda, Japan

Jean Williams Cacicedo
Berkeley, California
Education: B.F.A., Sculpture, Pratt Institute, New York, 1970
Awards/Honors: *Quilt National,* Cathy Ramussen Emerging Artist Memorial Award, 2005; Artist of the Year, Contemporary Crafts Committee of the Art Guild of the Oakland Museum, 1985; National Endowment for the Arts, Craftsman Fellowship Grant, 1976
Exhibitions (selected): Solo Retrospective, *Explorations in Cloth,* San Francisco Museum of Craft and Folk Art, San Francisco, 2000; Group, *Slash, Burn and Cut,* University of California Design Museum at Davis, 2005; *Fashion and Anti-Fashion,* Fine Arts Museum of San Francisco Legion of Honor, 2005; *Celebrating California Art of the 20th Century,* Los Angeles County Museum, Los Angeles, 2000; *Breaking Barriers,* National Touring Exhibition, American Craft Museum, New York, 1995

Dorothy Caldwell
Hastings, Ontario, Canada
Education: Tyler School of Fine Arts, Rome, Italy, 1969; Temple University, Tyler School of Art, Philadelphia, B.F.A., 1970; Banff Centre for Fine Arts, Banff, Alberta, Canada
Awards/Honors (selected): Saidye Bronfman Award for Excellence in the Crafts, 1990; nominee, Governor General's Award; recipient, Canada Council for the Arts Grants; elected member, Royal Canadian Academy of Arts
Exhibitions (selected): Solo: Belger Arts Center, Kansas City, Mo., 2007; Mobilia Gallery, Cambridge, Mass., 2005; *In Good Repair,* Textile Museum of Canada, Toronto, 2003; Group: *Of Time and Place,* Houston Center for Contemporary Craft, 2005; *Ragged Beauty,* Museum of Craft and Folk Art, San Francisco, 2005
Collections (selected): Museum of Art and Design, New York; Canadian Museum of Civilization, Quebec; Daphne Farago Collection of Contemporary Textiles, Rhode Island; Canadian Department of External Affairs; Ottawa International Museum; International Quilt Study Center, University of Nebraska, Lincoln
Related Professional Experience (selected): Juror, *Fiberart International,* 2007; Co-curator, *Stitching Women's Lives: Sujuni Quilts from Bihar, India,* Museum of Textiles, Toronto, Canada; Juror, *If Images Could Speak a Thousand Words,* Convergence Conference, 2002; Associate Fellow, International Quilt Study Center, University of Nebraska, Lincoln; Instructor; Lecturer

Kyoung Ae Cho
Milwaukee, Wisconsin
Education: B.F.A., Duksung Women's University, Seoul, South Korea, 1986; M.F.A., Cranbrook Academy of Art, Michigan, 1991
Awards/Honors: Wisconsin Arts Board Award Fellowship, Madison, 2006; University of Wisconsin–Milwaukee Foundation and Graduate School Research Award, 2004; Lillian Elliott Award, 1997; *Quilt National* Award of Excellence, 1997; Pollock–Krasner Foundation Grant, 1995
Exhibitions (selected): Solo: *Eloquent Silences,* Tweed Museum of Art, University of Minnesota–Duluth, 2006; *Continuation,* James Watrous Gallery, Madison, Wis., 2005; *Nature on the Grid,* Gallery at Montalvo, Saratoga, Calif., 2001; *Rearrangements,* Kemper Museum of Contemporary Art, Kansas City, Mo., 1998; *The Branch, The Leaf,* Sheehan Gallery, Whitman College, Walla Walla, Wash., 1998
Collections (selected): Pavilion, University of Wisconsin–Milwaukee; Tweed Museum

of Art, University of Minnesota–Duluth; Hawaii State Foundation on Culture and the Arts; Merck Pharmaceutical, Philadelphia; John M. Walsh III Collection, Martinsville, N.J.

Related Professional Experience: Associate Professor, University of Wisconsin–Milwaukee; Panel, Ohio Arts Council's Individual Excellence Award Fellowship in Craft, 2006; Panel, Mid Atlantic Fellowship, New Jersey State Council on the Arts and Crafts and Maryland State Council Crafts, 2002; Juror, Artists Fellowship, Illinois Arts Council, 1998

Nancy Crow

Baltimore, Ohio

Education: B.F.A., Ohio State University, 1965; M.F.A., Ceramics and Textiles, Ohio State University, 1969

Awards/Honors: Fellow, ACC, New York, 1999; Quilter's Hall of Fame, Marion, Ind., 1997; National Living Treasure Award, University of North Carolina at Wilmington, 1999; Ohio Arts Council Individual Artist's Fellowship, 2002, 1996, 1988, 1985, 1982, and 1980; Major Fellowship from the Ohio Arts Council, 1990; National Endowment for the Arts Craftsmen's Fellowship, 1980

Exhibitions (selected): *Nancy Crow Constructions: Color and Spatial Relationships*, Auckland Museum, Auckland, New Zealand, 2004–2005; Renwick Gallery of the Smithsonian Museum of American Art, Washington, D.C., 1995; Miami University Art Museum, Oxford, Ohio, 1995; American Craft Museum, New York, 1993; *Ohio Patchwork '76*, Bowling Green State University, Bowling Green, Ohio, 1976

Collections (selected): Renwick Gallery of the Smithsonian Museum of American Art; Museum of Arts and Design, New York; Museum of American Folk Art, New York; Miami University Art Museum, Oxford, Ohio; Indianapolis Museum of Art, Indianapolis

Related Professional Experience: Author (selected): *Nancy Crow*, 2006; *Nancy Crow: Improvisational Quilts*, 1995; *Nancy Crow: Quilts and Influences*, 1990; Exchange artist, Shaanxi Province, People's Republic of China, 1990; Co-founder, *Quilt National*, Quilt Surface Design Symposium, Art Quilt Network, Ohio; Founder and teacher, Timber Frame Barn Workshops, Ohio

Nancy Erickson

Missoula, Montana

Education: M.A., Painting, University of Montana, 1968; M.F.A., Painting, 1969

Awards/Honors: *Quilts=Art=Quilts*, Best of Show, Schweinfurth Memorial Art Museum, Auburn, N.Y., 2006–2007; *Quilt National*, Best of Show, 2003, Athens, Ohio

Exhibitions (selected): Solo: *Nancy Erickson: Recent Works*, Missoula Art Museum, Missoula, Mont., 2003; San Jose Museum of Quilts and Textiles, 2000; Group: 5 *Quilt National* exhibitions; *Quilt Visions*, 1999, 1998; Gross McCleaf Gallery, 2001, 2004; Art in Embassies, U.S. State Department, 2000, 2002; more than 500 exhibitions of quilts, paintings, and drawings

Collections (selected): Museum of Arts and Design, New York; Federal Reserve Bank of Minneapolis; Society for Contemporary Crafts, Pittsburgh; Washington State Art in Public Places Program, Seattle; Universities of Idaho and Montana, permanent collections; Rocky Mountain Quilt Museum, Golden, Colo.; numerous international exhibitions

Related Professional Experience: Montana Arts Council, 1988; Montana representative, Surface Design Association; Member, Northwest Designer Craftsmen and Art Quilt Network/New York; Lecturer

Carole Harris

Detroit, Michigan

Education: B.F.A., Wayne State University, Detroit, 1966

Awards/Honors: New Initiative for the Arts Exhibition Award, Michigan Council for Arts and Cultural Affairs, 1995, 1996; Kentucky Art and Craft Foundation, 1994

Exhibitions (selected): *Art Quilts: America at the Millennium,* Pavillon Josephine, Parc de l'Orangerie, Strasbourg, France, 2000; *Spirits of the Cloth: Contemporary Quilts by African American Artists,* American Craft Museum, New York (toured to 3 additional museums), 1999–2001; *Uncommon Beauty in Common Objects,* National African American Museum and Cultural Center, Wilberforce, Ohio, and the American Craft Museum, New York, 1993; *African American Quiltmaking in Michigan,* 1990; *Always There: The African American Presence in Quiltmaking,* Kentucky Quilt Project, Museum of History and Science, Louisville, Ky. (toured to 8 additional museums), 1992; *A Communion of the Spirits,* 1997, curated by Roland Freeman

Collections (selected): Michigan State University Folk Art Museum, Lansing; Montgomery Museum of Fine Art, Montgomery, Ala.; Lewis and Munday, Lansing, Mich.; Detroit Receiving Hospital; Strozier Hospital, Chicago; private collections

Related Professional Experience: President, Harris Design Group, LLC

Ana Lisa Hedstrom

La Honda, California

Education: B.A., Mills College, Oakland, California

Awards/Honors (selected): American Craft Council Fellow, 2003; National Endowment for the Arts Craftsman Grants, 1988, 1982; Ideacomo Award: Third International Textile Competition, Tokyo, 1988

Exhibitions (selected): Solo Exhibition: *Process = Pattern,* Robert Hillstad Gallery, University of Nebraska, 2004 and traveling through 2005; *Quilt National,* Athens, Ohio, 2005 and 2003; *Generations/Transformation: American Fiber Art,* American Textile History Museum, Lowell, Mass., 2003; *Fiberart International,* Pittsburgh, 2001; *Art, Image, and Identity,* Los Angeles County Museum, Los Angeles, 2001

Collections (selected): Museum of Art and Design, New York; Cooper Hewitt Museum, New York; De Young Museum, San Francisco; Oakland Museum, Oakland, Calif.

Related Professional Experience: Instructor, San Francisco State University, 2000–2006; Instructor, California College of the Arts, 2005–2006; Instructor, University of Minnesota, Split Rock Summer Program, Penland School of Craft, Haystack School of Craft

Marilyn Henrion

New York, New York

Education: Certificate, Cooper Union College of Arts and Sciences, 1952; B.A., Fordham University, 1972

Awards/Honors: New York Foundation for the Arts Fellowship Award, 2005; Brisons Veor Trust Fellowship Residency, England, 2003; New York State Craft Alliance Grant, 1999; Friends of Fiber Art International Grant, 1999; Artslink Partnership Grant (NEA, Open Society), 1995–1996

Exhibitions (selected): 3 solo exhibitions 2002–2006, Noho Gallery, New York; *Beyond Tradition: Contemporary Art Quilts,* Carl Solway Gallery, Cincinnati, Ohio, 2005; *Six Continents of Quilts: The American Craft Museum Permanent Collection,* UBS Paine Webber, New York, 2002; *Gallery Artists,* Thirteen Moons Gallery, Santa Fe, N.M., 2001; *Five Perspectives: American Art Quilts,* Museum of Decorative and Applied Arts, Moscow, Russia, 1996

Collections: Museum of Arts and Design, New York; Museum of the American Quilter's Society, Paducah, Ky.; U.S. Embassy, Pnom Penh, Cambodia; Lucent Technologies, Denver; Avaya Communication, Denver; Dana Farber Cancer Institute, Boston; Nihon Vogue, Tokyo

Related Professional Experience: Invited by the Smithsonian Institution Archives of American Art to donate all personal and professional papers, sketchbooks, journals to the archives for their permanent collection, 2002

Michael James

Lincoln, Nebraska

Education: B.F.A., University of Massachusetts–Dartmouth, 1971; M.F.A., Rochester Institute of Technology, Rochester, New York, 1973

Awards/Honors: NEA, Visual Artist's Fellowship, 1978, 1988; Artists' Foundation, Boston, Craftsmen's Fellowship, 1979, 1988; NEA, United States/France Exchange Fellowship, 1990; Honorary Doctorate in Fine Arts, University of Massachusetts–Dartmouth, 1992; Fellow of the American Crafts Council, 2001

Exhibitions (selected): Solo: *Material Response,* Racine Art Museum, Racine, Wis., 2006; *Questioning Convention: The Quilts of Michael James,* Fuller Craft Museum, Brockton, Mass., 2005; *Quilt National* (6 exhibitions); *Michael James Studio Quilts: Twenty-Five Years,* Museum of the American Quilter's Society, Paducah, Ky., 1999; Gallery Jonas, Petit-Cortaillod, Switzerland, 1988–2004; Invitational: International Trienniale of Tapestry, Lodz, Poland, 1995; *Poetry of the Physical,* Museum of Arts and Design, New York, 1986

Collections (selected): Newark Museum, Newark, N.J.; Renwick Gallery of the Smithsonian Museum of American Art; Museum of Arts and Design, New York; Mint Museum of Craft and Design, Charlotte, N.C.; Robert and Ardis James Collection of the International Quilt Study Center, Lincoln, Neb.; John M. Walsh III Collection, Martinsville, N.J.

Related Professional Experience: Ardis James Professor of Textiles, Clothing and Design, College of Education and Human Sciences, University of Nebraska–Lincoln; Faculty Fellow of the International Quilt Study Center, Lincoln, Neb.; Author: "The Digital Quilt," *Fiberarts* (November/December 2003); "Orchestrating an Elusive Element: Approaches to the Study of Color," *Surface Design Journal* 20:4 (Summer 1996); *The Second Quiltmaker's Handbook: Creative Approaches to Contemporary Quilt Design,* 1981; *The Quiltmaker's Handbook: A Guide to Design and Construction,* 1978

Jan Myers-Newbury

Pittsburgh, Pennsylvania

Education: B.A., St. Olaf College, Northfield, Minn., 1972; M.A., University of Minnesota, St. Paul, 1979

Awards/Honors: *Ophelia's Dream* added to permanent collection of International Quilt Study Center, University of Nebraska–Lincoln, 2006; *Precipice* added to the permanent collection of Museum of the American Quilter's Society, Paducah, Ky., 2000; *Depth of Field* selected as one of the 20th century's 100 best quilts, 1999; *Quilt National,* Best of Show Award, 1993; Pennsylvania Council on the Arts Fellowship in Crafts, 1989; First Annual Minnesota Governor's Award in the Crafts, 1985

Exhibitions (selected): *Quilt National,* 12 exhibitions, Athens, Ohio, 1993 Best of Show; 1999 Juror's Choice Award; 2001 Surface Design Award; *Textilkunst and Quilts,* Invitational, Konstanz, Germany, 2004; *Pioneers: Teaching the World to Quilt,* New England Quilt Museum, Lowell, Mass., 2003; *30 Distinguished Quilt Artists of the World,* Tokyo International Quilt Festival, 2002; *The 20th Century's 100 Best Quilts,* International Quilt Market, Houston, 1999

Collections (selected): Museum of Arts and Design, New York; Minneapolis Institute of Arts, Minneapolis; Art in Embassies, U.S. State Department; Goldstein Gallery Collection, University of Minnesota, St. Paul; Museum of the American Quilter's Society, Paducah, Ky.; International Quilt Study Center, Lincoln, Neb.

Related Professional Experience (selected): Jurying Committee Chair, *Fiberart International,* Fiberarts Guild of Pittsburgh, 1994–2006; Board of Directors, Pittsburgh Fiberarts Guild, 1994–2001; Board of Directors, Society for Contemporary Crafts, Pittsburgh, 1989–1994

Risë Nagin

Pittsburgh, Pennsylvania

Education: B.F.A., Painting, Carnegie Mellon University, Pittsburgh, 1972

Awards/Honors: Professional Development Grant, Creative Capital Foundation, 2005; Nihon Vogue *Quilt Visions* Quilts Japan Prize, 1994; Artist of the Year, Pittsburgh Center for the Arts, 1993; *Quilt National,* Best of Show, 1991; Pennsylvania Council for the Arts, Individual Fellowship, 1987

Exhibitions (selected): Invitational: *High Fiber,* Renwick Gallery of the Smithsonian Museum of American Art, Washington, D.C., 2005; *Miniatures 2000,* Museum of Art and Design, Helsinki, Finland; Helen Drutt Gallery, Philadelphia, 2000; *The Kimono Inspiration: Art and Art to Wear in America,* Textile Museum, Washington, D.C., Parish Art Museum, Southampton, New York, 1996; *Contemporary American Quilts,* Crafts Council Gallery, London, England, 1993; *Craft Today: Poetry of the Physical,* Museum of Art and Design, New York, 1986, traveled through 1989

Collections (selected): Heinz Endowments, Pittsburgh; Helen Drutt English, Philadelphia; KPMG Peat Marwick, Pittsburgh; Museum of Arts and Design, New York; Nijon Vogue, Inc., Tokyo; Philadelphia Museum of Art; Renwick Gallery of the Smithsonian Museum of American Art, Washington, D.C.

Related Professional Experience (selected): Independent studio artist; Exhibition Project Director, *Fiberart International 2001,* 1999–2001; Board of Directors, Pittsburgh Center for the Arts, 1998–2003; Costume Design, Mary Miller Dance Company, 1986; Crafts Advisory Panel, Pennsylvania Council for the Arts, 1981–1985

Joy Saville

Princeton, New Jersey

Education: RN, University of Nebraska and Lincoln General Hospital School of Nursing, 1957; drawing course, Julian Ashton School of Art, Sydney, Australia, 1990

Awards/Honors: New Jersey State Council on the Arts Fellowship, 1996, 1987, 1982; *Chautauqua International for Fiber Art,* Juror's Commendation, Dunkirk, N.Y., 1994; *Quilt Connection All-Stars,* Judge's Choice Award, Museum of American Folk Art, New York, 1993

Exhibitions (selected): Solo: *Fleisher Art Memorial Challenge Exhibition,* Philadelphia, 1994; Newark Museum, Newark, N.J., 1992, 1983; Group: *Material Difference, Too,* Friends of Fiber Art International, SOFA Chicago, 2006; Jane Sauer, Thirteen Moons Gallery, Santa Fe, N.M., 2005; *Quilt National,* 4 exhibitions, Athens, Ohio; Art in Embassies Program, U.S. State Department; *Fiberart International,* Pittsburgh, 1997, 1979

Collections (selected): Museum of Arts and Design, New York; Newark Museum, Newark, N.J.; John M. Walsh III Collection, Martinsville, N.J.; GoodSmith Gregg Unruh, Chicago; Bristol-Myers Squibb, Princeton, N.J.; Time Warner Inc., HBO, New York; Wilmington Trust, Wilmington, Del.; Johnson and Johnson, New Brunswick, N.J.; private collections

Related Professional Experience: Instructor, Quilt/Surface Design Symposium, 2005, 1996, 1993; Curator, Russian Fiber Art, Rider University, Lawrenceville, N.J., 1998; Lecturer, American Center, Moscow, Russia, 1996; James A. Michener Art Museum, Doylestown, Pa., 1995; Co-chairman, Princeton Artists Alliance, Princeton, N.J., 1994–1997

Joan Schulze

Sunnyvale, California

Education: B.S., Education, University of Illinois, 1958; design and art history course, De Anza College, Cupertino, Calif., 1974

Exhibitions (selected): Solo: National Exhibition Centre, Festival of Quilts, England, 2005; Invitational: *International Fiber Exhibition,* Shanghai, People's Republic of China, 2004; *Six Continents of Quilts: The Museum of Arts and Design Collection,* New York, N.Y., 2002; Group: *Quilt Visions,* Oceanside Art Museum, Oceanside, Calif., 2006; *Quilted Constructions: The Spirit of Design,* American Folk Art Museum, New York, N.Y., 2001; *Renwick at 25,* Smithsonian Museum of American Art, Washington, D.C., 1996

Collections (selected): Museum of Arts and Design, New York; Oakland Museum, Oakland, Calif.; Adobe Systems, Inc., San Jose, Calif.; Renwick Gallery, Smithsonian Museum of American Art, Washington, D.C.; John M. Walsh III, Martinsville, N.J.; private collections

Related Professional Experience: Cultural Specialist, U.S. Information Agency, U.S. Embassy, Luxembourg, The Hague; Textile Museum, The Netherlands; Visiting Professor, Shandong Province, People's Republic of China, 2006; Exhibition Consultant and Juror, International Fiber Exhibitions, Beijing 2000, 2002; Shanghai 2004; Suzhou 2006

Julie John Upshaw

Dallas, Texas

Education: B.F.A., Visual Arts Studies, University of Texas, Austin, 1990

Awards/Honors: *Masterpieces: A Voyage of Self Discovery,* Husqvarna/Viking Gallery, International Quilt Festival, First Place, 2002; Husqvarna/Viking Award of Excellence for the Most Innovative Use of the Medium, *Quilt 21,* Lowell, Mass., 2002

Exhibitions (selected): Solo: *Thread Drawn Work in Fiber,* Southern Methodist University Women's Center, Dallas; Dual: *Insecurity,* San Jose Museum of Quilts and Textiles, San Jose, Calif., 2006; Invitational: Second Miniature Art Textile Exhibition, Ocean County Artists' Guild, Island Heights, N.J., 2005; *Special Interests: The Art of Politics,* San Jose Museum of Quilts and Textiles, 2004

Collections (selected): John M. Walsh III Collection, Martinsville, N.J.; Husqvarna/Viking Collection, Sweden; private collections

INDEX

Page numbers in italics refer to illustrations.

Photo by Spectrum Studio Inc.

Kate Lenkowsky has been quilting since the early 1990s. Her *Call to Service,* a large narrative quilt depicting volunteers serving their communities, hangs in the entryway of the Corporation for National and Community Service at its headquarters in Washington, D.C. *To Everything There Is a Season* hangs in the sanctuary of Congregation Shaarey Tefilla in Indianapolis. Other quilts have won regional awards. She is a member of the Studio Art Quilt Associates, Surface Design Association, the Alliance for American Quilts, Fiber Art Study Group (Washington, D.C.), and the Charm Club (Indianapolis), whose members hold a biennial exhibit of their quilts.